Spanish
Vocabulary
Handbook

Mike Zollo

Berlitz Publishing
New York   Munich   Singapore

Spanish Vocabulary Handbook

Copyright © 2009 Mike Zollo

CONTACTING THE EDITORS
Every effort has been made to provide accurate information in this publication, but changes are inevitable. The publisher cannot be responsible for any resulting loss, inconvenience, or injury. We would appreciate it if readers would call our attention to any errors or outdated information by contacting Berlitz Publishing, 193 Morris Avenue, Springfield, NJ 07081, USA. Fax: 1-908-206-1103. email: comments@berlitzbooks.com

Published by Berlitz Publishing/Apa Publications GmbH & Co. Verlag KG, Singapore Branch, Singapore

Berlitz Trademark Reg. U.S. Patent Office and other countries.
Marca Registrada.
Used under license from Berlitz Investment Corporation.

Printed in Singapore by Insight Print Services (Pte) Ltd., April 2009

Cover Photo © Age Fotostock/Corbis

The Author:
Written by **Mike Zollo**, an experienced teacher, author and chief examiner. He is the chairman of the Association for Language Learning Spanish and Portuguese Committee.

The Series Editor:
Christopher Wightwick is a former UK representative on the Council of Europe Modern Languages Project and principal inspector of Modern Languages for England.

CONTENTS

C   Appendices

D   Subject Index

How to Use This Handbook

This Handbook is a carefully ordered work of reference covering all areas of Spanish vocabulary and phrasing. It is based on the thesaurus structure of the Council of Europe's Threshold Level, expanded to include other major topics, especially in the fields of business, information technology, and education. Unlike a dictionary, it brings together words and phrases in related groups. It also illustrates their usage with contextualized sample sentences, often in dialogue form. This enables learners and users of the language to:

- refresh and expand their general knowledge of vocabulary;
- review systematically, using the word groups to test their knowledge from Spanish to English and vice versa;
- extend their knowledge of authentically Spanish ways of saying things by studying the sample sentences;
- support their speaking and writing on a given topic, when the logical arrangement of the sections will often prompt new ideas as well as supply the means of expressing them.

THE STRUCTURE OF THE HANDBOOK

The Handbook is divided into four parts:

A   Introduction: The Vocabulary of the Spanish Language

A concise account of the ways in which Spanish creates compound words and phrases in order to express more complex ideas. (For a more extensive treatment of this topic, see the Berlitz *Spanish Grammar Handbook*.)

B   Vocabulary Topics

Ninety-six Vocabularies, grouped under twenty-seven major areas of experience. Most Vocabulary Topics are divided into a number of sections, so that words and phrases are gathered together into closely related groups. Almost all sections contain sample sentences showing the vocabulary in use. Wherever it makes sense to do so, these sentences are linked together to form short narratives or dialogues that help to fix them in memory. In some Vocabularies the lists of words and phrases are both extensive and more independent of context, so that the role of the sample sentences is reduced.

C   Appendices

Lists of specific terms such as the names of countries or musical instruments. These are linked to the Vocabularies by clear cross-references.

D   Subject Index

An alphabetical index of topics and themes, enabling you to locate quickly the area you are interested in.

LOCATING THE RIGHT SECTION

The Handbook can be approached in two ways.

• If you are not sure which topic will be best suited to your needs, start with the Contents on page iii. This will give you a general picture of the areas covered. You can then browse through the sections until you find the one you want.

• Alternatively, if you have a specific topic in mind, look it up in the Subject Index at the end of the book. This will take you directly to the relevant Vocabulary Topic or Appendix. To help you find what you are looking for, topics are often listed more than once, under different headings. Within most sections there are cross-references to other, related areas.

A

INTRODUCTION

The Vocabulary of the Spanish Language

Conventions Used in This Handbook

The Vocabulary of the Spanish Language

1   *The Origins of Spanish*

Modern Castilian Spanish (**castellano**) is derived from Vulgar Latin, the Latin spoken by ordinary Romans, which also gave rise to other Romance languages, including other languages and dialects of the Iberian Peninsula. The Castilians won political and military dominance over much of Spain, so it was their dialect that eventually became the national language of Spain. Thus, Spanish comes from the same source as, for example, Italian, French, and Portuguese, and almost all other Iberian Peninsular languages, such as **catalán, valenciano,** and **gallego.**

Much vocabulary in English also comes from Latin, either via Norman French or other Romance languages; and in more recent times (largely in the fields of science or culture), directly from Latin. Hence, Spanish and English have a lot of vocabulary in common, and many words new to you in Spanish will be recognizable from English or any other Romance language you may know.

Spanish has also imported words from many other languages over the centuries, among them Arabic (e.g., **algodón** 'cotton'), French (e.g., **boutique**), English (e.g., **márketing**) and Latin American Indian languages (e.g., **tomate** 'tomato'). Many of the more recent importations are from English, mostly in the fields of sports, pop music, business, science, and computing. It is worth noting that verbs based on imported words are almost always in the **-ar** verb family, e.g., **dopar, esnifar, xerocopiar.**

Some imported words more or less keep their original spelling, but with pronunciation adapted to Spanish: this is usually the case with words adopted in written form (e.g., 'iceberg'). Words imported through spoken language on the other hand tend to do the opposite, and have spelling adapted to keep the pronunciation similar, such as is the case with **fútbol.** It is interesting to compare two words with similar meanings — **jersey** and **suéter:** the former was probably adopted from written English and is now usually pronounced in Spanish as something like 'hersei'; the latter was obviously adopted in spoken form, and a form of spelling was evolved to produce the right sound when said aloud.

2   *Important Grammatical Features*

Awareness of these will help you to categorize words and get to their base form. (For full treatment of Spanish structures, consult the Berlitz *Spanish Grammar Handbook*.)

2a   *The Noun Phrase*

(i)   *Gender*

All Spanish nouns are either **masculine** or **feminine** in gender. As a general rule:

• most words for female people or animals are in the **feminine** group, and most male people or animals are in the **masculine** group.

• most masculine words end in **-o**, and most words ending in **-o** are masculine

• most feminine words end in **-a**, and most words ending in **-a** are feminine

BUT there are exceptions:

el **taxista**, *el* **mapa**, *la* **radio**, *la* **foto**

(ii)   *Number*

All nouns and adjectives ending in a vowel add **s** to form their plural, those ending in a consonant add **-es.**

el niño → los niños	**la carta → las cartas**
el papel → los papeles	**la mujer → las mujeres**

There are a few exceptions. For these, consult the Berlitz *Spanish Grammar Handbook.*

(iii)   *Articles*

There are four words for 'the' in Spanish:

el = masculine singular	**el chico, el perro, el papel**
la = feminine singular	**la chica, la vaca, la verdad**
los = masculine plural	**los chicos, los gatos, los taxis**
las = feminine plural	**las chicas, las ratas, las fotos**

Nouns listed in this Handbook are accompanied by **el/la, los/las,** to show you which gender they belong to.

INTRODUCTION

There are four words for 'a / some' in Spanish:

un = masculine singular	**un chico, un perro, un papel**
una = feminine singular	**una chica, una vaca, una verdad**
unos = masculine plural	**unos chicos, unos gatos, unos taxis**
unas = feminine plural	**unas chicas, unas ratas, unas fotos**

(iv)   Agreement of adjectives

Adjectives have to match the noun they describe in **gender** and **number.** Therefore, they can have four forms: masculine singular and plural, feminine singular and plural. Those ending in **-e**, however, have the same form for masculine and feminine. This often gives rise to apparently rhyming phrases — learn the following as useful examples to remind you:

el niño malo	**un*os* tor*os* brav*os***
un*a* paloma blanc*a*	**l*as* isl*as* bonit*as***

BUT

un hombre inteligent*e*	**unas casas grand*es***

Note that the masculine singular form is usually listed in this Handbook.

2b   Verb Forms

Different verb forms exist for each person referred to and for each tense, and the verb ending is crucially important. On the whole, Spanish does not use subject pronouns — words such as **yo** 'I,' **él** 'he,' **nosotros** 'we,' and so on — because the actual verb form reveals who is doing the action as well as what is being done and when. Since Spanish pronunciation is very faithful to its spelling and vice versa, Spanish has never really developed the need to use subject pronouns all the time, and it reserves them for emphasis or to avoid ambiguity.

• Here are the six forms of a typical regular verb of the **-ar** verb family in the present tense, with the subject pronouns given in brackets. You will see that the verb forms are all clearly different and that most end in a vowel, an **n,** or an **s.**

hablar	to speak
(yo) habl*o*	I speak
(tú) habl*as*	you speak (familiar singular)
(él / ella / usted) habl*a*	he / she / speaks, you speak (formal singular)

4

(nosotros / as) habl*amos*	we speak
(vosotros / as) habl*áis*	you speak (familar plural)
(ellos / ellas / ustedes) habl*an*	they speak, you speak (formal plural)

• Some verbs are affected by the spelling change described as vowel stretching (see Section 4). Here is an example — note that not all forms are affected.

pensar	to think
(yo) p*i*enso	I think
(tú) p*i*ensas	you think (familiar singular)
(él / ella / usted) p*i*ensa	he / she / thinks, you think (formal singular)
(nosotros / as) pensamos	we think
(vosotros / as) pensáis	you think (familar plural)
(ellos / ellas / ustedes) p*i*ensan	they think, you think (formal plural)

Apart from the **-ar** verb family, other regular verbs belong to the **-er** and **-ir** verb groups. For other forms and for more information, consult the Berlitz *Spanish Verb Handbook*.

• In this Handbook, verbs are usually given in the 'I' form of the present tense (e.g., '*I* speak' **hablo**). If you come across a particular verb form, you need to work back to this form to find it in this Handbook, or to the infinitive part of the verb to find it in a dictionary.

3   Guessing Unknown Words

For various reasons, several letters or combinations of letters changed in written form in the transition from Latin to modern Castilian Spanish. If you are aware of these, you can quite easily work out the meanings of many words that are similar in English but not otherwise easily recognizable. Often the changed Castilian form and a form closer to Latin exist side by side, though sometimes with slightly different meanings.

(i)   'vowel stretching' of *e*, *o*, and *u*

e → ie, and o → ue; and in addition, sometimes e → i, o → u and, u → ue.

e → ie: b*i*en	= well; cf. Latin / Italian 'bene,' English 'beneficial'
o → ue: b*ue*no	= good; cf. French 'bon,' English 'bounty'
e → i: p*i*do	= I ask for, from **pedir**; cf. 'petition'

o → u: d*u*rmió

= he slept, from **dormir;** cf. 'd*o*rmitory'

u → ue: ag*üe*ro

= aug*ur*

(ii) *sc, sp, st*

You may notice that some native speakers of Spanish speaking English tend to put an 'e-' at the beginning of words starting with 'sc-,' 'sp-,' 'st-.' This is because many such words in English, French, and so on, tend to begin in Spanish with **esc-, esp-, est-;**

e + sc: *esc*uela

= *sc*hool

e + sp: *esp*añol

= *Sp*anish

e + st: *est*udiante

= *st*udent

(iii) *ll*

Castilian Spanish often uses **ll** instead of 'cl,' 'fl,' and 'pl' at the beginning of words.

cl → ll: *ll*amar

= to call; cf. *cl*aim (call)

fl → ll: *ll*ama

= *fl*ame (also the South American animal)

pl → ll: *ll*ano

= *fl*at, *pl*ain

(iv) *f / h*

Castilian Spanish often uses **h** instead of 'f,' and two words with similar meanings but different spellings often coexist.

h ↔ f: *h*ogar

= hearth +

  *f*uego

= fire; cf. '*fo*cus'

  *h*ijo

= son; cf. '*f*ilial' and French '*f*ils'

(v) *w / g*

Especially at the beginning of words, Spanish tends to use **g** or **gu** instead of 'w.'

w ↔ g: (el País de) *G*ales

= *W*ales; cf. **Galicia**

  *gu*erra

= *w*ar; cf. **g**uerrilla / **g**uerrillero

Note: *w*hisky is often pronounced or written **gu**isky.

(vi) *x / j*

Spanish usually uses **j** where English uses '**x**.'

x → j: **Mé*j*ico**   = Mexico   fi*j*o   = fi*x*ed

(vii)   g/h

Spanish sometimes begins words with **h** instead of 'g.'

g → h: *h*ermano   = brother; cf. '*g*ermane'

> *Note:* G with **e** and **I** sounds like h.

(viii)   ph/f

Spanish does not allow 'ph' spellings, and uses **f** instead.

pro*f*eta	= pro*ph*et
geografía	= geogra*ph*y
farmacia	= *ph*armacy

(ix)   Double consonants

Spanish has fewer double consonants than English. However, **cc, ll, rr** are all very common and; **nn** occurs in a few words, usually ones beginning with the prefix **in-.**

*inn*ecesario   = unnecessary (**in-** negating/opposite)

*inn*ovar   = to innovate (**in-** meaning into)

4   Cognates and Derivatives

Many Spanish words can be identified in a straightforward way, either because of their similarity to known words in other languages (*cognates*), or by being derived from known words in Spanish itself with bits added at the beginning or end of the word (*derivatives*). In the case of the latter, you can often derive a word by knowing how similar words are built from a base word, and you can work out the meaning of a word by 'undressing' it to get back to the base word at its core. Beware though of **amigos falsos** — words that look the same but have different meanings.

4a   Cognates

(i)   English words absorbed into Spanish without change of meaning.

álbum, récord, líder, fútbol, mánager

> *Note:* Many have spellings adapted into Spanish as we have seen before.

INTRODUCTION

(ii) Spanish words with common equivalents in English or ones that English has borrowed from Spanish.

paella, matador, fiesta, aficionado

(iii) Words identical in form to their English equivalent.

casual, panorama

(iv) Words similar in form to their English equivalent.

documento, militar, sistema, clima, movimiento, millón

(v) Verbs whose stem is identical or similar in form to the English equivalent.

admirar, contener, consistir, aplaudir

(vi) Words with frequently occurring suffixes with English equivalents.

libertad, posibilidad, indicación, potencia

Note the equivalent English and Spanish suffixes:

-dad	= '-ty,' e.g., **ciudad** 'city'; **capacidad** 'capacity'
-ción	= '-tion,' e.g., **acción** 'action'; **elección** 'election'
-ía, -ia	= '-y,' e.g., **energía** 'energy'; **farmacia** 'pharmacy'

4b *Derivatives: Word Building and Undressing*

(i) Words whose meaning is determined by common prefixes or suffixes, but whose base element is already known or easily identifiable.

con-: contener	**des-: deshacer, desnudo**
dis-: disuadir	**in-/im-: incorrecto, imposible**
re-: revolver	**sub-: submarino, subcontinente**
-able: salud > saludable	**-ería: zapatero > zapatería**
-miento: pensar > pensamiento	**-oso: arena > arenoso**

(ii) Nouns denoting people and other concepts, with endings such as **-ero/a, -or/a, -ista**.

-ero/-era: zapatero, niñera
-ista: pianista, taxista
-or/-ora: pintor, pescador

These are mostly based on another noun or a verb.

(iii)   Adverbs formed by adding the ending **-mente** to adjectives.

totalmente, activamente

> *Note:* In Spanish most adverbs end in **-mente,** just as in English most end in '-ly.' This ending is usually added to the feminine form of the adjective.

(iv)   Adjectives with ending **-able,** equivalent to English '-able' or '-ible.'

imaginable, admirable

(v)   Adjectives with ending **-oso / -osa,** equivalent to English '-ous.'

religioso, furioso, vigoroso, vicioso

(vi)   Adjectives with ending **-és / esa, -(i)ense, -eno / a, -eño / a,** equivalent to English '-ese' or '-(i)an,' usually indicating place of origin.

inglés, japonesa, canadiense, chileno, brasileña

(vii)   Diminutives ending in **-ito, -illo, -ico**

señorito, panecillo, casita, perico

(viii)   Augmentative and pejorative suffixes such as **-ón / ona, -azo, -ucho.**

hombrón, mujerona, manotazo, casucha

(ix)   Compound nouns, consisting of combinations of known words.

abrelatas, sacacorchos, cortacésped

(x)   Words derived from adjectives.

tranquilizar, ensuciar, limpieza

(xi)   Words mainly derived from verbs, with endings **-ante** or **-ente, -iente.**

cantante, oyente, comiente

(xii)   Common acronyms and initials, often in a different order.

UNO	**ONU - Organización de las Naciones Unidas**
NATO	**OTAN - Organización del Tratado del Atlántico del Norte**
Note:	
USA	**EEUU - los Estados Unidos** (Plural words have doubled-up letters when given as acronyms.)

Conventions Used in This Handbook

a) Nouns
Nouns are given in the singular form preceded by the definite article.

el (pl. **los**) indicates masculine gender
la (pl. **las**) indicates feminine gender
Feminine words beginning with stressed **a-** or **ha-** are usually used with **el.**

Nouns referring to professions are generally given in the masculine form only, except for the list of professions in App. 14b, where the feminine is included.

b) Verbs
Verbs are in the first person, except when inappropriate. In the sample sentences both familiar and polite forms of 'you' are used as appropriate in that particular context. Sometimes both are given.

c) Adjectives
Adjectives are in the masculine singular form.

Abbreviations

adj	adjective	m	masculine
adv	adverb	pl	plural
f	feminine		

Symbols

( )	a part of a translation that is optional: **el juzgado (de lo) penal**
/	alternative word(s): **la historia / el cuento de terror** = **la historia de terror** or **el cuento de terror**
,	an alternative translation: 'I resign' **dimito, renuncio**
[ ]	an alternative used in Latin American Spanish: 'computer' **el ordenador, [la computadora]**
➤	a cross-reference to a vocabulary or chapter

B

VOCABULARY TOPICS

Functional Words

Articles

a	**un, una**
the	**el, la, los, las**
some	**unos, unas**
	algunos, algunas

Demonstrative adjectives / pronouns*

this	**este, esta**
that	**ese, esa, aquel, aquella**
these	**estos, estas**
those	**esos, esas, aquellos, aquellas**
this one	**éste, ésta**
that one	**ése, ésa**
these	**éstos, éstas**
those	**ésos, ésas, aquéllos, aquéllas**

Emphatic subject pronouns*

I	**yo**
you *(fam sing)*	**tú**
(fam pl)	**vosotros / as, [ustedes]**
(formal sing)	**usted**
(formal pl)	**ustedes**
he	**él**
she	**ella**
it	**ello**
we	**nosotros / as**
they	**ellos / as**

Personal object pronouns (accusative & dative)

me	**me**
you *(fam sing)*	**te**
(fam pl)	**os, [les]**
(formal sing)	**lo, la, le**
(formal pl)	**los, las, les**
him	**lo, le**
her	**la, le**
it	**lo, la, le**
us	**nos**
them	**los, las, les**
one	**lo, la, le**

Reflexive pronouns

myself	**me**
yourself *(fam sing)*	**te**
(fam pl)	**os, [les]**
(formal sing / pl)	**se**
him / herself	**se**
itself	**se**
ourselves	**nos**
themselves	**se**
oneself	**se**
each other	**se**

Prepositional pronouns*

me	**mí**
you *(fam sing)*	**ti**
(fam pl)	**vosotros / as, [ustedes]**
(formal sing)	**usted**
(formal pl)	**ustedes**
him	**él**
her	**ella**
it	**ello**
. . . self, . . . selves	**sí** *(reflexive)*
us	**nosotros / as**
them	**ellos / as**
one	**uno**

Possessive adjectives*

my	**mi, mis**
your *(fam sing)*	**tu, tus**
(fam pl)	**vuestro / a / os / as, [su, sus]**
(formal sing / pl)	**su, sus**
his	**su, sus**
her	**su, sus**
its	**su, sus**
our	**nuestro / a / os / as**
their	**su, sus**

one's   **su, sus**

*Possessive pronouns**

mine   **el mío, la mía, los míos, las mías**
yours *(fam sing)*   **el tuyo,** etc.
   (fam pl)   **el vuestro,** etc., [**el suyo,** etc.]
   (formal sing/pl)   **el suyo,** etc.
his/hers   **el suyo,** etc.
ours   **el nuestro,** etc.
theirs   **el suyo,** etc.
this is mine   **este/a es mío/a**
mine is better   **el mío/la mía es mejor**

*Relative pronouns**

who   **que**
   quien, quienes
   el/la que, los/las que
   el/la cual, los/las cuales
which   **que**
   el/la que, los/las que
   el/la cual, los/las cuales
that   **que**
   quien, quienes
   el/la que, los/las que
   el/la cual, los/las cuales
what   **lo que, lo cual**
what you say is true   **lo que dices es verdad**

Indefinite pronouns

somebody/one   **alguien**
no one   **nadie**
anybody/one(s)   **cualquiera;** (pl) **cualesquiera**
nobody   **nadie**
each   **cada (uno/a)**
everybody/one   **todos/as**
something   **algo**
anything   **algo, alguna cosa, cualquier cosa**
   (after negative) **nada**
nothing   **nada**
everything   **todo**

all (of them)   **todos/as**
both (of them)   **los/las dos, ambos/as**
some (of them)   **algunos/as**

Questions

when?   **¿cuándo?**
where?   **¿dónde?**
how?   **¿cómo?**
how much?   **¿cuánto/a?**
how many?   **¿cuántos/as?**
how far?   **¿a qué distancia?,** [**¿qué tan lejos?**]
how long?   **¿durante cuánto tiempo?**
how hot?   **¿qué temperatura?**
why?   **¿por qué?**
who?   **¿quién(es)?**
whom?   **¿a quién(es)?**
to whom?   **¿a quién(es)?**
whose?   **¿de quién(es)?**
what?   **¿qué?**
what...?   **¿qué ...?, ¿cuál(es) ...?**
which (one)?   **¿cuál?**

Common prepositions and conjunctions

about   **a eso de, acerca de**
also   **también**
although   **aunque**
and   **y**
as *(since)*   **puesto que**
because   **porque**
but   **pero**
if   **si**
in   **en**
in order that/so that   **para que**
on   **en, sobre**
only   **sólo, solamente**
or   **o**
since   **puesto que**
so   **pues**
too   **también**
until   **hasta (que)**
with   **con**
without   **sin**

2 Where? — Position & Movement

2a Position

about **alrededor de**
  about *(adv)* **por todas partes**
above **encima de**
across **a través (de)**
after **después (de)**
against **contra**
ahead **delante, [adelante]**
ahead of **delante de**
along **a lo largo de**
among **entre**
anywhere **en cualquier sitio**
around *(adv)* **alrededor de, por**
  around the garden **por el jardín**
as far as **hasta**
at **en**
  at home **en casa**
  at school **en el colegio**
  at work **en el trabajo**
back **detrás, atrás**
  at the back (of) **detrás (de), a la espalda (de), [atrás, en la parte trasera]**
  to the back **hacia atrás**
backwards **hacia atrás**
behind **detrás (de)**
below **debajo (de)**
  below **debajo, [abajo]**
beside **al lado de, [junto a]**
between **entre**
beyond **más allá (de)**
bottom **el fondo**
  at the bottom (of) **al fondo (de)**
center / centre **el centro**
  in the center / centre **en el centro (de)**
direction **la dirección**
  in the direction of Murcia **en la dirección de Murcia**
distance **la distancia**

in the distance **a la distancia**
distant **distante, distanciado, lejano**
down there **allí abajo**
downstairs **abajo**
edge **el borde**
  at the edge **al borde (de)**
end **el final**
  at the end **al final (de)**
everywhere **en todas partes, por todas partes, en todos los sitios**
far **lejos**
  far away (from) **lejos (de)**
first **primero**
  first (of all) **primero (de todo)**
  I am first **estoy primero**
from **de, desde**
front **el frente**
  at the front **al frente**
  I am in front **estoy al frente**
  in front of **delante de, al frente de**
  to the front **hacia delante, al frente**
here **aquí**
  here and there **aquí y allí**
in **en**
  in there **allí dentro**
inside **dentro**
  inside **adentro**
into **dentro**
last **último**
  last of all **por último**
  last of all *(adv)* **últimamente**
  I am last **soy el último**
left **izquierda**
  on the left **a la izquierda**
  to the left **hacia la izquierda**

middle **medio**
  in the middle (of) **en (el) medio (de)**
I move **me muevo**
movement **el movimiento**
near **cerca**
near(by) **cercano**
neighborhood / neigbourhood **el vecindario, las cercanías**
  in the neighborhood / neigbourhood of **en las cercanías (de)**
next **próximo, al lado**
  next *(adv)* **próximamente**
  next to **al lado de**
nowhere **en ningún sitio**
on **en, sobre**
onto **en**
opposite **opuesto (a), en frente (de)**
out of **fuera de**
  out there **allí fuera, [allá atuera]**
outside **fuera**
  outside **afuera**
over **encima**
  over there **allí, [allá]**
past **pasado**

right **derecho**
  the right **la derecha**
  to the right **a la derecha**
round / around **alrededor (de)**
  round / around the tree **alrededor del árbol**
side **lado**
  at the side **al lado**
  at both sides of **a ambos lados de**
somewhere **en alguna parte, en algún sitio**
there **allí**
to **a, hacia**
top **arriba, encima**
  top *(of mountain)* **la cima**
  at the top **encima**
  on top **encima**
towards **hacia**
under **debajo (de), bajo**
up there **allí arriba**
upstairs **arriba**
where? **¿dónde?**
where from? **¿de dónde?**
where to? **¿hacia dónde?, ¿adónde?**
with **con**

Over there in the distance is the river. It's not far—about 1 km from our house.
Opposite the houses is the church, and nearby are the shops / stores.

At the top of the hill is a farm, and in the middle of the village is the bank.
The first house on the main / high street is near the river. Our house is the last one. The next village is about five kilometers / kilometres away.

Allá a lo lejos está el río. No es lejos—**a un kilómetro más o menos de nuestra casa.**
Enfrente de la casa está la iglesia, y las tiendas están cerca.

En lo alto de la colina hay una granja, y en el centro del pueblo está el banco.
La primera casa de la calle principal está cerca del río. Nuestra casa es la última. El pueblo mas cercano está a unos cinco kilómetros.

WHERE? — POSITION & MOVEMENT

2b Directions & Location

Points of the compass

atlas **el atlas**
east **el este, [el oriente]**
   east *(adj)* **del este, oriental**
   in the east **en el este**
   to the east **al este**
compass **la brújula**
latitude **la latitud**
location **la situación, la posición,
   la ubicación**
longitude **la longitud**
map **el mapa**
north **el norte**
   north *(adj)* **del norte, nórdico**
   in the north **en el norte**
   to the north (of) **al norte (de)**

northeast **el nordeste**
northnortheast **el nornordeste**
northwest **el noroeste, el
   norueste**
northnorthwest **el nornoroeste, el
   nornorueste**
point of the compass **la cuarta**
south **el sur**
   south *(adj)* **del sur, sureño**
   in the south **en el sur**
   to the south **al sur**
southeast **el sudeste, el
   sureste**

Santiago is south of La Coruña.
Right in the south is Pontevedra.
I prefer the south of Galicia to
the north.

**Santiago está al sur de La Coruña.
Precisamente en el sur está
Pontevedra. Prefiero el sur de
Galicia al norte.**

Look on the map. You go
north(wards).

**Mire el mapa. Usted sigue hacia
el norte.**

To the south of the woods you can
see the church spire.

**Hacia el sur del bosque se puede
ver la aguja de la iglesia.**

"How do I get to Pamplona?"
"Go straight on to the second
intersection / crossroads.
Turn right at the lights and take the
road to Vitoria. It's twenty-five
kilometers / kilometres from here."

**— ¿Cómo se va a Pamplona?
— Siga todo derecho hasta el
segundo cruce.
Doble a la derecha en el
semáforo y tome la carretera
para Vitoria. Está a veinte y cinco
kilómetros de aquí.**

"Is there a bank nearby?"
"It's behind the supermarket."
"Where is the tourist office?"

**— ¿Hay un banco cerca de aquí?
— Está detrás del supermercado.
— ¿Dónde está la oficina de
turismo?**

"Opposite the town hall."

— En frente del ayuntamiento.

southsoutheast **el sudsudeste**
southwest **el sudoeste, el suroeste**
southsouthwest **el sudsudoeste**
west **el oeste, [el occidente]**
    west *(adj)* **del oeste, occidental**
    in the west **en el oeste, [al occidente]**
    to the west (of) **al oeste (de), [al occidente de]**

Location & existence

I am **soy, estoy**
    there is, there are **hay**
    there isn't (any), there aren't (any) **no hay (ninguno)**

it is ready **está listo, está preparado**
it amounts to **hace, [asciende a]**
I become **llego a ser**
I exist **existo**
existence **la existencia**
I have got / I have **tengo**
it lies **está situado**
I possess **poseo**
possession **la posesión**
present **el presente**
    I am present **estoy presente**
    I am present at **estoy presente en**
I am situated **estoy situado**

The town lies at a longitude of 32°. **La ciudad está en la longitud de 32°.**

"Are you lost?" **— ¿Se ha perdido usted?**
"Yes. Can you tell me the quickest way to the post office?" **— Sí. ¿Me puede decir el camino más corto para ir al correo [a la oficina de correos]?**

"It's down there on the left." **— Está allí abajo a la izquierda.**

How do you get to the other side? **¿Cómo se va al otro lado?**

"Who's that?" **— ¿Quién es?**
"It's me." **— Soy yo.**

"How many children are present?" **— ¿Cuántos niños asisten?**
"There are twenty-five. Five of them are at home." **— Hay veinte y cinco. Cinco de ellos están en casa.**

"Is there any cake? Are there still any cookies / biscuits?" **— ¿Hay torta / pastel? ¿Quedan galletas?**
"I am sorry, there is no cake, but there are some sandwiches." **— Lo siento, no hay pastel, pero sí hay unos bocadillos [emparedados / sándwiches].**

I have been to Madrid. I was at a concert. **He estado en Madrid. Fui a un concierto.**

WHERE? — POSITION & MOVEMENT

2c Movement

I arrive **llego**	I go out **salgo, voy fuera**
I bring **traigo**	I go round **doy vueltas, doy la vuelta a**
by car **en coche**	
I carry **llevo**	I go up **subo, voy arriba**
I climb **escalo, subo**	I hike **hago auto(e)stop**
I come **voy, vengo**	I hurry **me apresuro**
I come down **bajo, voy abajo**	I hurry up **me doy prisa**
I come in **entro**	I jump **salto**
I come out **salgo**	I leave **salgo**
I come up **subo, voy arriba**	I leave (something) **dejo (algo)**
I creep **ando a gatas, [gateo]**	I lie down **me echo, me acuesto**
I drive **conduzco**	I march **desfilo**
I drive on the right **conduzco por la derecha**	I move **me muevo, me cambio**
	on foot **a pie**
I fall **caigo**	I pass **paso**
I fall down **me caigo**	I pass (in car) **paso en coche, [rebaso en carro]**
I follow **sigo**	
I get in **subo en / a**	I pull **tiro**
I get out **bajo de, salgo de**	I push **empujo**
I get up **me levanto**	I put **pongo**
I go **voy**	I ride a horse **monto a caballo**
I go down **bajo, voy abajo**	I run **corro**
I go for a walk **voy a pasear**	I run away **echo a correr**
I go in **entro, voy dentro**	I rush **voy de prisa**

Put the picnic lunch in the car! Don't forget to bring your umbrella.	**Pon (la comida d)el picnic en el coche [el carro]! No te olvides de traer el paraguas.**
I will take you as far as the river. Then you must get out and walk.	**Te llevaré hasta el río. Luego tendrás que bajar y continuar a pie.**
Keep to the left. Be careful not to fall into the river.	**Anda a la izquierda. Ten cuidado de no caerte al río.**
We go down the hill, along the river, and then turn left towards the woods.	**Bajamos la cuesta, seguimos al lado del río, y luego torcemos a la izquierda hacia el bosque.**
You pass a farm.	**Se pasa delante de una granja.**

I sit down   **me siento**
I sit up   **me levanto**
I slip   **resbalo**
I am standing   **estoy de pie**
  I stand still   **(me) estoy quieto**
I stop   **paro**
straight   **derecho, seguido, recto**
  straight ahead   **todo derecho, todo seguido, todo recto, [derecho]**
I stroll   **me paseo**
I take   **cojo**
I turn   **tuerzo**
  I turn left   **tuerzo a la izquierda**
  I turn off   **me desvío**
  I turn round   **me vuelvo, doy la vuelta**
walk   **el paseo**
I walk   **ando, camino**
I wander   **voy sin rumbo**
way   **el camino**

Here and there

Come here!   **¡Ven aqui!**
I go there   **voy allí**

I rush there   **voy allí de prisa**
I travel there   **viajo allí**

Up and down

Stand up!   **¡Levántate!**
I climb the mountain   **subo la montaña**
I climb the stairs   **subo las escaleras**
I climb the wall   **subo por la pared**
I fall down   **me caigo**
I lie down   **me echo, me acuesto**
Do sit down!   **¡Siéntate!, ¡Siéntese!**
I go down the path   **bajo por el camino**

Round

I go round the town   **me paseo por la ciudad**
I run round in the garden   **corro alrededor del jardín**
I run around   **corro alrededor**
I turn round   **doy la vuelta**

"Where are you going?"
"To town. Are you coming?"

"No, I am going to my mother's."
"Which direction is that?"
"I take the first road on the left, then straight ahead up to the marketplace, then I turn right."

"I will follow you as far as the market."
I am going by car but some of us will go on foot. John is going by bike.

— ¿Adónde vas / va usted?
— Al pueblo. ¿Vienes / Viene usted?

— No, voy a casa de mi madre.
— ¿En qué dirección es eso?
— Tomo la primera calle a la izquierda, luego sigo todo recto hacia la plaza del mercado, luego tuerzo a la derecha.
— Te / le seguiré hasta el mercado.
Voy en coche, pero algunos iremos a pie. John irá en bicicleta.

When? — Expressions of Time

3a Past, Present & Future

about **alrededor de**
after **después**
    after *(conj)* **después (de) que**
    afterwards **después, más tarde**
again **otra vez**
    again and again **una y otra vez**
ago **hace**
    a short time ago **hace poco tiempo**
already **ya**
always **siempre**
anniversary **el aniversario**
annual **anual**
as long as *(conj)* **siempre que, siempre cuando**
as soon as *(conj)* **tan pronto como**
at once **inmediatamente, ahora mismo**
before **antes (de)**
    before, beforehand **de antemano**
I begin **empiezo, comienzo**
beginning **el principio, el comienzo**

birthday **el cumpleaños**
brief **breve, corto**
briefly **brevemente**
by (next month) **al (mes próximo)**
calendar **el calendario, el almanaque**
centenary **el centenario**
century **el siglo**
    in the twentieth century **en el siglo veinte**
continuous **continuo**
daily **diariamente**
date **la fecha**
dawn **el amanecer**
    at dawn **al amanecer**
day **el día**
    by day **por día**
    every day **todos los días, cada día**
    one day (when) **un día (cuando)**
    the days of the week **los días de la semana**
decade **la década**

"Last Friday the train was late and you didn't get there till a quarter to three."
"I'll make it by three at the latest. If I'm late, you can have a coffee till I get there."

"I don't want to spend all afternoon drinking coffee. Then there will be no time left for shopping."

—El viernes pasado el tren llevaba un retraso y no llegaste antes de las tres menos cuarto.
—Llegaré a las tres como más tarde [a más tardar]. Si llego tarde, puedes tomar un café mientras esperas mi llegada.
—No quiero pasar toda la tarde bebiendo café. Luego no quedará tiempo para hacer las compras.

delay **el retraso, la posposición**
   delayed **retrasado, aplazado**
during **durante**
early **temprano, pronto**
   I am early **llego pronto**
end **el fin, el final**
   I end (something) **termino, finalizo**
   it ends **termina, finaliza**
ever **siempre**
every **todo, cada**
   every time **todas las veces, cada vez**
exactly **exactamente**
fast **rápido, adelantado**
   my watch is fast **mi reloj va adelantado**
finally **finalmente**
I finish **termino, finalizo**
first **el primero, primero**
   at first **primero, al principio**
   in the first place **primeramente, en primer lugar**
for **para, a, por**
for a day *(duration)* **por (un) día**
forever / for good **para siempre, por siempre**
formerly **anteriormente**
frequent **frecuente**
frequently **frecuentemente**

from **de, desde**
   as of / from (today) **de (hoy) en adelante**
   from now on **de ahora en adelante, desde ahora**
I go on **continúo**
half **la mitad**
   half **medio, media**
   one and a half **uno y medio, una y media**
it happens **sucede, ocurre**
hurry **la prisa, [el afán]**
   I hurry up **me apresuro, me doy prisa**
   I am in a hurry **tengo prisa [afán]**
instant **el instante**
just **justo**
   just now **justo ahora**
last / final **el último, el pasado**
   last night **anoche**
   last / previous **el último**
   it lasts a long / short time **dura mucho / poco tiempo**
late **tarde**
   I am late **llego tarde**
   lately **últimamente**
   later (on) **más tarde, después**
long **largo**
   in the long term **a largo plazo**

"You're sometimes late, too."

   — A veces tú también llegas tarde.

"Only in winter or in bad weather."

   — Sólo en invierno o con (el) mal tiempo.

"Last month I had to wait for twenty minutes."

   — El mes pasado tuve que esperar veinte minutos.

"Perhaps it would be better to meet another time. I'll call next week."

   — Quizás sería mejor reunirnos en otra ocasión. Llamaré la semana que viene.

WHEN? — EXPRESSIONS OF TIME

many **muchos, muchas**
many times **muchas veces**
meanwhile **mientras tanto**
in the meanwhile **mientras tanto**
middle **medio**
moment **el momento**
at the moment **al momento**
at this moment *(right now)* **en este momento**
at that moment **en aquel momento**
in a moment **en un momento**
month **el mes**
monthly **mensualmente**
much **mucho/a**
never **nunca**
next *(adj)* **próximo**
next *(adv)* **próximamente**
not till/until **no hasta**
now **ahora**
nowadays **hoy en día**
occasionally **a veces, ocasionalmente**
often **a menudo, con frecuencia**
on and off **de vez en cuando**
once **una vez**
once upon a time **érase una vez, en tiempos de**
once in a while **de vez en cuando**
once a day **una vez al día**

one day **un día**
only **sólo**
past **el pasado**
per (day) **por (día)**
present **el presente**
present *(adj)* **presente, actual**
presently **en el momento presente**
at present **en este momento**
previous(ly) **anterior(mente)**
prompt **pronto, con prontitud, sin dilación**
promptly at (two) **a (las dos) en punto**
rarely **raramente**
recent **reciente**
recently **recientemente**
I remain **me quedo**
right away **en seguida, ahora mismo**
saint's day **el santo, el día del santo, la fiesta del santo**
season **la estación**
in season *(fruit)* **en sazón**
seldom **rara vez, raramente**
several **algunos, varios**
several times **algunas veces, varias veces**
short **corto**
(in the) short term **(a) corto plazo**
shortly **dentro de poco**

"Hello, John, Peter speaking/here. Thank you for yesterday's call. Sorry I couldn't call then. I had only gotten back from Madrid a quarter of an hour before."

—Hola, John, soy Peter. Gracias por haber llamado ayer. Siento que no pude llamar entonces. Sólo había llegado un cuarto de hora antes de Madrid.

After getting back I spent a long time with Anna; she thinks the project will take all month.

Después de volver pasé mucho tiempo con Ana; ella cree que hará falta todo el mes para terminar el proyecto.

since **desde**
slow **lento**
  my watch is slow **mi reloj va retrasado [está atrasado]**
sometimes **algunas veces**
soon **pronto**
  sooner or later **más tarde o más temprano, antes o después**
  the sooner the better **cuanto antes mejor**
I stay **me quedo**
still **todavía**
I stop (doing) **dejo (de hacer)**
suddenly **de repente**
sunrise **la salida del sol, el amanecer**
sunset **la puesta del sol**
I take (an hour) **me lleva, [gasto] (una hora)**
  it takes (an hour) **lleva (una hora)**
then (next) **luego, después**
  then (at that time) **entonces**
(one) thousand years **mil años**
till **hasta**
time (in general) **el tiempo**
time (occasion) **la vez**
  at any time **en cualquier momento**
  at the same time **al mismo tiempo**
  from time to time **de vez en cuando**
  for a long time **durante mucho tiempo**
  in good time **a tiempo**
  a long time ago **hace mucho tiempo**
  the whole time **todo el tiempo**
time zone **el huso horario**
twice **dos veces**
two weeks / fortnight **la quincena**
until **hasta**
usually **generalmente, usualmente**
vacation / holiday **las vacaciones**
I wait **espero**
week **la semana**
  weekly **semanalmente, por semana**
  weekday **el día de entre semana, el día laboral**
  weekend **el fin de semana**
when **cuando**
whenever **siempre que, cuandoquiera que**
while (conj) **mientras**
year **el año**
  yearly **anualmente**
yet **aún, todavía**
  not yet **todavía**

We should start on the work at the beginning of June, before the summer vacations / holidays start. We can then get it done in good time.
"Hello Peter, John Brown speaking/ here. I have been working on the project for a few days. Have you finished yours yet? Call me this afternoon. We must meet sometime."

Deberíamos empezar el trabajo a principios de junio, antes del comienzo de las vacaciones de verano. Entonces podremos terminarlo a tiempo.
—Hola Peter, soy John Brown. Llevo varios días trabajando en el proyecto. ¿Ya has terminado el tuyo? Llámame esta tarde. Deberíamos reunirnos alguna vez.

WHEN? — EXPRESSIONS OF TIME

3b The Time, Days & Dates

Time of day

a.m. **de la mañana**
morning **la mañana**
  in the morning(s) **por la(s) mañana(s)**
noon **el mediodía**
at noon **al mediodía**
afternoon **la tarde**
  in the afternoon(s) **por la(s) tarde(s)**
p.m. **de la tarde**
evening **la tarde, la noche**
  in the evening(s) **por la(s) tarde(s), por la(s) noche(s)**
night **la noche**
  at night **por la noche**
midnight **las doce de la noche, medianoche**
  at midnight **a las doce de la noche, a medianoche**
today **hoy**
  in a week **dentro de una semana**
  tomorrow **mañana**
  tomorrow morning **mañana por la mañana**
  tomorrow afternoon **mañana por la tarde**
  tomorrow evening **mañana por la tarde, mañana por la noche**

the day after tomorrow **pasado mañana**
tonight **esta noche**
yesterday **ayer**
  yesterday afternoon **ayer por la tarde**
  yesterday morning **ayer por la mañana**
  yesterday evening **ayer por la tarde, ayer por la noche**
the day before yesterday **anteayer**

Telling time

second **el segundo**
minute **el minuto**
hour **la hora**
  half an hour **media hora**
  in an hour's time **dentro de una hora**
  hourly **cada hora**
quarter **un cuarto**
  quarter of an hour **un cuarto de hora**
  three quarters of an hour **tres cuartos de hora**
  quarter past / after (two) **(dos) y cuarto**
  quarter to / of (two) **(dos) menos cuarto**

"What's the date today?"
— **¿A cuántos estamos? [¿Qué fecha es hoy?]**

"The twenty-first of January."
— **Estamos a veintiuno de enero.**
"And what's the time, please?"
— **¿Y qué hora es por favor?**
"Ten past ten."
— **Son las diez y diez.**
"What time does the movie / film start this evening?"
— **¿A qué hora empieza la película esta tarde / noche?**
"20:00 hours."
— **A las veinte horas.**
"How long does it last?"
— **¿Cuánto dura?**
"One and a half hours."
— **Dura una hora y media.**

➤ HOLIDAYS & RELIGIOUS FESTIVALS App. 13b; NUMBERS 4c

half past (two)   **(dos) y media**
17:45   **las seis menos cuarto, las cinco y cuarenta y cinco**
five past / after six   **las seis y cinco**
five to / of six   **las seis menos cinco**
12:00 noon   **las doce del mediodía, el mediodía**
12:00 midnight   **las doce de la noche, la medianoche**

The days of the week

Monday   **el lunes**
Tuesday   **el martes**
Wednesday   **el miércoles**
Thursday   **el jueves**
Friday   **el viernes**
Saturday   **el sábado**
Sunday   **el domingo**

The months *

January   **enero**
February   **febrero**
March   **marzo**
April   **abril**
May   **mayo**
June   **junio**
July   **julio**
August   **agosto**
September   **septiembre / setiembre**
October   **octubre**
November   **noviembre**
December   **diciembre**

The seasons

spring   **la primavera**
summer   **el verano**
autumn / fall   **el otoño**
winter   **el invierno**

The date

last Friday   **el viernes pasado**
on Tuesday   **el martes**
on Tuesdays   **los martes**
by Friday   **para el viernes**
the first of January   **el uno de enero, [el primero de enero]**
on the third of January   **el tres de enero**
in 2000   **en el año dos mil**
January 1st / 1st January, 1998   **el uno de enero de 1998**
at the end of 1999   **a finales de 1999**
by the end of 1999   **para finales de 1999**
at the beginning (of July)   **a primeros de (julio)**
by the beginning (of July)   **para primeros de (julio)**
in December   **en diciembre**
in mid / the middle of January   **a mediados de enero**
at the end of March   **al final de marzo**
in spring   **en primavera**

"I am going shopping tomorrow morning. Would you like to come too?"
"I'd prefer to go in the afternoon. And let's go on Tuesday. I always have so much to do on Mondays."

"All right, I'll leave home at two o'clock and meet you at half-past two at the station."

— **Voy de compras mañana por la mañana. ¿Te gustaría ir conmigo?**
— **Preferiría ir por la tarde. Y vayamos el martes. Siempre tengo mucho que hacer los lunes.**

— **Vale, saldré de casa a las dos y te veré a las dos y media en la estación.**

➤ All months in Spanish are masculine.

How Much? — Expressions of Quantity

4a Length & Shape

angle	**el ángulo**
area	**el área, la superficie**
big	**grande**
center / centre	**el centro**
concave	**cóncavo**
convex	**convexo**
curved	**curvo**
deep	**profundo, hondo**
degree	**el grado**
depth	**la profundidad**
diagonal	**diagonal**
distance	**la distancia**
I draw	**dibujo**
height	**la altura**
high	**alto**
horizontal	**horizontal**
large	**grande**
length	**la longitud**
line	**la línea**
long	**largo**
low	**bajo**
it measures	**mide**
narrow	**estrecho**
parallel	**paralelo**

perpendicular	**perpendicular**
point	**el punto**
room *(space)*	**el espacio, el sitio**
round	**redondo**
ruler	**la regla**
shape	**la forma, la figura**
short	**corto**
size	**el tamaño, la talla, la medida**
small	**pequeño**
space	**el espacio**
straight	**derecho**
tall	**alto**
thick	**grueso, espeso**
thin	**fino, delgado**
wide	**ancho**
width	**la anchura**

Shapes

circle	**el círculo**
circular	**circular**
cube	**el cubo**
cubic	**cúbico**
cylinder	**el cilindro**
hectare	**la hectárea**

You need a ruler and pencil. Measure the space and then draw a plan.

Necesita una regla y un lápiz. Mida el espacio, luego dibuje un plano.

Leave room for the vegetable garden. The distance from the house to the fence is twelve meters / metres. The garden is not wide enough for a pool.

Deja sitio para el huerto. La distancia entre la casa y la tapia es doce metros. El jardín no es bastante ancho para un estanque.

"How high is the tree?"
"About five meters / metres."

— ¿Qué altura tiene el árbol?
— Unos cinco metros.

pyramid   la pirámide
rectangle   el rectángulo
  rectangular   rectangular
sphere   la esfera
  spherical   esférico
square   el cuadrado
  square   cuadrado
triangle   el triángulo
  triangular   triangular

Units of length

centimeter / centimetre   el
  centímetro
foot   el pie
inch   la pulgada
kilometer / kilometre   el kilómetro
meter / metre   el metro
mile   la milla
millimeter / millimetre   el milímetro
yard   la vara, la yarda

Expressions of quantity

about   alrededor,
  aproximadamente
almost   casi
approximate   aproximado
approximately   aproximadamente
as much as   tanto como
at least   al menos
capacity   la capacidad, el
  volumen

it contains   contiene
cubic capacity   la capacidad
  cúbica
it decreases   disminuye
difference   la diferencia
empty   vacío
I empty   vacío
enough   bastante, suficiente
I fill   lleno
full (of)   lleno (de)
growth   el aumento
hardly   difícilmente, casi
increase   el aumento
it increases   aumenta
little   pequeño
  a little   un poco
a lot (of)   mucho (de)
I measure   mido
measuring tape   la cinta métrica,
  [el metro]
more   más
nearly   casi
number   el número
part   la parte
quantity   la cantidad
sufficient   suficiente
too much   demasiado
volume   el volumen
whole   la totalidad, el todo
  whole *(adj)*   todo

The shed will be at an angle of about forty degrees to the house, diagonally across from the gate.

El cobertizo estará a un ángulo de unos cuarenta grados con relación a la casa, en sentido diagonal con relación a la puerta.

The area of our garden is one hundred square meters / metres. It is ten meters / metres long and ten wide.

El área de nuestro jardín es cien metros cuadrados. Tiene diez metros de largo y diez metros de ancho.

We put in a round pond, only eighty to one hundred centimeters / centimetres deep.

Introdujimos un estanque redondo, de una profundidad de ochenta a cien centímetros.

HOW MUCH? — EXPRESSIONS OF QUANTITY

4b Measuring

Expressions of volume

bag   **el saco, la bolsa**
bar   **la barra**
bottle   **la botella**
box   **la caja**
container   **el recipiente, [el contáiner]**
cup   **la copa, la taza**
gallon   **el galón**
glass   **el vaso**
liter / litre   **el litro**
   centiliter / centilitre   **el centilitro**

milliliter / millimetre   **el mililitro**
pack   **el paquete, la cajetilla**
pair   **el par, la pareja**
piece   **la pieza**
   a piece of cake   **una porción de tarta**
pint   **la pinta**
portion   **la porción**
pot   **la olla**
sack   **el saco, [el costal]**
tube   **el tubo**

"How many centiliters / centilitres are there in the bottle?"
"Seventy-five, but you can also get it in liter / litre bottles."

— **¿Cuántos centílitros hay en la botella?**
— **Setenta y cinco, pero también se puede obtener en botellas de litro.**

"Would you like a cup of tea?"
"No, I would prefer a glass of water."

— **¿Desea una taza de té?**
— **No, preferiría un vaso de agua.**

May I have two packets of tissues and a packet of aspirin please?

Quisiera dos paquetes de pañuelos de papel y un paquete de aspirina, por favor.

"How much wood do you want?"
"Enough for the whole fence. I must not buy too much. Yes, that should be sufficient. Give me a bag of cement too."

— **¿Cuánta madera desea?**
— **Lo suficiente para toda la valla. No debería comprar demasiado. Sí, eso será suficiente. Deme también un saco de cemento.**

"How many cubic meters of concrete do you need?"
"About two."

— **¿Cuántos metros cúbicos de hormigón necesita?**
— **Dos, más o menos.**

Temperature

it boils	**hierve**
I chill	**enfrío**
cold	**el frío**
cold *(adj)*	**frío**
cool	**fresco**
I cool it down	**lo enfrío**
degree	**el grado**
I freeze	**congelo**
heat	**el calor**
I heat	**caliento**
hot	**caliente**
temperature	**la temperatura**
I warm it (up)	**lo caliento**
warmth	**el calor**

Weight and density

balance / scales	**el peso, la balanza**
dense	**denso**
density	**la densidad**
gram / gramme	**el gramo**
heavy	**pesado**
kilo	**el kilo**
light	**ligero**
mass	**la masa**
ounce	**la onza**
pound *(lb)*	**la libra**
ton(ne)	**la tonelada**
I weigh	**peso**
weight	**el peso**

It's so hot! What's the temperature? It must be nearly thirty centigrades. I am too hot.

¡Qué calor hace! ¿Cuál es la temperatura? Serán unos treinta centígrados. Tengo demasiado calor.

In winter it's cold here. We all freeze in this house and have to put on the heating in September.

En el invierno hace frío aquí. Todos pasamos frío en esta casa y tenemos que poner la calefacción en setiembre.

When the temperature reaches zero we have to light two fires.

Cuando la temperatura baja a cero grados, tenemos que encender dos fuegos.

"Would you weigh the ingredients?" "How many grams of sugar do we need?"
"I want a pound—that must be about five hundred grams / grammes. I need a little flour and a lot of sugar. Give me a piece of butter. About one hundred grams / grammes. I will need several eggs "

— ¿Podría pesar los ingredientes?
— ¿Cuántos gramos de azúcar necesitamos?
— Quiero una libra—que serán unos quinientos gramos. Necesito un poco de harina y mucho azúcar. Póngame un trozo de mantequilla. Unos cien gramos. Necesitaré unos huevos.

"That's too little. We need even more cakes. Make a bit more."

— No basta así. Vamos a necesitar más pasteles aun. Haz un poco más.

HOW MUCH? — EXPRESSIONS OF QUANTITY

4c Numbers

Cardinal numbers

zero	**cero**
one	**uno**
two	**dos**
three	**tres**
four	**cuatro**
five	**cinco**
six	**seis**
seven	**siete**
eight	**ocho**
nine	**nueve**
ten	**diez**
eleven	**once**
twelve	**doce**
thirteen	**trece**
fourteen	**catorce**
fifteen	**quince**
sixteen	**dieciséis**
seventeen	**diecisiete**
eighteen	**dieciocho**
nineteen	**diecinueve**

twenty	**veinte**
twenty-one	**veintiuno**
twenty-two	**veintidós**
twenty-nine	**veintinueve**
thirty	**treinta**
thirty-one	**treinta y uno**
forty	**cuarenta**
fifty	**cincuenta**
sixty	**sesenta**
seventy	**setenta**
eighty	**ochenta**
ninety	**noventa**
a hundred	**cien, ciento**
a hundred and one	**ciento uno**
two hundred	**doscientos**
a thousand	**mil**
two thousand	**dos mil**
million	**el millón**
two million	**dos millones**
billion	**el billón**
billion / milliard	**mil millones**

Half of the house belongs to my brother. We divided it between us. However, he only pays a quarter of the costs as I rent my half out in summer.

La mitad de la casa pertenece a mi hermano. La dividimos entre los dos. Sin embargo, sólo paga la cuarta parte de los gastos, pues yo dejo mi mitad en alquiler durante el verano.

"What is the volume of water in the swimming pool?"
"Ten thousand gallons, that is about forty-five thousand liters / litres."

— ¿ Cuánta agua hay en la piscina?
— Diez mil galones, es decir unos cuarenta y cinco mil litros.

Ordinal numbers

first	el primero
second	el segundo
third	el tercero
fourth	el cuarto
nineteenth	el décimonoveno
twentieth	el vigésimo
twenty-first	el vigésimo primero
hundredth	el centesimo

Nouns

one	el uno
unit	la unidad
a pair / couple of	un par (de)
ten	el diez
about ten (of)	una decena (de)
tens	las decenas
dozen	la docena
about twenty	una veintena (de)
hundred	el cien
hundreds of	cientos de
about a thousand	un millar
thousands (of)	millares / miles (de)
million	el millón
millions of	millones de

Writing numerals

1,000	1.000
1,500	1.500
1st	1°
2nd	2°
1.56	1,56 (uno coma cincuenta y seis)
.05	,05 (coma cero cinco)

Fractions

half	la mitad, el medio
a half	una mitad, un medio
one and a half	uno y medio
two and a half	dos y medio
quarter	el cuarto
a quarter	un cuarto
three quarters	tres cuartos
third	el tercio
fifth	el quinto
five and five sixths	cinco y cinco sextos
tenth	el décimo
sixth	el sexto
hundredth	el centésimo
thousandth	el milésimo
millionth	el millonésimo

"You cannot all have half a bar of chocolate.	—No todos podéis tener media tableta de chocolate.
There is only enough for a quarter each.	Sólo hay suficiente para una cuarta parte para cada uno.
And a quarter of a liter / litre of apple juice."	Y un cuarto de litro de zumo de manzana.
"I don't want a quarter, I want a half."	—No quiero una cuarta parte, quiero una mitad.

4d Calculations

addition **la suma, la adición**
I add **sumo, adiciono**
average **la media, el medio, el promedio**
I average out **saco la media**
on average **como media**
I calculate **calculo**
calculation **el cálculo**
calculator **la calculadora**
I correct **corrijo**
I count **cuento**
data **el dato, los datos**
piece of data **el dato**
decimal **el decimal**
decimal point **el punto decimal**
diameter **el diámetro**
digit **el dígito, la cifra**
two digit **de dos dígitos**
I double **multiplico por dos, doblo**
division **la división**

I divide by **divido entre / por**
six divided by two **seis dividido entre / por dos**
it equals **es igual a**
equation **la ecuación**
it is equivalent to **es equivalente a**
I estimate **estimo**
even **el par**
figure **la cifra**
graph **el gráfico**
is greater than **es mayor que**
is less than **es menor que**
maximum **el máximo**
maximum **máximo**
up to a maximum of **hasta un máximo de**
medium **la media**
medium *(adj)* **medio**
minimum **el mínimo**
minimum *(adj)* **mínimo**
minus **menos**

An inch is the same as 2.54 cm, and there are twelve inches in a foot, thirty-six in a yard. A mile is 1760 yards. A kilometer / kilometre is 1000 meters / metres.

Una pulgada equivale a 2,54 centímetros, y hay doce pulgadas en un pie, treinta y seis en una vara. Una milla tiene 1.760 varas. Un kilómetro tiene 1.000 metros.

What is fourteen plus eight? It equals twenty-two. Did you get the right result?

¿Cuántos son catorce más ocho? Son veinte y dos. ¿Obtuviste el resultado correcto?

Twenty minus five is fifteen, twenty divided by five equals four.

Veinte menos cinco son quince, veinte dividido por cinco son cuatro.

Work out twelve times twenty-two. That is an easy sum.

Calcula doce por veinte y dos. Es un cálculo fácil.

Two to the power of three is eight. Three squared equals nine.

Dos a la potencia de tres son ocho [dos al cubo son ocho]. Tres al cuadrado son nueve.

mistake / error **el error**
multiplication **la multiplicación**
  I multiply **multiplico**
  three times two **tres por dos**
negative **el negativo**
number **el número**
  cardinal / ordinal numbers **los números cardinales / ordinales**
numeral **el numeral**
odd **el impar**
percent **el por ciento**
  ten percent **el diez por ciento**
percentage **el porcentaje**
plus **más**
  two plus two **dos más dos**
positive **el positivo**
power **la potencia**
  to the power of five **a la quinta potencia**
problem **el problema**
quantity **la cantidad**
ratio **la proporción**
  a ratio of 100:1 **una proporción de cien a uno**

result **el resultado**
similar **similar**
solution **la solución**
  I solve **resuelvo**
square **el cuadrado**
square root **la raíz cuadrada**
  three squared **la raíz cúbica**
statistic **la estadística**
statistics **las estadísticas**
statistical **estadístico**
sum **la suma**
subtraction **la resta, la sustracción**
  I subtract **resto, sustraigo**
symbol **el símbolo**
I take away **resto**
total **el total**
  in total **en total**
I treble **triplico**
triple **el triple**
I work out **saco, calculo**
wrong **mal, equivocado**

"I estimate that we have about five hundred visitors a year."
"What percentage of visitors are local?"
"Twenty percent."

—**Calculo que recibimos a unos quinientos visitantes al año.**
— **¿Qué porcentaje de los visitantes son de esta misma región?**
—**Veinte por ciento.**

Have you got any statistics about it?

— **¿Tiene estadísticas sobre ello?**

A snail travels at an average speed of 0.041 kilometers / kilometres per hour.

Un caracol viaja a una velocidad de 0,041 kilómetros por hora.

"In this game you add up your score over the week."
"What was the total score?"
"I have a total of five hundred points."
To calculate the average you add up the totals and divide by the number of games.

—**En este juego, se hace la puntuación total de la semana.**
— **¿Cuál fue la puntuación final?**
—**Tengo un total de quinientos puntos.**
Para calcular el promedio, sumas los totales y lo divides por el número de juegos.

What Sort Of? — Descriptions & Judgments

5a Describing People

appearance **la apariencia**	fat **gordo**
attractive **atractivo**	feature **la facción, el rasgo**
average **medio**	female **la mujer**
he is bald **es calvo**	feminine **femenino**
beard **la barba**	figure **la figura, el tipo**
bearded **con barba**	fit **en forma**
beautiful **guapo, bello**	I frown **frunzo el ceño**
beauty **la belleza**	glasses **las gafas**
beauty mark **el lunar**	good-looking **guapo**
with beauty marks **con lunares**	I grow **crezco**
blond **rubio**	hair **el pelo, el cabello**
broad **ancho**	hairstyle **el peinado**
build **la constitución**	handsome **hermoso, bello,**
chic **chic, de moda**	**distinguido**
cleanshaven **afeitado**	heavy **pesado, grueso**
clumsy **torpe**	height **la altura**
complexion **la constitución**	large **grande**
curly **rizado, crespo**	I laugh **río, me río**
dark **oscuro, moreno**	laugh **la risa**
I describe **describo**	I am left-handed **soy zurdo**
description **la descripción**	light **claro**
different (from) **diferente de,**	I look like **soy, mi apariencia es**
distinto de	I look good **soy guapo**
elegant **elegante**	male **el varón, el hombre**
energy **la energía, el vigor**	masculine **masculino**
expression **la expresión**	mustache **el bigote**
farsighted / longsighted **présbite,**	nearsighted / shortsighted **miope**
hipermétrope	neat **limpio, acicalado, pulcro**

adolescence **la adolescencia**	older / elder **mayor**
adolescent **el / la adolescente**	teenager **el adolescente**
age **la edad**	young **joven**
elderly **viejo, mayor, anciano**	young person **el joven, la**
grown up **el adulto**	**persona joven**
grown up **adulto**	young people **los jóvenes**
middle-aged **de mediana edad**	youth **la juventud**
old **viejo, mayor**	youthful **lleno de juventud**

neatness la limpieza, el aseo
obese obeso
overweight el sobrepeso, el exceso de peso
part of body la parte del cuerpo
paunch la barriga, la panza
physical físico
pimple el grano
pimply con granos
plump rechoncho
pretty guapo, bonito
red-haired pelirrojo
I am right-handed soy diestro
I scowl pongo mal gesto, frunzo el ceño, hago mala cara
sex/gender el sexo, el género
short bajo, corto
similar (to) parecido a, similar a
similarity la similaridad
size el tamaño, la talla

slim/slender delgado, esbelto
small pequeño, bajo
I smile sonrío
smile la sonrisa
stocky rechoncho, bajo pero fuerte
strength la fuerza
striking impresionante, imponente
strong fuerte, robusto
tall alto
thin delgado, flaco
tiny pequeño
trendy moderno
ugliness la fealdad
ugly feo
walk el andar, el paso
wavy ondulado
I weigh peso
weight el peso

"What's your uncle like? Can you describe him?"
"He looks a lot like my father, but he wears glasses. Look, who's that tall fellow?"
"That's my brother, with the beard. He's mad about keeping fit."

"What a pretty girl! Is that your cousin?"
"Yes, she's blonde with blue eyes. She's very slim, with a good figure and a beautiful smile."
"Little Ben now has dark hair and is about one meter/metre tall.

He looks very well, but he's very thin."
"Yes, he only weighs sixteen kilos."

—¿Cómo es tu tío? ¿Puedes describirlo?
—Se parece mucho a mi padre, pero lleva gafas. Mira, ¿quién es ese tipo alto?
—Es mi hermano con la barba. Es muy aficionado a mantenerse en forma.

—¡Qué chica más bonita! ¿Es tu prima?
—Sí, es rubia con ojos azules. Es muy esbelta, con un buen físico y una sonrisa hermosa.
—Ahora el pequeño Ben tiene el pelo oscuro y mide aproximadamente un metro.
Tiene buena cara, pero es muy delgado.
—Sí, sólo pesa diez y seis kilos.

5b The Senses

bitter **amargo**
bright **claro, luminoso**
   bright *(harsh)* **brillante**
cold **el frío**
   cold **frío**
color / colour **el color**
colorful / colourful **lleno de color**
dark **oscuro**
darkness **la oscuridad**
delicious **delicioso**
disgusting **desagradable**
dull **apagado, sombrío**
I feel . . . **siento**
   it feels **es**
I hear **oigo**
hot **caliente**
light *(color / colour)* **claro, pálido**
I listen **oigo, escucho**
I look **miro, veo**
   I look at **miro**
loud **alto, ruidoso**
noise **el ruido**
noisy **ruidoso**
odor / odour **el olor**
opaque **opaco**
perfume **el perfume**
perfumed **perfumado**

quiet **quieto, tranquilo, callado**
rough **rugoso, áspero**
salty **salado**
I see **veo**
sense **el sentido**
silence **el silencio**
silent **silencioso**
   I am silent **estoy silencioso,**
   estoy en silencio
smell **el olor**
   I smell **huelo**
   it smells (of) **huele a**
   smelly **oloroso, apestoso**
soft *(sound)* **bajo, flojo, suave**
   soft *(texture)* **suave**
sound **el sonido**
it sounds **suena**
   it sounds like **suena como**
sour **agrio**
sticky **pegajoso**
   it is sticky **es pegajoso**
sweet **dulce**
taste **el sabor**
I taste **saboreo**
it tastes (of) **sabe a**
tepid **tibio**
I touch **toco**

"What color / colour is your new coat?"
"Well, it's sort of red."
"Dark or light red?"
"It is more maroon."

— ¿De qué color es tu abrigo nuevo?
— Bueno, es una especie de rojo.
— ¿Rojo oscuro o claro?
— Es más bien rojo oscuro.

The jam tastes of fruit but is very bitter.

La mermelada sabe a fruta, pero está muy amarga.

Don't touch that book, your hands are all sticky.

No toques ese libro, tienes las manos todas pegajosas.

transparent **transparente**
visible (in-) **(in)visible**
warm **caliente**
warmth **el calor**

Common parts of the body

arm **el brazo**
back **la espalda**
body **el cuerpo**
    part of the body **la parte del cuerpo**
chest **el pecho**
ear **la oreja**

eye **el ojo**
face **la cara**
hand **la mano**
head **la cabeza**
leg **la pierna**
mouth **la boca**
neck **el cuello**
neck (back of) **la nuca**
nose **la nariz**
shoulder **el hombro**
stomach **el estómago**
tooth **el diente**

Colors / Colours

beige **beige**
black **negro**
blue **azul**
brown **marrón, café**
brownish **amarronado**
cream **crema**
gold *(metal)* **el oro**
  gold *(adj)* **de oro, dorado**
green **verde**
gray / grey **gris**
maroon **rojo oscuro**
orange *(fruit)* **la naranja**

orange *(adj)* **anaranjado**
pink **rosa, rosado**
purple **purpúreo, [morado]**
red **rojo**
scarlet **escarlata** *(invar)*
silver *(metal)* **la plata**
  silver *(adj)* **plateado**
turquoise **la turquesa**
  turquoise *(adj)* **aturquesado**
violet **violeta** *(invar)*
white **blanco**
yellow **amarillo**

"What's in that bag? It feels hard."

"Let me feel—it's a bottle. What's in it?"
"I don't know. It looks like orange juice."
"I'll taste it ... It's disgusting. It tastes of oranges, but it's too sweet."

"What a beautiful smell."
"Yes, that's the flowers; they are so bright and colorful."

— ¿Qué hay en esta bolsa? Parece ser algo duro.

— Déjame palparlo—es una botella. ¿Qué tiene dentro?
— No sé. Se parece a zumo de naranja.
— Lo voy a probar ... Es asqueroso. Sabe a naranjas, pero es demasiado dulce.

— ¡Qué olor más agradable!
— Sí, son las flores; están tan llenas de colores vivos.

5c Describing Things

appearance **la apariencia**	dirt **la suciedad**
big **grande**	dirty **sucio**
broad **ancho**	dry **seco**
broken **roto**	empty **vacío**
clean **limpio**	enormous **enorme**
closed **cerrado**	fashionable **de moda**
color / colour **el color**	fat **gordo**
colored / coloured **de color**	firm **firme**
colorful / colourful **de muchos**	flat **plano**
colores	flexible **flexible, elástico**
damp **húmedo**	fresh **fresco**
deep **hondo, profundo**	full (of) **lleno (de)**
depth **la hondura, la**	genuine / real **genuino, auténtico**
profundidad	hard **duro**

Ten questions

What's that thingamajig? **¿Qué es ese chisme?, [¿Qué es esa cosa?]**

What's it for? **¿Para qué sirve?**

What do you use it for? **¿Para qué lo utilizas?**

Can you see it? **¿Lo ves?**

What's it like? **¿Cómo es?**

What does it look like? **¿A qué se parece?**

What does it sound like? **¿A qué suena?**

What does it smell of? **¿A qué huele?**

What color / colour is it? **¿De qué color es?**

What kind of thing is it? **¿Qué tipo de cosa es?**

"What's that over there?"
"That thing there? It's a new kind of bottle opener."
"Does it work?"
"Yes, indeed. It's the best there is."

This is a genuine natural material, soft and thick. That is a synthetic material, it's smooth, but the colors / colours are harsh.

— **¿Qué es aquello que está allí?**
— **¿Aquello allí? Es un nuevo tipo de abrebotellas.**
— **¿Funciona?**
— **Claro. Es el mejor que existe.**

Éste es un tejido genuinamente natural, blando y espeso. Aquel es un tejido sintético, es liso, pero los colores son chillones.

height **la altura**
it looks like **se parece a**
it matches **hace juego con**
kind **agradable**
large **grande**
liquid **líquido**
little **pequeño**
long **largo**
low **bajo**
main **principal, importante**
material **material**
matter **la materia**
moist **mojado, húmedo**
moldy / mouldy **mohoso, enmohecido**
narrow **estrecho**
natural **natural**
new **nuevo**
open **abierto**
out-of-date **pasado de moda**
painted **pintado**
pale **pálido, claro**
pattern **el diseño**
patterned **modelado**
plump **lleno, rechoncho**
resistant **resistente**
rotten **podrido**
shade **el tono, el matiz**

shallow **poco profundo**
shiny **brillante**
short **corto**
shut **cerrado**
small **pequeño**
smooth **liso**
soft *(texture)* **suave**
solid **sólido, compacto**
soluble **soluble**
sort **la clase, el tipo**
spot **el lunar, la mota**
spotted **a lunares, moteado**
stain **la mancha**
stained **manchado**
stripe **la raya**
striped **a rayas, rayado**
subsidiary **secundario**
substance **la substancia**
synthetic **sintético**
thick **espeso**
thing **la cosa, el objeto**
thingamajig **la cosa**
tint **el tinte**
varied **variado**
waterproof **a prueba de agua**
wet **mojado**
wide **ancho**

"I'm looking for something big to stand on." — **Busco algo grande en que subirme.**
"Will anything do?" — **¿Bastará cualquier cosa?**
"Well, it must be something solid." — **Bueno, tiene que ser algo sólido.**

"What about this?" — **¿Qué te parece esto?**
"Is there nothing bigger?" — **¿No hay nada más grande?**
"Stand on the chair." — **Levántate en la silla.**
"It's too soft." — **Es demasiado blanda.**
"All the other chairs are too low." — **Todas las demás sillas son demasiado bajas.**

"Both the cupboards are too high." — **Ambos armarios son demasiado altos.**

5d Evaluating Things

abnormal **anormal, raro**	I enjoy **disfruto**
I adore **adoro**	easy **fácil**
all right **muy bien, bueno**	essential (un-) **(no) esencial**
it is all right **está bien**	excellent **excelente**
appalling **espantoso, horroroso**	expensive **caro, costoso**
bad **malo**	I fail **fallo, fracaso**
beautiful **bonito**	failure **el fallo, el fracaso**
better / best **mejor, el mejor**	false **falso**
cheap **barato**	fine **bueno, fino, delicado**
correct **correcto**	good **bueno**
it costs **cuesta**	good value **buen precio**
delicious **delicioso**	great / terrific **magnífico,**
I detest **detesto**	**estupendo, tremendo**
difficulty **la dificultad**	I hate **odio, detesto**
difficult / hard **difícil, duro**	high **alto, bueno**
disgusting **repugnante,**	important (un-) **(no) importante**
asqueroso	incorrect **incorrecto**
I dislike **no me gusta**	interesting (un-) **(no) interesante**

a bit **un poco**	not at all **nada en absoluto**
enough **bastante, suficiente**	particularly **particularmente,**
extremely **extremadamente**	**especialmente**
fairly **bastante**	quite **bastante**
hardly ... at all **difícilmente**	rather **muy, bastante**
little **pequeño, poco**	really **realmente**
a little **un poco**	so **así, de esta manera**
a lot **mucho**	too (good) **demasiado (bueno)**
much (better) **mucho mejor**	very **muy**

How do you like our neighbor's / neighbour's garden / yard? We do not like it at all.	**¿Qué te parece el jardín de nuestro vecino? A nosotros no nos gusta nada.**
I wish he would throw away that broken seat.	**Me gustaría que tirara [botara] aquella silla rota.**
It is only plastic anyway. We always buy the best! Our garden furniture is made of wood.	**Sólo es de plástico. ¡Siempre compramos lo mejor! Nuestros muebles de jardín son de madera.**
And his lawn mower is out of order.	**Y su cortacésped no funciona.**

I like **me gusta**
mediocre **mediocre**
necessary (un-) **(in)necesario**
normal **normal, común**
order **el orden**
    in order **en orden**
    out of order **sin orden**
out-of-date **fuera de fecha,
    caducado**
ordinary **ordinario, normal,
    común**
pleasant **agradable**
poor **pobre**
practical (im-) **(no) práctico**
I prefer **prefiero**
quality **la calidad**
    top quality **la mejor calidad, la
    alta calidad**
    poor quality **la mala calidad, la
    baja calidad**

right **bueno**
strange **extraño, raro**
I succeed **consigo**
success **el éxito, la consecución**
successful **exitoso**
true **verdadero**
I try **intento, pruebo**
ugly **feo**
unpleasant **desagradable**
unsuccessful **sin éxito, fracasado**
I use **uso, utilizo**
use **el uso, la utilización**
useful **útil**
well **bien**
worse / worst **peor, el peor**
I would rather **prefiero, preferiría**
wrong **equivocado**

He never puts it away, and now
he'll have to get it fixed / mended.
I fear he's not a very successful
gardener. His vegetables are a
complete failure.

**Nunca la guarda, y ahora tendrá
que hacerla reparar.
Por desgracia no tiene mucho
éxito como jardinero. Sus
legumbres han fallado [se
perdieron] por completo.**

I do like to keep the garden / yard
tidy / neat.
People always say our garden /
yard is the best on the street.

**Me gusta mucho mantener el
jardín en buen estado.
La gente siempre dice que
nuestro jardín es el mejor de la
calle.**

I tried to call / ring you yesterday,
but the telephones were out of
order.

**Traté de llamarte ayer pero no
funcionaban los teléfonos.**

"Would you like to try this wine?"
"Thank you, it is quite delicious."

**— ¿Te gustaría probar este vino?
— Gracias, está muy delicioso.**

"Do you enjoy going to the
movies / cinema?"
"Yes, I particularly enjoyed last
week's movie / film."

— ¿Te gusta ir al cine?

**— Sí, me gustó sobre todo la
película de la semana pasada.**

5e Comparisons

Regular comparatives & superlatives*

easy **fácil**
   easier **más fácil**
   easiest **el más fácil**

Irregular comparatives and superlatives*

bad **malo**
   worse **peor**
   worst **el peor**

big **grande**
   bigger **mayor, más grande**
   biggest **el mayor, el más grande**
good **bueno**
   better **mejor**
   best **el mejor**
small **pequeño**
   smaller **menor, más pequeño**
   smallest **el menor, el más pequeño**

Look at the children! Peter, our eldest son, is now the tallest. He's best at soccer, too. That's what he enjoys best.

¡Mira a los niños! Pedro, nuestro hijo mayor, ya es el más alto. Es el que juega mejor al fútbol también. Es lo que a él le gusta más hacer.

John is now fairly large, almost as tall as Peter, and he really is too fat. He prefers to swim.

Juan ya es bastante grande, casi tan alto como Pedro, y la verdad es que es demasiado gordo. Prefiere nadar.

The smallish boy over there is David. He is quite small compared to the others, but on the other hand very confident. He behaves less well than his brother.

El chico pequeño que está allá es David. Es bastante pequeño en comparación con los demás, pero por otra parte está muy seguro de sí mismo. Se comporta menos bien que su hermano.

John has eaten the largest cake. He gets larger and larger.

Juan ha comido el pastel más grande. Se pone cada vez más grande.

 ▶ For further details see Berlitz *Spanish Grammar Handbook* 22d

5f Materials

acrylic el acrílico
brick el ladrillo
cashmere la cachemira, el
  cachemir
cement el cemento
china la porcelana
concrete el hormigón
cotton el algodón
Dacron / Terylene el dacrón,
  el terilene
denim el dril, la tela vaquera
gas el gas
glass el vidrio, el cristal
gold el oro
iron el hierro
leather la piel, el cuero
linen el lino, el lienzo, [el hilo]
metal el metal
mineral el mineral
nylon el nilón, el nailon

oil el aceite, el petróleo
paper el papel
plastic el plástico
polyester el poliéster
pottery la cerámica
satin el raso
silk la seda
  silky sedoso
silver la plata
steel el acero
  steel (adj) de acero, acerado
stone la piedra
  stone (adj) de piedra
velvet el terciopelo
viscose la viscosa
wood la madera
wooden de madera
wool la lana
  woolen / woollen de lana

Have you seen our latest products? They are just as cheap as the competition.

¿Ha visto usted nuestros últimos productos? Son tan baratos como los de la competencia.

We cannot ask a higher price, as the greatest demand is for the cheaper product.

No podemos pedir un precio más alto, pues la demanda más grande es la del producto más barato.

Which dress would you like? Silk is softer than wool, but it costs a lot. Nylon is cheapest.

¿Qué vestido preferirías? La seda es más suave que la lana, pero cuesta mucho dinero. El nilón es el más barato.

The most beautiful dress is the one made of cotton.
The colors / colours are brighter and I think the cut is better, although it is not as warm as the woolen / woollen dress.
It is not at all expensive. I prefer it to the others.

El vestido más bello es el que está hecho de algodón.
Los colores son más vivos y creo que el corte es mejor, aunque no es tan abrigado como el vestido de lana.
No es caro de ninguna manera.
Lo prefiero a los demás.

The Human Mind & Character

6a Human Character

active **activo**
I adapt **me adapto**
amusing **divertido**
I annoy **molesto, importuno**
bad **malo**
bad-tempered **de mal temperamento / genio**
I behave **me comporto, me porto**
behavior / behaviour **la conducta, el comportamiento**
I boast **presumo, fanfarroneo**
calm **tranquilo, calmado**
care **el cuidado**
careful **cuidadoso**
careless **descuidado**
character **el carácter**
characteristic **la característica**
  characteristic *(adj)* **característico**
charming **encantador, atractivo**
cheerful **alegre**
clever **listo, despierto**
confident **seguro de sí mismo**
discipline **la disciplina, el orden**
dreadful **terrible, espantoso, horrible**

evil **el mal**
  evil *(adj)* **maligno**
foolish **tonto**
forgetful **olvidadizo**
friendly (un-) **(poco) amistoso**
fussy **quisquilloso, exigente**
generous **generoso**
I get on with **me llevo bien con, [me entiendo con]**
gifted **con talento, dotado**
good **bueno**
good-tempered **amistoso, afable**
habit **la costumbre, el hábito**
hard-working **trabajador, laborioso**
I help **ayudo**
helpful **atento, servicial**
honest (dis-) **(des)honesto**
humor / humour **el humor, el estado de ánimo**
humorous **humorístico**
immorality **la inmoralidad**
innocent **inocente**
intelligence **la inteligencia**
intelligent **inteligente**
kind (un-) **(poco) amable**

Don't be so suspicious. Please trust me.	**No seas tan desconfiado. Por favor, fíate de mí [confía en mí].**
Our neighbor / neighbour is a lazy fellow, but very gifted. He has a good sense of humor but is very pretentious.	**Nuestro vecino es un tipo perezoso, pero tiene mucho talento. Tiene un buen sentido de humor, pero es muy presumido.**
His wife is very pleasant and helpful.	**Su esposa es muy simpática y amable.**
The children are lively characters. They never obey their mother.	**Los niños son muy enérgicos. Nunca le obedecen a su madre.**

kindness **la amabilidad**
lazy **perezoso, holgazán**
laziness **la pereza, la holgazanería**
lively **animado, alegre, vivo**
mad **loco**
manners **los modales, las maneras**
mental(ly) **mental(mente)**
moral (im-) **(in)moral**
morality **la moralidad**
nervous **nervioso, agitado**
nice **agradable, bonito**
I obey (dis-) **(des)obedezco**
optimistic **optimista**
patient (im-) **(im)paciente**
personality **la personalidad**
pessimistic **pesimista**
pleasant **agradable, placentero**
polite (im-) **(mal) educado, (des)cortés**
popular **popular**
quality **la calidad**
reasonable (un-) **(ir)razonable**
respect **el respeto**
I respect **respeto**
rude **grosero, descortés**
sad **triste**
self-confident **seguro de sí mismo**
self-esteem **la autoestima**
sense **el sentido**
  common sense **el sentido común**
  good sense **el buen sentido**

sensible **sensato, prudente**
serious **serio, formal**
shy **tímido, retraído**
skill **la habilidad**
skillful **habilidoso**
sociable (un-) **(in)sociable**
strange **extraño, raro**
stupid **tonto, estúpido**
stupidity **la estupidez**
suspicious **suspicaz, desconfiado**
sympathetic **comprensivo, compasivo**
sympathy **la simpatía, la solidaridad, la comprensión**
tactful **discreto, con tacto**
tactless **indiscreto, sin tacto**
talented **con talento, dotado**
temperament **el temperamento, el carácter**
temperamental **temperamental, con mucho temperamento**
I trust **confío, me fío de**
trusting **confiado**
warm **cálido, efusivo**
well-known **conocido, sabido**
wise **prudente, cauteloso**
wit **el ingenio, la agudeza mental**
witty **ingenioso, agudo, ocurrente**

The pupils here are hardworking and well-behaved.
We encourage self-confidence and discipline.
Bad behavior/behaviour and laziness are punished.

Los alumnos de aquí son muy trabajadores y formales.
Fomentamos la confianza en sí mismo y la disciplina.
Castigamos a los que se comportan mal y a los perezosos.

Mr. B is a serious person, but rather pessimistic.

El señor B es un hombre muy serio, pero bastante pesimista.

THE HUMAN MIND & CHARACTER

6b Feelings & Emotions

I am afraid (of) **tengo miedo (de)**
I am amazed **estoy asombrado**
amazement **el asombro, la sorpresa, la estupefacción**
I amuse **divierto, entretengo**
  I am amused by **me divierte, me hace gracia**
amusement **la diversión**
anger **la furia, la ira, la cólera**
angry **enfadado, furioso**
I am annoyed (at / about) **estoy molesto (por / con)**
anxiety **la ansiedad**
anxious **ansioso**
I approve (of) **apruebo, tengo buen concepto (de)**
I am ashamed (of) **estoy avergonzado (de)**
I am bored **estoy aburrido**
boredom **el aburrimiento**
content (with) **contento (con), satisfecho (de)**
cross (with) **enfadado (con)**
delighted (about) **encantado (con)**
I dislike **no me gusta**

dissatisfaction **el descontento, la insatisfacción**
dissatisfied (with) **descontento (con), insatisfecho (de)**
embarrassed (about) **desconcertado (con), avergonzado (por)**
embarrassment **el desconcierto, la turbación, la vergüenza**
emotion **la emoción**
emotional(ly) **emocional(mente)**
I enjoy **disfruto**
envy **la envidia**
envious (of) **envidioso (de)**
fear **el miedo**
I feel **siento**
I forgive **perdono**
forgiveness **el perdón**
I am frightened (of) **estoy asustado (de), tengo miedo (a)**
furious (about) **furioso (acerca de)**
fussy **quisquilloso, exigente**
grateful (to) **agradecido (a)**
gratitude **la gratitud**
guilty **culpable**

I like our neighbor / neighbour a lot but worry about his wife. She cares for her old mother, who has not adapted to life in the city. She is often in a bad temper and very fussy.

Me gusta mucho nuestro vecino, pero me preocupa su esposa. Cuida a su madre anciana quien no se ha adaptado a la vida de la ciudad. Muchas veces tiene [está de mal] genio y es muy quisquillosa.

"I am really ashamed of my behavior / behaviour yesterday. I was so upset and worried."
"It really doesn't matter. I am thankful that you feel better."

—De verdad estoy avergonzado de mi comportamiento de ayer. Quedé tan trastornado y preocupado.
—La verdad es que no importa. Estoy agradecido de que te sientas mejor.

happiness la alegría, la felicidad
happy (about) contento (con)
hate el odio
I hate odio, detesto
I have a grudge against him le tengo rencor, le tengo inquina
hope la esperanza
I hope espero
hopeful optimista, esperanzado
idealism el idealismo
indifference la indiferencia
indifferent (to) indiferente (a)
   I am indifferent (to) soy indiferente (a)
interest el interés
I am interested (in) me interesa, estoy interesado (en)
jealous celoso
jealousy los celos
joy la alegría, el júbilo, el gozo
joyful alegre, jubiloso
I like me gusta
   I would like quisiera
love el amor
I love amo
miserable (about) triste (por)
misery el sufrimiento, la tristeza, la aflicción

mood el humor, el estado de ánimo
in a good / bad mood de buen / mal humor
I'm pleased / glad that estoy contento / satisfecho que
I prefer prefiero
I regret me arrepiento de, lamento
satisfaction la satisfacción
satisfied (with) satisfecho (de)
surprise la sorpresa
I am surprised (at) estoy sorprendido (de)
thankful agradecido
unhappy infeliz, desdichado
unhappiness la infelicidad, la desdicha
upset (about) desconcertado, perturbado, molesto (por)
I wonder (at) me pregunto
   I wonder if me pregunto si
worried (about) preocupado (por)
worry la preocupación
I worry (about) me preocupo (por)
   it worries me me preocupa

I am so glad you are not angry with me.

Me alegro / Me alegra tanto que no estés enfadado conmigo.

We are very fond of our uncle. He has many good qualities. However, he is often somewhat temperamental. He hates it when we thank him. It makes him embarrassed.

Le tenemos mucho cariño a nuestro tío. Tiene muchas buenas cualidades. Sin embargo, a menudo es algo caprichoso. Lo odia cuando le expresamos nuestra gratitud. Le hace sentirse desconcertado.

The boss is in a bad mood. He is cross with his secretary. She is bored with the work and indifferent to his annoyance.

El jefe está de mal humor. Está enfadado con su secretaria. A ella le aburre su trabajo, y no le importa nada el enojo de él.

THE HUMAN MIND & CHARACTER

against **en contra de**
   I am against it **estoy en contra de ello**
I analyze **analizo, estudio**
analysis **el análisis, el estudio**
I assume **asumo, me hago cargo de**
assuming that . . . **asumiendo que, suponiendo que**
attention **la atención**
aware of (un-) **enterado de, (in)consciente de**
I base **baso**
basic **básico**
basically **básicamente**
basis **la base**
belief **la creencia**
I believe **creo, pienso**
   I believe in **creo en**
certainty **la seguridad, la certeza**
certain, sure **cierto, seguro**
coherent (in-) **(in)coherente**
complex **el complejo**
   inferiority complex **el complejo de inferioridad**
I comprehend **entiendo**
comprehensible **comprensible**
I concentrate **concentro**
   I concentrate on **me concentro en**
I conclude (that) **concluyo (que)**
conscience **la conciencia**
with a clear conscience **con la conciencia limpia**
I consider . . . (to be) **considero**
consideration **la consideración**
   I take into consideration **tengo en consideración / cuenta, tomo en consideración**
   taking everything into consideration **considerándolo todo**
I contemplate **pienso**
context **el contexto**

on the contrary **por el contrario**
controversial **controvertido, conflictivo**
I decide **decido**
decision **la decisión**
I deduce **deduzco que**
I delude myself **me engaño**
delusion **el engaño, la ilusión**
I determine **determino**
I disbelieve **no creo**
I distinguish **distingo**
doubt **la duda**
I doubt **dudo**
doubtful **dudoso**
doubtless / without a doubt **sin duda**
exception **la excepción**
evidence **la evidencia**
evidently **evidentemente**
fact **el hecho**
   in fact **de hecho**
false **falso**
fantasy **la fantasía**
fiction **la ficción**
for **por, para**
   I am for it **estoy por ello, [estoy a favor de ello]**
I forbid **prohibo**
I forget **olvido, no me acuerdo de**
genius (for) **el genio (para)**
I grasp **comprendo**
hypothesis **la hipótesis**
I imagine **imagino**
imagination **la imaginación**
implication **la implicación**
interesting **interesante**
I invent **invento**
invention **el invento, la invención**
issue **el asunto, la materia**
I judge **juzgo**
judgment **el juicio**
justice **la justicia**
I justify **justifico**
I know **sé, conozco**

knowledge el conocimiento, el saber
logic la lógica
logical lógico
I go mad me vuelvo loco
madness la locura
meaning el sentido
it means quiere decir
I meditate (on) medito
memory la memoria
metaphysics la metafísica
mind la mente, la inteligencia
 a great mind el sabio
I misunderstand no entiendo
misunderstanding el malentendido
motive el motivo
philosophy la filosofía
point of view el punto de vista
I ponder reflexiono, medito
premise la premisa
I presume presumo, supongo
principle el principio
 in/on principle en principio
problem el problema
proof la prueba
I prove pruebo
psychology la psicología
psychoanalysis el psicoanálisis
rational (ir-) (thinking) (ir)racional, (i)lógico
reality la realidad
I realize me doy cuenta
I reason razono
 I reason (conclude) concluyo

reason (faculty) la razón
I recognize reconozco
I reflect reflexiono
relevant pertinente, conexo, relacionado
I remember me acuerdo
right correcto, verdadero
 I am right tengo razón
 it is right es verdad, está bien
I see veo
I solve resuelvo
solution la solución
I speculate especulo
subconscious el subconsciente
I suppose supongo
theoretical teórico
theory la teoría
 in theory en teoría
I think pienso, creo
thought el pensamiento
true verdadero
truth la verdad
I understand entiendo, comprendo
understanding el entendimiento, la comprensión
valid (in-) (in)válido
view la opinión
 in my view en mi opinión
wrong equivocado
 I am wrong estoy equivocado
 it is wrong está equivocado

He is partly right about the reasons for our difficulties, but there is probably much more behind it.

Even if he is right, there is virtually nothing we can do about it.

En parte tiene razón cuando se refiere a las causas de nuestras dificultades, pero habrá otras razones que no son tan obvias. Aun si tiene razón, no hay casi nada que podamos hacer para remediarlo.

THE HUMAN MIND & CHARACTER

6d Expressing Views

I accept **acepto**
I agree (with / about) **estoy de acuerdo (con / sobre)**
I answer **contesto, respondo**
answer **la respuesta**
I argue **arguyo, discuto**
argument **el argumento, la discusión**
I ask *(a question)* **pregunto**
I contradict **contradigo**
I criticize **critico**
I define **defino**
definition **la definición**
I deny **niego**
I describe **describo**
description **la descripción**
I disagree (with / about) **no estoy de acuerdo (con / sobre)**
I discuss **discuto**
discussion **la discusión**
I maintain **mantengo, [sostengo]**
I mean **quiero decir**
opinion **la opinión**

in my opinion **en mi opinión, a mi modo de ver**
question **la cuestión, el caso**
a thorny question **una cuestión espinosa**
it is a question of **es una cuestión de**
I question **me cuestiono**
I say **digo**
I state **afirmo**
statement **la afirmación**
suggestion **la sugerencia**
I suggest **sugiero**
I summarize **resumo**
summary **el sumario, el resumen**
I think (of / about) **pienso (en)**
thought **el pensamiento**

Giving examples

as is known **como es sabido**
etc. / and so on **y así sucesivamente**
example **el ejemplo**

"In my opinion, he did not consider the basic problem. I would have liked to ask more questions."
"In principle, I agree with his views. On the one hand he proved the need for new housing. On the other hand he discussed the problems of finding a site."

"I suggest we try to analyze the problem carefully. Then we shall be able to judge the situation and come to a sound conclusion."

— En mi opinión no consideró el problema básico. Querría haber preguntado algo más.
— En principio estoy de acuerdo con sus opiniones. Por una parte, ha demostrado la necesidad de construir casas nuevas. Por otra parte habló de los problemas de encontrar un solar [lote] apropiado.
— Sugiero que tratemos de analizar el problema con cuidado. Luego podremos juzgar la situación y llegar a una conclusión razonable.

➤ COMMENTS & INTERJECTIONS 15b; COMPARISONS 5e

for example **por ejemplo**
i.e. **a saber**
namely **es decir**
I quote **cito**
such as **como**

Comparing and contrasting

advantage **la ventaja**
I compare **comparo**
comparison **la comparación**
  in comparison with **en comparación con**
it contrasts with **contrasta con**
contrast **el contraste**
  in contrast **en contraste**
I differ **difiero**
difference **la diferencia**
different (from) **diferente de, distinto de**
disadvantage **la desventaja**
dissimilar **distinto**
I distinguish **distingo**
pros and cons **los pros y los contras**
relatively **relativamente**

same **el mismo**
similar **similar, igual**

Expressing reservations

even if **aun cuando**
even so **aun así**
to some extent **en alguna medida**
at first sight **a primera vista**
hardly **con dificultad, difícilmente**
in general **en general**
in the main **en general, en su mayoría**
in part / partly **en parte**
perhaps **quizás**
presumably **posiblemente**
probably **probablemente**
relatively **relativamente**
reservation **la reserva, [la reservación]**
unfortunately **desafortunadamente**
virtually **virtualmente**
in a way **de algún modo**

beginning **el principio, el comienzo**
from the beginning **desde el principio, desde el comienzo**
I am brief **soy breve, soy lacónico**
  in brief **en resumen**
I conclude **concluyo**
conclusion **la conclusión**
  in conclusion **en conclusión**
final **final**
finally **finalmente**
first **el primer, el primero**
in the first place **en primer lugar**
furthermore **más aun**
on the one hand **por una parte, de una parte**

on the other hand **por otra parte**
initially **inicialmente**
last **el último**
lastly **útimamente**
  at last **por fin**
next **el próximo**
place **lugar**
  in the first place **en primer lugar**
  in the second place **en segundo lugar**
secondly **en segundo lugar**
in short **en breve, próximamente**
I sum up **resumo**

THE HUMAN MIND & CHARACTER

Arguing a point

admittedly **se reconoce que, es verdad que, [se sabe que]**

all the same **de cualquier manera**

although **aunque**

anyway **de todas formas, de cualquier modo**

apart from **aparte de**

as for **en cuanto a, en lo que concierne a, en lo que se refiere a**

as I see it **como yo lo veo**

as well **también**

despite this **a pesar de esto**

in effect **en efecto**

however **sin embargo**

incidentally **incidentalmente**

instead **en cambio**

instead of **en vez de, en lugar de**

just as important **tan importante**

likewise **asimismo, además**

no matter whether **sin que importe que**

that may be so **puede ser así**

nevertheless **sin embargo, no obstante**

otherwise **de otra manera**

in reality **en realidad**

in many respects **en muchos respectos**

in return **en cambio**

as a rule **como regla (general)**

so to speak **para decirlo así**

in spite of **a pesar de**

still . . . **aun así**

to tell the truth **para decir la verdad, [para ser franco]**

whereas **mientras, visto que**

on the whole **en general, por regla general**

Cause & effect

all the more (because) **tanto más (porque)**

as **como**

because **porque**

cause **la causa**

consequence **la consecuencia**

consequently **consecuentemente, por consecuencia**

effect **el efecto**

it follows that **se deduce que**

how? **¿cómo?**

if **si**

"How did he break his leg?"
"When he went to get the ladder, he did not notice that it was broken. So he fell off it."
"Why did he want the ladder?"

"Because he wanted to paint the house."

"What are the reasons for his behavior / behaviour?"
"Maybe he is cross with me and that is why he went away."

— ¿Cómo se rompió la pierna?
— Al ir a buscar la escalera, no se fijó en que estaba rota. Por lo tanto se cayó de ella.
— ¿Por qué necesitaba la escalera?

— Porque quería pintar la casa.

— ¿Cuáles son las causas de su comportamiento?
— A lo mejor está enfadado conmigo y por eso se fue.

reason **la razón**
   for this reason **por esta razón**
result **el resultado, la**
   consecuencia
   as a result **como resultado**
provided that **suponiendo que**
since **desde que, en vista de que**
so long as **con tal que**
therefore, so **por lo tanto**
thus **de este modo, así es que**
whether **si**
why? **¿por qué?**

Emphasizing

above all **sobre todo**
in addition **además**
all the more **tanto más**
also **también**
certainly **desde luego, por**
   supuesto, naturalmente
clearly **claramente**
under no circumstances **bajo**
   ninguna circunstancia
completely **completamente**
especially **especialmente**
even (more) **aun**
without exception **sin excepción**

I emphasize **enfatizo**
extremely **extremadamente**
far and away **con mucho**
fortunately **afortunadamente**
honestly **honestamente,**
   honradamente
just when **sólo cuando**
mainly **principalmente**
moreover **más aun**
naturally **naturalmente**
not at all **para nada, de ninguna**
   manera
not in the least **en lo más mínimo**
both . . . and **tanto ... como**
obviously **obviamente**
in particular **en particular**
particularly **particularmente**
in every respect **en todos los**
   respectos
I stress **acentúo**
thanks to **gracias a**
undeniably **innegablemente**
very **muy**
and what is more **y lo que es más**

Honestly I'm extremely angry with him. Thanks to his carelessness we missed the plane.

De verdad, estoy muy enfadada con él. Gracias a su descuido perdimos el avión.

Fortunately, there was another, but we got to Chicago completely exhausted.

Afortunadamente hubo otro, pero llegamos completamente agotados a Chicago.

And what is more, he clearly didn't care at all.

Y lo que es más, no le preocupaba a él de ninguna manera.

Obviously, I shall tell his firm exactly what I think of him. Under no circumstances will I employ him again.

Claro que informaré a su compañía lo que pienso de él. No lo emplearé otra vez bajo ninguna circunstancia.

7 Human Life & Relationships

7a Family & Friends

Friendship

acquaintance **el conocido**
boyfriend **el amigo, el novio**
buddy / mate **el compañero, el camarada, [el compinche]**
classmate **el compañero de clase**
companion **el compañero**
friend (close) **el íntimo**
friend **el amigo**
friendship **la amistad**
gang **la pandilla, la cuadrilla**
we get on well together **nos llevamos bien**
we get together **nos reunimos**
I get to know **llego a conocer ..., concozco**
girlfriend **la amiga, la novia**
I introduce **presento a ...**
pal / chum **el compañero, el compinche**
pen pal / penfriend **el amigo por correspondencia**
relationship **la relación**
schoolfriend / pal **el amigo de clase**

The family and relatives

adopted **adoptivo**
ancestor **el antepasado**
aunt **la tía**
baby **el bebé, el nene, la nena, [el / la guagua]**
brother **el hermano**
brother-in-law **el cuñado, el hermano político**
brothers and sisters **los hermanos**
children **los niños, los hijos**
close relative **el pariente cercano**
common-law husband **el marido en una unión consensual**
common-law wife **la mujer en una unión consensual**
cousin **el primo**
dad **el papá, el papaíto, [el papito]**
daughter **la hija**
daughter-in-law **la nuera, la hija política**
distant relative **el pariente lejano**
elder **mayor**
family **la familia**
family tree **el árbol genealógico**

We are good friends. We get on well together. We do a lot together.	**Somos buenos amigos. Nos llevamos bien. Hacemos muchas cosas juntos.**
We are more open with one another. We settle conflicts.	**Somos más sinceros el uno con el otro. Resolvemos los conflictos.**

father   el padre
father-in-law   el suegro, el padre político
fiancé(e)   el novio, (la novia), el prometido, (la prometida)
forebear   el antepasado
foster *(adj)*   adoptivo
foster mother   la madre adoptiva
genealogy   la genealogía
godchild / son   el ahijado
goddaughter   la ahijada
godfather   el padrino
godmother   la madrina
grandad / pa   el abuelito
grandchildren   los nietos
granddaughter   la nieta
grandfather   el abuelo
grandma / granny   la abuelita
grandmother   la abuela
grandparents   los abuelos
grandson   el nieto
great-aunt   la tía abuela
great grandchild   el bisnieto
great-grandfather   el bisabuelo
great-grandmother   la bisabuela
great-nephew   el sobrinonieto
great-niece   la sobrinanieta
great-uncle   el tío abuelo
guardian   el tutor, la tutora
half-brother   el medio hermano
half-sister   la media hermana
husband   el marido

mom / mum   la mamá
mother   la madre
mother-in-law   la suegra, la madre política
nephew   el sobrino
niece   la sobrina
only (child)   (el hijo) único
parents   los padres
partner   el cónyuge, la pareja, el compañero
related   emparentado
relation   el pariente
relationship   el parentesco, la parentela, el trato, la relación
relative   el pariente
second cousin   el primo segundo
sister   la hermana
son   el hijo
son-in-law   el yerno, el hijo político
spouse   el cónyuge
stepbrother   el hermanastro
stepdaughter   la hijastra
stepfather   el padrastro
stepmother   la madrastra
stepsister   la hermanastra
stepson   el hijastro
twin brother   el (hermano) gemelo
twin sister   la (hermana) gemela
uncle   el tío
wife   la mujer, la esposa
younger   menor

I come from a large family. We just don't get on well.	**Vengo de una familia grande. Es que no nos llevamos bien.**
There are family problems.	**Hay problemas familiares.**
It runs in the family.	**Viene de familia.**
She's very difficult to get along with. I fell out with her.	**Es muy difícil llevarse bien con ella. Me reñí con ella.**

➤ LOVE, MARRIAGE, CHILDREN 7b; GROWING UP, DEATH 7c

HUMAN LIFE & RELATIONSHIPS

7b Love & Children

Love & marriage

affair   la aventura amorosa, el amorío
bachelor   el soltero
best man   el padrino de boda
betrothal   el noviazgo, los desposorios
betrothed   prometido
bride   la novia
bridegroom   el novio
bridesmaid   la dama de honor
couple   la pareja
   married couple   el matrimonio
I court   cortejo, hago la corte a ...
courtship   el cortejo, el noviazgo
divorce   el divorcio
divorced   divorciado
divorcé(e)   el divorciado, la divorciada
engaged   prometido
engagement   el compromiso, el noviazgo
I fall for   me enamoro de
I fall in love (with)   me enamoro (de)
I get divorced (from)   me divorcio (de)

I get engaged (to)   me prometo, [me compremeto] (con)
I get married (to)   me caso (con)
I go out with   salgo con
honeymoon   la luna de miel
lover   el amante, la amante, el querido, la querida
marriage / matrimony   el matrimonio
married   casado
I marry   me caso con
mistress   la querida, la amante
newly married couple   los recién casados
I separate from   me separo de
separated   separado
separation   la separación
I have sex (with)   tengo relaciones sexuales (con)
unmarried   soltero
unmarried mother   la madre soltera
wedding   la boda, las bodas, el casamiento
widow   la viuda
widower   el viudo

We are madly in love. It was love at first sight.	**Estamos enamorados perdidamente. Fue un flechazo [Fue amor a primera vista].**
Are you married?	**¿Estás casado?**
She doesn't understand me. She is always nagging.	**No me entiende. Siempre me importuna con sus quejas.**
We have nothing to say to each other.	**Ya no tenemos nada que decirnos.**
Our relationship is breaking up.	**Nuestras relaciones se están rompiendo.**

Birth & children

abortion   **el aborto**
I have an abortion   **me hago un aborto**
I adopt   **adopto**
adoption   **la adopción**
au pair   **la chica au pair, [la niñera]**
baby   **el bebé, el nene / la nena, [el / la guagua]**
baby food   **la comida para niños**
babysitter   **el canguro, la niñera**
baptism   **el bautizo, el bautismo**
bib   **el babero, el babador**
birth   **el nacimiento, el parto**
birthrate   **(la tasa de)** natalidad
birthday   **el cumpleaños**
I was born   **nací**
boy   **el niño, el muchacho, el chico, el joven, el mozo, el chaval, el zagal**
I breast feed   **crío a los pechos, amamanto, doy el pecho**
I bring up a child   **crío / educo a un niño**
caesarian section   **la operación cesárea**
child, children   **el niño, los niños**
childhood   **la niñez, la infancia**
christening   **el bautizo, el bautismo**
condom   **el condón**
contraception   **la contracepción, [la anticoncepción]**
contraction   **la contracción**
crib   **la cuna**
I deliver (a baby)   **asisto en el nacimiento, parto**
I am expecting a baby   **estoy encinta / embarazada**
feeding bottle   **el biberón**
fertile (in-)   **(in)fecundo (estéril)**

fertility   **la fecundidad**
fetus   **el feto**
I foster   **crío**
fostering   **el acogimiento familiar**
I get pregnant   **quedo embarazada**
I give birth   **doy a luz**
girl   **la niña, la muchacha, la chica, la joven, la moza, la chavala, la zagala**
incubator   **la incubadora**
infancy   **la infancia**
infant   **el niño, la criatura**
infantile   **infantil**
I am in labor   **estoy de parto**
live birth   **el nacimiento vivo**
I have a miscarriage   **malparo, aborto**
nanny   **la niñera**
diaper   **el pañal**
newborn child   **el (bebé) recién nacido**
orphan   **el huérfano**
pacifier   **el chupete**
period   **el período, la regla**
pill   **la píldora**
pregnant   **encinta, embarazada**
saint's day   **el santo, el día del santo, la fiesta del santo**
sibling   **el hermano, la hermana**
stillbirth   **el nacimiento de un niño muerto**
stillborn   **nacido muerto, mortinato**
stroller / perambulator   **el cochecito de niño**
I take after   **salgo a, me parezco a**
toddler   **el pequeñito (que da sus primeros pasos)**
triplets   **los trillizos**
twin   **gemelo**

7c Life & Death

Growing up

adolescent **adolescente**
adult **el adulto, el mayor**
   adult *(adj)* **adulto, mayor**
age **la edad**
aged **viejo, anciano**
centenarian **el centenario**
he comes from **es de**
I come of age **llego a la mayoría de edad**
elderly **de edad, mayor, anciano, viejo**
eldest **el / la mayor**
female **la hembra**
   female *(adj)* **femenina**
foreigner **el extranjero**
generation **la generación**
generation gap **la barrera generacional**
life **la vida**
life insurance **el seguro de vida**
I look my age **represento los años que tengo**
male **el macho, el varón**
   male *(adj)* **masculino, macho**
man **el hombre**
manhood **la virilidad, la masculinidad**

manly **varonil, viril, masculino**
mature **maduro**
maturity **la madurez**
menopause **la menopausia**
middle age **de mediana edad**
name **el nombre**
nickname **el apodo, el mote**
octogenarian **el octogenario**
old **viejo, anciano**
old age **la vejez**
old man, woman **el viejo, la vieja, el anciano, la anciana**
old age home **el asilo de ancianos**
pension **la pensión**
pensioner **el jubilado, la jubilada, el pensionado, la pensionada, el / la pensionista**
people **la gente**
permissive society **la sociedad permisiva**
person **la persona**
present **el regalo**
I prosper **prospero**
responsible **responsable**
retired **jubilado**
single **soltero**
spinster **la soltera**

He respects his elders.	**Respeta a sus mayores.**
I learn from my own experience.	**Aprendo por mi propia experiencia.**
"How old are you?"	**—¿Cuántos años tienes?**
"I'm twenty-five."	**—Tengo veinte y cinco años.**

stranger   el forastero
surname   el apellido
underage   menor de edad
woman   la mujer
womanhood   la feminidad
young   joven
young person   el / la joven
younger   más joven
youngest   el / la más joven
youth   la juventud
youth *(persons)*   el / la joven

Death

afterlife   la vida futura
angel   el ángel
ashes   las cenizas
autopsy   la autopsia, [la necropsia]
body   el cadáver
burial   el entierro
I bury   entierro
cemetery / graveyard   el cementerio
corpse   el cadáver
he is cremated   es incinerado
cremation   la incineración, la cremación
crematorium / crematory   el horno crematorio
dead   muerto
death   la muerte

death certificate   la partida de defunción
he dies   muere
epitaph   el epitafio
eulogy   el elogio, el encomio
funeral   el entierro, los funerales
he goes to heaven   sube al cielo
grave   la sepultura
heaven   el cielo
hell   el infierno
I inherit   heredo
inheritance   la herencia
last rites   las exequias
he lies in state   está expuesto en capilla ardiente
mortuary   el depósito de cadáveres
I mourn   estoy de luto
mourning   la lamentación, el luto
I am in mourning for   llevo luto por
neonatal death rate   la (tasa de) mortalidad neonatal
obituary   la necrología
he passes away   fallece
remains   los restos
tomb   la tumba
tombstone / gravestone   la lápida
undertaker   el director de pompas fúnebres
will   el testamento

The baby was born in the early hours of the morning but died an hour later.

El nene nació por la madrugada pero murió una hora después.

Daily Life

8a The House

---

amenities **las comodidades, las conveniencias**

apartment / flat **el piso, el apartamento**

apartment house / block of flats **el bloque de pisos, [el edificio de apartamentos]**

(of) brick **de ladrillo**

I build **construyo**

building **el edificio**

building plot **el solar (para construcción), [el lote]**

building site **el solar (para construcción), la obra**

bungalow **el chalet, el bungalow**

caretaker **el conserje, el portero, el vigilante**

chalet **el chalet, el chalé**

detached house **la casa independiente, el chalet**

furnished apartment / flat **el piso / apartamento amueblado**

furnished house **la casa amueblada**

freehold **propiedad absoluta**

I have an extension built **hago construir un ensanche**

garbage / refuse collection **la recolección de basuras**

house **la casa**

housing **la vivienda**

landlord **el propietario, el dueño**

lease / leasehold **el arrendamiento**

leased / leasehold property **el inmueble arrendado**

lodger / roomer **el huésped**

I modernize **modernizo**

mortgage **la hipoteca**

mortgage rate **el tipo de interés hipotecario**

I move (house) **me mudo (de casa)**

I occupy **ocupo**

I own **poseo**

owner-occupied apartment / flat **el piso / apartamento ocupado por el propietario**

The whole house needs painting before we sell it. We are buying a new detached house.	**Tenemos que pintar la casa entera antes de venderla. Compramos un nuevo chalet.**
We are having a house built.	**Hacemos construir una casa.**
I live in a rented, furnished apartment.	**Vivo en un apartamento amueblado, alquilado.**
Her penthouse is for rent.	**Su ático está disponible para alquilar.**

owner-occupied house **la casa ocupada por el propietario**

penthouse **el ático, la casa de azotea**

partly furnished **amueblado en parte**

prefabricated house **la casa prefabricada**

premises **el local, la propiedad**

public housing **el piso de protección oficial, la casa protegida, [el apartamento estatal]**

rent **el alquiler, el arriendo**

I rent **alquilo**

semi-detached house **la casa semi-separada**

sewage disposal **la depuración de aguas residuales**

(of) stone **de piedra**

street light **el farol**

I take out a mortgage **obtengo una hipoteca**

tenancy **el inquilinato, la ocupación**

tenant **el inquilino, el arrendatario**

unfurnished **sin muebles**

unfurnished apartment / flat **el piso / apartamento desamueblado**

Rooms

attic **el ático, el desván, la buhardilla**

basement **el sótano**

backdoor **la puerta trasera**

bathroom / lavatory **el cuarto de baño, el retrete, el lavabo, el inodoro, el excusado, [el baño]**

bedroom **el dormitorio**

breakfast room **la habitación del desayuno**

cellar **el sótano, la bodega**

corridor **el pasillo, el corredor**

dining room **el comedor**

hall(way) **el hall, el vestíbulo, el pasillo**

landing **el descanso, el rellano**

kitchen **la cocina**

living room / sitting-room **el cuarto de estar, el living, el salón**

loft **el desván**

lounge **el cuarto de estar, el living, el salón**

restroom / W.C. **el retrete, el lavabo, el inodoro, el excusado, [el baño]**

shower **la ducha**

study **el despacho, el estudio**

utility room **la trascocina**

veranda **la veranda, la terraza, la galería**

My tenancy has two weeks to run. | **Quedan dos semanas de mi arrendamiento.**

We moved two years ago. | **Mudamos de casa hace dos años.**

The house has a fairly pleasant view: it grows on you after a while. | **La casa tiene un panorama bastante agradable: después de un rato le gusta a uno cada vez más.**

▶ DAILY ROUTINE 8d

8b The Household

aerial **la antena**
backdoor **la puerta trasera**
balcony **el balcón**
baseboard **el rodapié, la cenefa**
blind **la persiana**
boiler **la caldera, el calentador**
burglar alarm **la alarma antirrobo**
carpet **la moqueta, la alfombra**
ceiling **el techo**
chimney / smokestack **la chimenea**
central heating **la calefacción**
clean **limpio**
comfortable **cómodo**
cozy **cómodo, acogedor**
curtain **la cortina**
desk **el escritorio, la mesa de trabajo**
dirty **sucio**
door **la puerta**
doorhandle **el tirador (de puerta), el puño, [el porno]**
doorknob **el tirador (de puerta), el pomo (de puerta)**
doormat **el felpudo, la estera, la alfombrilla, [el tapete]**
downstairs **abajo, en el piso de abajo**
electric **eléctrico**
electric plug **el enchufe,**
electric socket **el enchufe, la toma (de electricidad), el toma-corriente**

electricity **la electricidad, la luz**
elevator / lift **el ascensor**
extension cord **el cable, el cordón (de la luz)**
fire alarm **la alarma de incendio**
fire extinguisher **el extintor de incendio**
fireplace **el hogar, la chimenea**
floor **el suelo**
floor (story / storey) **el piso, la planta**
frontdoor **la puerta principal, la puerta de entrada**
furnished **amueblado**
furniture **los muebles**
item of furniture **el mueble**
garage **el garaje, la cochera**
gas **el gas**
glass (material) **el vidrio, el cristal**
ground floor **la planta baja, [el primer piso]**
handle **el puño**
(on jug, etc.) **el asa** (f), **el asidero**
(drawer, etc.) **el tirador, la manija**
hearth **el hogar, la chimenea**
included **incluido**
key **la llave**
keyhole **el ojo de la cerradura**
lamp **la lámpara**
lampshade **la pantalla de lámpara**
letterbox **el buzón**

The bed has not been changed. | **La cama no ha sido cambiada.**

I have just bought a compact disc player. | **Acabo de comprar un reproductor de discos compactos.**

lever   **la palanca**
light   **la luz**
lightbulb   **la bombilla**
lightswitch   **el interruptor, el conmutor**
lock   **la cerradura**
it looks onto   **da a**
mantelpiece   **el manto (de chimenea), la repisa de chimenea**
mat   **la estera, la esterilla**
mezzanine floor   **el entresuelo**
modern   **moderno**
new   **nuevo**
nice   **bonito, ameno**
off *(switches, electrical appliance)*   **desconectado, desenchufado, apagado**
off *(tap)*   **cerrado**
old   **viejo**
on *(switches, electrical appliance)*   **conectado, enchufado, encendido, puesto**
on *(tap)*   **abierto**
on the first floor   **en el primer piso**
own   **propio**
passage   **el pasillo**
radiator   **el radiador**
rent   **el alquiler, el arriendo**
roof   **el tejado, el techo**
room   **la habitación, el cuarto**
shelf   **el estante, la tabla, el anaquel, [la repisa]**
shutter   **la contraventana**

situation   **la situación, el emplazamiento**
skylight   **el tragaluz, la claraboya**
small   **pequeño**
spacious   **espacioso, amplio**
staircase   **la escalera**
stairs   **la escalera**
step   **el peldaño, el escalón, la grada**
terrace   **la terraza**
tile *(floor)*   **la baldosa**
roof tile   **la teja**
toilet   **el retrete, el inodoro, el lavabo, el wáter, el excusado, [el baño]**
trashcan / dustbin   **el cubo de basura, [el balde], [la caneca]**
upper floor   **el piso superior, el piso de arriba**
upstairs   **arriba**
view   **la vista, el panorama**
wall   **el muro**
inside wall   **la pared**
partition wall   **el tabique**
garden wall   **la tapia**
wastepaper basket / litter bin   **la papelera**
water   **el agua** *(f)*
window   **la ventana**
windowsill   **el alféizar, el antepecho**
wire   **el alambre**
wiring   **el alambrado**
with bath   **con baño adjunto**
wood   **la madera**

The washing machine doesn't work! Can you repair it?	**¡La lavadora no funciona! ¿Puede usted repararla?**
Come into the dining room.	**Pase al comedor.**

8c Furnishings

Lounge

armchair **la butaca, la silla**
ashtray **el cenicero**
bookcase **la librería, el estante**
bookshelf **el estante, la estantería**
bureau **el escritorio**
closet / cupboard **el armario**
coffee table **la mesita baja**
cushion **el cojín**
easy chair **la butaca, la silla**
ornament **el adorno, el ornamento**
picture **el cuadro, la pintura**
 picture *(portrait)* **el retrato**
photo **la foto**
poster **el cartel, el póster**
rocking chair **la mecedora**
rug **el tapete, la alfombrilla**
sofa / settee **el sofá**

Kitchen

bottle opener **el abrebotellas**
bowl **el plato, el tazón**
clothesline **la cuerda de tendedero, la tendedera**
clothespin **la pinza**
coffee machine **la máquina de café, la cafetera**
coffeepot **la cafetera**
colander **el colador, el escurridor**
crockery **la vajilla, los platos**
cup **la taza**
cupboard **el armario**
 wall cupboard **la alacena**
cutlery **los cubiertos, la cuchillería**
deepfreeze **el (ultra)congelador**
dish **el plato**
dishcloth **el trapo de fregar, el paño de cocina, el limpión**
dishwashing detergent **el detergente líquido, el lavavajillas**
draining board **el escurreplatos, la escurridera, el escurridor**

faucet / tap **el grifo, [la llave]**
fork **el tenedor**
frying pan **la sartén**
garbage can / rubbish bin **el cubo [la caneca] de la basura, el basurero**
glass **el vaso, la copa, la copita**
knife **el cuchillo**
oven **el horno**
plate **el plato**
saucepan **la cacerola, el cazo**
saucer **el platillo**
scouring pad **el estropajo**
sink **el fregadero, la pila**
sink unit **el lavadero, el fregadero**
spoon **la cuchara**
stove / gas cooker **la cocina / estufa de gas**
teapot **la tetera**
tea towel **el paño de cocina, [el trapo de cocina]**
tray **la bandeja**
washing powder **el jabón en polvo**

Dining room

candle **la vela**
candlestick **el candelero**
chair **la silla**
chandeliers **la araña, el candelero**
dresser **el aparador, la rinconera**
serviette **la servilleta**
sideboard **el aparador**
table **la mesa**
tablecloth **el mantel**
table mat **el salvaplatos, el salvamanteles**
table napkin **la servilleta**

Bedroom

alarm clock **el despertador**
bed **la cama**

bunk bed   la litera, la cama camarote
double bed   la cama doble
bedclothes   la ropa de cama
bedding   la ropa de cama
bedside table   la mesa de noche
bedspread   el sobrecama, el cobertor, el cubrecama
blanket   la manta, la cobija
chest of drawers   la cómoda
dressing table   el tocador
duvet   el edredón, la colcha
mattress   el colchón
pillow   la almohada
quilt   la colcha, el edredón
sheet   la sábana
wardrobe   el guardarropa, el armario (ropero)

Bathroom

bath   el baño, la bañera
bathmat   la estera de baño
bidet   el bidet, el bidé
clothes brush   el cepillo de la ropa
faucet / tap   el grifo, [la llave]
flannel   la manopla, el paño
laundry basket   el cesto de la ropa sucia
mirror   el espejo
nailbrush   el cepillo para las uñas
plug   el tapón
scales   la balanza
shampoo   el champú
shower   la ducha
sink   el lavabo
soap   el jabón
toilet   el retrete, el inodoro, el lavabo, el excusado, el wáter
toilet paper   el papel higiénico
toothbrush   el cepillo de dientes
toothpaste   la pasta dentífrica
towel   la toalla
towel rail   el toallero
washbasin   el lavabo, la jofaína, la palangana, [el lavamanos]

*Electrical goods

cassette player   el casete, el cassette, el tocacintas
cassette recorder   la grabadora de cassette
clothes dryer   la secadora
compact disc player   el reproductor de discos compactos
dishwasher   el lavaplatos, el lavavajillas
electric appliance   el (aparato) electrodoméstico
electric stove   la cocina / estufa eléctrica
electric razor / shaver   la afeitadora (eléctrica), la rasuradora
freezer   el (ultra)congelador, [la congeladora]
hi-fi   el equipo de hi-fi / de alta fidelidad, [el equipo de sonido]
iron   la plancha, el planchador
microwave oven   el horno de microonda, el microondas
mixer   la batidora, la mezcladora, la licuadora
record player   el tocadiscos
refrigerator / fridge   la nevera, el frigo, [la refrigeradora]
sink   el lavabo, [el lavamanos]
spin dryer   el secador centrífugo
stereo system   el estéreo, [el equipo de sonido]
tape player   el casete
tape recorder   la grabadora
trouser press   la prensa para pantalones
TV set   el televisor
television (TV)   la televisión
vacuum cleaner   la aspiradora
video recorder   la videograbadora
walkman®   el Walkman®
washing machine   la lavadora

TOILETRIES 9b; PLANTS 24c; VEGETABLES & FRUIT 10c; TOOLS App. 8b

8d Daily Routine

bath **el baño, [la tina]**
bed **la cama**
breakfast **el desayuno**
clean **limpio**
daily routine **la rutina diaria**
dinner **la cena**
dressed **vestido**
evening meal **la cena**
garbage / rubbish **la basura, los desperdicios** *(pl)*, **los desechos** *(pl)*
home **la casa, el hogar**
  at home **en casa**
housework **los quehaceres domésticos** *(pl)*
lunch **el almuerzo, la comida**
maid / housekeeper **la criada**
school **la escuela**
shop **la tienda**
shower **la ducha**
sleep **el sueño**
spare time **el tiempo libre, las horas libres**
supper **la cena**
tea **el té, la merienda**
time *(commodity)* **el tiempo**
  time (of day) **la hora**
undressed **desnudo, desvestido**
vacuum cleaner **la aspiradora**
washing **el lavado, el lavar**
  dirty washing **ropa sucia, ropa por lavar**

washing *(hung to dry)* **el tendido, la colada**
dishwashing / washing up *(act)* **el fregado, el fregar, [el lavado de platos]**
  dishes *(to be washed)* **los platos para lavar**
work **el trabajo**

Actions

I bathe **me baño**
I break **rompo**
I bring **traigo**
I build **construyo**
I buy **compro**
I carry **llevo**
I change (clothes) **me cambio (de ropa)**
I chat **charlo**
I clean **limpio**
I clear away **quito (los platos, la mesa)**
I clear the table **quito la mesa**
I cook **cocino**
I close **cierro**
I darn **zurzo**
I dig **cavo, cultivo**
I do **hago**
I drink **bebo**
I drop **dejo caer**
I dry up **seco (los platos)**
I dust **quito (el polvo), limpio**
I eat **como**

We usually get up at seven o'clock and have breakfast at eight.

Solemos levantarnos a las siete y desayunamos a las ocho.

Who is going to wash the dishes?

¿Quién va a lavar los platos?

I'll do the drying.

Voy a secar los platos.

Sweep up that mess right now!

¡Barre ese revoltijo ahora mismo!

I empty **vacío**
I fasten **abrocho**
I fill **lleno**
I get dressed **me visto**
I get undressed **me desnudo**
I get up **me levanto**
I go to bed **me acuesto**
I go to sleep **me duermo**
I go to the toilet **voy al lavabo / baño / wáter**
I take a bath **tomo un baño**
I have breakfast **desayuno**
I have lunch **como, almuerzo**
I have a snack / tea **meriendo**
I heat **caliento**
I hire / rent **alquilo**
I hire / rent out **alquilo**
I iron / press **plancho**
I knit **hago punto, [tejo]**
I set the table **pongo la mesa**
I let *(allow)* **dejo**
I live **vivo**
I lock **cierro con llave**
I make **hago**
I polish **limpio, saco brillo a ...**
I prepare **preparo**
I press *(button)* **aprieto, pulso**
I put on *(clothes)* **me pongo**
   I put on *(radio, TV)* **pongo, conecto, enchufo, enciendo**
I rest **descanso**
I call *(telephone)* **llamo por teléfono**
I ring *(doorbell)* **toco el timbre**
I scrub **friego**

I sew **coso**
I shine **saco brillo a, limpio**
I shop **hago las compras**
I shower **me ducho**
I sit down **me siento**
I sit **me siento, me quedo sentado, estoy sentado**
I sleep **duermo**
I speak **hablo**
I stand **estoy de pie**
I stand up **me levanto**
I start **empiezo, comienzo**
I stop **(me) paro**
I sweep **barro**
I take off *(clothes)* **me quito**
I take **cojo**
I throw away **tiro, echo, [boto]**
I tidy / straighten up **arreglo, pongo en orden, limpio**
I tie **ato, lío**
I trim **arreglo, ajusto**
I turn / switch off **apago, desenchufo, desconecto**
I turn / switch on **pongo, enchufo, enciendo**
I unblock **desatasco**
I use **utilizo, uso**
I wake up **me despierto**
I wallpaper **empapelo**
I wash the dishes **lavo los platos**
I wash **(me) lavo**
I watch TV **veo la televisión**
I water **riego**
I wear **llevo**

The table has not been cleared! **¡Aún no se ha quitado la mesa!**

She does the dusting and cleaning for us on Fridays. **Los viernes quita el polvo y hace la limpieza en nuestra casa.**

My husband cooks on Saturdays. Dinner will be at nine p.m. **Mi marido cocina los sábados. La cena será a las nueve.**

Shopping

9a General Terms

article **el artículo**
assistant **el dependiente, la dependienta**
automatic door **la puerta automática**
bargain **la ganga, el artículo de ocasión**
business **el comercio, la empresa**
cash register / desk **la caja registradora**
cash machine **la caja electrónica**
change *(money)* **la moneda suelta, el suelto, el vuelto**
cheap **barato**
checkout **la caja**
choice **la elección, la selección**
closed / day off **cerrado (por vacaciones)**
coin **la moneda**
contents **el contenido**
costly **costoso, caro**
credit **el crédito**
credit card **la tarjeta de crédito**
customer information **el servicio de información para clientes**
customer service **el servicio de asistencia posventa**
dear **caro, costoso**

department **el departamento, la sección**
discount **la rebaja**
elevator / lift **el ascensor**
entrance **la entrada**
escalator **la escalera mecánica**
exit **la salida**
expensive **caro, costoso**
fashion **la moda**
fire door **la puerta contra / de incendios**
fire exit **la salida de incendios**
fitting room **el probador, el vestidor**
free **gratis**
free gift **el regalo (gratuito)**
it is good value **bien vale lo que pagué**
handbag **el bolso, la bolsa, [la cartera]**
instructions for use **el modo de empleo**
item **el artículo**
mail order **las ventas por correo**
manager **el director / gerente, la directora / gerente**
market **el mercado**
money **el dinero**

Expressions you hear

Anything else? / Is that all?	**¿ Algo más / Es todo?**
Can I help you?	**¿ En qué puedo servirle?**
Do you want anything in particular?	**¿ Desea algo en concreto?**
What would you like?	**¿ Qué desea usted?**
Who's next?	**¿ Quién sigue?**
Whole or sliced?	**¿ Entero o en trozos?**

bill *(money)* el billete
open abierto
opening hours las horas de abrir
packet el paquete
pocket el bolsillo
pound *(weight)* la libra
PULL tira, tire, hale
purse el monedero
PUSH empuja, empuje
quality la calidad
real / genuine verdadero, genuino, auténtico
receipt el recibo
reduction la reducción
refund el reembolso, la devolución
sale las rebajas, la liquidación, el saldo, [la promoción]
salesperson / shop-assistant el dependiente, el vendedor
security guard / store detective el guarda jurado
self-service autoservicio
shopkeeper el tendero / la tendera
shoplifter la mechera, el ratero de tiendas
shopping las compras
  I go shopping voy de compras
shopping basket la cesta de compras
shopping cart el carrito de la compra
shopping list la lista de compras
shut cerrado
slice el trozo, la tajada
special offer la oferta especial

stairs la escalera
summer sale las rebajas de(l) verano, [la promoción]
trader el comerciante, el traficante, el vendedor
traveler's check / cheque el cheque de viaje / de viajero
wallet la cartera, [la billetera]
way in la entrada
way out la salida

Actions

I change cambio
I choose escojo, elijo
I decide decido
I exchange cambio
I have on / wear llevo, [me pongo]
I line / queue up hago cola
I order pido, encargo
I pay pago
I put on me pongo
I select elijo, selecciono, escojo
I sell vendo
I serve sirvo
I shop hago las compras
I shoplift hurto / robo en tiendas
I show (de)muestro, enseño
I spend *(money)* gasto
I steal robo
I take off me quito
I try on (me) pruebo, [me mido]
I wait espero
I wear llevo, me pongo
I weigh peso
I wrap up envuelvo

Is there a dairy around here?	¿Hay una lechería por aquí?
Where is the nearest bakery?	¿Dónde está la panadería más cercana?
Can I pay by check / cheque?	¿Puedo pagar por cheque?

9b Household Goods & Toiletries

Toiletries

after-shave **la loción para después del afeitado**
antiperspirant **el antiperspirante**
blusher **el colorete**
brush **el cepillo**
comb **el peine, la peinilla**
condom **el condón, el preservativo**
cotton **el algodón, el hidrófilo**
deodorant **el desodorante**
dental floss **el hilo de higiene dental**
eyeliner **el lápiz de ojos**
face cream **la crema de belleza**
glasses **las gafas**
hairbrush **el cepillo para el pelo**
lipstick **la barra de labios, el lápiz labial**
makeup **el maquillaje, los cosméticos**
nailfile **la lima para las uñas**
paper handkerchief **el pañuelo de papel**
perfume **el perfume**
razor **la afeitadora, la maquinilla de afeitar**
razor blade **la hoja de afeitar, la cuchilla de afeitar**
rouge **el colorete**
sanitary napkin **el paño higiénico, la compresa (higiénica), [la toalla higiénica]**
shampoo **el champú**
soap **el jabón**
spray **el aerosol, el atomizador**
sunglasses **las gafas de sol**
suntan lotion **el bronceador**
talcum powder **(los polvos de) talco**
tampon **el tampón, el tapón**
tissues **los pañuelos de papel**

toilet water **el agua *(f)* de colonia, la colonia**
toilet paper **el papel higiénico**
toothbrush **el cepillo de dientes**
toothpaste **la crema dental, la pasta dentífrica**
tweezers **las pinzas**

Household items

bottle **la botella**
bowl **la fuente, la escudilla, el tazón**
cleanser **el jabón en polvo**
clothespin **la pinza**
cup **la taza**
dish **el plato, la fuente**
dishwashing / washing-up liquid **el detergente líquido, el lavavajillas**
foil / aluminum foil **el aluminio doméstico, el papel de aluminio**
fork **el tenedor**
glass **el vaso**
jar **el tarro, el pote, el frasco, la jarra, el bote**
jug **el jarro, la jarra**
kitchen roll **el rollo de cocina**
knife **el cuchillo**
matches **los fósforos, las cerillas**
paper napkin / serviette **la servilleta de papel**
paper towel **la toallita de papel**
plastic wrap **el plástico para envolver**
plate **el plato**
pot **la olla, la cacerola, la cazuela, el cazo**
saucer **el platillo**
scouring pad **el estropajo**
spoon **la cuchara**
string **la cuerda, el cordel**

Basic foodstuffs

bacon **el tocino, el bacón**
beans **las habas, las judías**
beef **la carne de vaca**
beer **la cerveza**
biscuits **las galletas, los bizcochos**
bread **el pan**
butter **la mantequilla**
cakes **los pasteles**
carrots **las zanahorias**
cereals **los cereales**
chocolate spread **la pasta de chocolate**
cola **la cola**
coffee **el café**
custard **las natillas, la crema instantánea (en polvos)**
fish **el pescado**
fruit **la fruta**
ham **el jamón**
jam **la confitura, la mermelada**
juice **el zumo, el jugo**
lemonade **la limonada, la gaseosa**
loaf **el pan, la barra de pan**
macaroni **los macarrones**
margarine **la margarina**
marmalade **la mermelada**
mayonnaise **la mayonesa**
meat **la carne**

milk **la leche**
mustard **la mostaza**
oil **el aceite**
olive oil **el aceite de oliva**
pasta **las pastas alimenticias**
pâté **el pâté, el pastel (de carne)**
peanut butter **la mantequilla de cacahuete, [la mantequilla de maní]**
peas **los guisantes, [las arvejas]**
pepper **la pimienta**
peppers **los pimientos**
pork **el cerdo, la carne de cerdo**
potatoes **las patatas, [las papas]**
pudding **el púding, el pudín**
salt **la sal**
sardines **las sardinas**
sauce **la salsa**
sausage **la salchicha, el embutido**
soup **la sopa**
spaghetti **los espaguetis, los fideos**
sugar **el azúcar**
tea **el té**
tea bag **la bolsita de té**
tortilla **la tortilla**
vegetables **las legumbres, las verduras, los vegetales**
vinegar **el vinagre**
wine **el vino**

Expressions of quantity

a bar of . . . **una pastilla de ...**
a bottle of . . . **una botella de ...**
a box of . . . **una caja de ...**
a hundred gram(me)s of . . . **cien gramos de ...**
a kilo of . . . **un kilo de ...**
a liter / litre of . . . **un litro de ...**

a packet of . . . **un paquete de ...**
a slice of . . . **un trozo de ..., una tajada de ...**
a can / tin of . . . **una lata de ...**
half a pound of . . . **media libra de ...**

9c Clothing

artificial **artificial**
beautiful **hermoso**
belt **el cinturón**
big **grande**
bikini **el bikini**
blouse **la blusa**
boot **la bota**
bra **el sostén**
brand new **flamante, completamente nuevo**
cagoule **el canguro, el chubasquero**
cap **el gorro, la gorra**
cardigan **la rebeca, el cardigán**
checked **a cuadros**
clothes **la ropa, los vestidos**
clothing **la ropa, los vestidos**
coat **el abrigo, [el saco]**
colorfast / colourfast **no desteñible**
colorful / colourful **vivo, animado**
corduroy **la pana**

cravat **la corbata de fantasía, el fular, el foulard**
dress **el vestido**
elegant **elegante**
embroidered **bordado, recamado**
fashionable **de moda**
glove **el guante**
handkerchief **el pañuelo**
hat **el sombrero**
high-heeled **de tacones altos**
in the latest fashion **de última moda**
jacket **la chaqueta, la americana**
jeans **el(los) vaquero(s), el(los) tejano(s)**
jersey **el jersey, el suéter**
jewelry / jewellery **las joyas, las alhajas**
jumper **el jersey, suéter**
knitted **de punto, [tejido]**
knitwear **los géneros de punto**
ladies' wear **la ropa de señora**
lingerie **la lencería**

Expressions in clothes shops / stores

Can I try it on? **¿Puedo probarlo?**
Do you have the same in red? **¿Tiene usted uno / a parecido / a en rojo?**
I like it. **Me gusta.**
I take / wear size *(clothes)* **Llevo el ..., [Me llevo una talla ...]**
I take / wear size *(shoes)* **Calzo el ...**
I would like a ... **Quiero un / una ...**
I would like to change ... **Quisiera cambiar ...**
I would rather have ... **Preferiría ...**
I'll take it. **Me lo / la llevo.**
I'll take the big one. **Me llevo el / la grande.**

I'd like it two sizes bigger. **Lo quisiera dos números más grande.**
I'm next. **Me toca a mí.**
It suits me. **Me va bien. Me sienta bien.**
That's not quite right. **No es del todo correcto. / Eso no está del todo bien.**
They don't go together. **No armonizan., No hacen juego.**
What color / colour? **¿De qué color?**
What's it made of? **¿De qué está hecho?**
Will it shrink? **¿[Se] encogerá?**

long **largo**
long-sleeved **con mangas largas**
loose **suelto**
loud / brash **chillón, charro, cursi**
low-heeled **de tacones bajos**
man-made fiber / fibre **las fibras sintéticas**
matching **acompañado, a tono, que hace juego con**
men's wear **la ropa de caballero**
no-iron **de no planchar, que no necesita planchado**
pair **el par**
pajamas **el pijama, la pijama**
panties **las bragas, la braga, las braguitas, [los pantys]**
pants **los pantalones**
parka / anorak **el anorak / anorac, el chubasquero**
plain **sencillo, llano, sin adornos**
printed **impreso, estampado**
pure **puro**
raincoat **el impermeable, la gabardina**
sandal **la sandalia, la alpargata**
scarf **la bufanda**
shirt **la camisa**
shoe **el zapato**
shoelace **el lazo, el cordón**
short-sleeved **de mangas cortas**
size **el tamaño, la talla, el número**
skirt **la falda**
slip **las enaguas, la combinación**
small **pequeño**
smart **elegante, pulcro**
sneakers **los zapatos de lona / deportivos, las zapatillas**
sock **el calcetín, [la media]**
soft **blando**
stocking **la media**
striped **listado, rayado, a rayas**
suit **el traje**
sweater **el suéter, el jersey**
sweatshirt **la sudadera**
swimming trunks **el bañador, [el traje de baño]**

swimsuit / bathing suit **el traje de baño, el bañador**
synthetic **sintético**
tie **la corbata**
tight **estrecho, apretado, ajustado, ceñido**
tights **el panti, las medias**
too big / small **demasiado grande / pequeño**
toweling **la felpa**
training shoes **las zapatillas de deporte**
trousers **el pantalón, los pantalones**
T-shirt **la camiseta, el niki, [la playera], [la remera]**
ugly **feo**
umbrella **el paraguas**
underpants **los calzoncillos**
undershirt **la camiseta**
underwear **la ropa interior**
unfashionable **fuera de moda, pasado de moda**
velvet **el terciopelo**
vest / waistcoat **el chaleco**

Alterations & repairs

I alter **arreglo**
buckle **la hebilla**
button **el botón**
heel **el tacón**
hem **el dobladillo**
hole **el roto**
I knit **tricoto**
knitting needle **la aguja de hacer calceta**
material **el tejido**
patch **el remiendo**
pin **el alfiler**
pocket **el bolsillo, [la bolsa]**
I repair / mend **remiendo, [zurzo]**
I sew **coso**
stain **la mancha**
tailor **el sastre**
tailored **hecho por sastre**
thread **el hilo**
zipper **la cremallera**

Food & Drink

10a Drinks & Meals

Drinks

alcoholic **alcohólico**
aperitif **el aperitivo**
beer **la cerveza**
brandy **el brandy, el coñac**
champagne **el champán**
chocolate (drinking) **el chocolate (para beber)**
cider **la sidra**
cocktail **el cóctel**
coffee **el café**
cola **la cola**
draught beer **la cerveza al grifo**
drink **la bebida**
dry **seco**
juice (fruit) **el zumo / [el jugo] (de fruta)**
lemonade **la limonada**
low alcohol **de baja graduación de alcohol**
orange / lemon crush **la naranjada / la limonada**
milk **la leche**
milk shake **el batido, [la malteada]**
mineral water **el agua** *(f)* **mineral**
nonalcoholic **sin alcohol**
sherry **el vino de jerez, el jerez**

sparkling **espumoso**
spirits **los licores, las bebidas alcohólicas**
sweet **dulce**
tea **el té**
water **el agua**
noncarbonated / still water **el agua sin gas**
with ice **con hielo**
whisky **el whisky**
wine **el vino**

Drinking out

bar **el bar**
bartender **el barman**
beer hall **la cervecería**
bottle **la botella**
café **el café**
coffee shop / bar **la cafetería**
cellar **la bodega**
counter / bar **la barra**
cup **la taza, la copa**
I drink **bebo**
glass **el vaso**
refreshments **los refrescos**
sip **el sorbo**
straw **la pajita**
tavern / pub **el pub, la taberna**

---

cafeteria **la cafetería**
canteen **la cantina**
stall **el puesto**
ice cream parlor / parlour **la heladería**
pizza parlor / parlour **la pizzería**
restaurant **el restaurante**

self-service **el autoservicio**
snack bar **el bar de aperitivos, el snack-bar**
take out / take-away **para llevar**
take out / take-away restaurant **el restaurante con comida para llevar**

---

teaspoon **la cucharita**
wine cellar **la bodega**
wineglass **el vaso de vino**
wine tasting **el catamiento de vino**

Meals

appetizer / starter **el entremés, la entrada**
breakfast **el desayuno**
course **el plato**
dessert **el postre**
I dine **ceno**
dinner **la cena**
I eat **como**
I have a snack **tomo un aperitivo, tomo una tapa**
I have breakfast **desayuno**
I have dinner **ceno**
I have lunch **como, almuerzo**
lunch **la comida, el almuerzo**
main **principal**
meal **la comida**
snack **el aperitivo, la tapa, el refrigerio**
supper **la cena**

Eating out

I add up the bill **hago la cuenta**
bowl **el cuenco, la fuente**
charge **el precio**
cheap **barato**
check / bill **la cuenta**
I choose **elijo, escojo**

it costs **cuesta**
I decide **decido**
expensive **caro**
first course **el primer plato**
fixed price **el precio fijo**
fork **el tenedor**
inclusive **incluido, inclusive**
knife **el cuchillo**
main course **el plato principal**
menu **el menú**
menu of the day **el menú del día**
napkin **la servilleta**
I order **pido**
order **el pedido**
place setting **la colocación de la mesa**
plate **el plato**
portion **la porción**
reservation **la reserva**
I serve **sirvo**
service **el servicio**
set menu **el menú prefijado**
side dish **el plato adicional**
spoon **la cuchara**
table **la mesa**
tablecloth **el mantel**
tip / gratuity **la propina**
I tip **doy propina**
toothpick **el palillo de dientes**
tourist menu **el menú turístico**
tray **la bandeja**
waiter **el camarero**
waitress **la camarera**
wine list **la lista de vinos**

Can you tell me where the nearest café is, please?

¿Me puede decir dónde está el café más cercano, por favor?

Where can we get a drink around here?

¿Dónde podemos tomar algo por aquí?

I'd like a chocolate milk shake, please.

Un batido [Una malteada] de chocolate, por favor.

➤ VEGETABLES, FRUIT, DESSERT 10c; COOKING & EATING 10d

10b Fish & Meat

Fish & seafood

anchovy **la anchoa**
clam **la almeja**
cockles **los berberechos**
cod **el bacalao**
crab **el cangrejo**
crayfish **el cangrejo de río**
eel **la anguila**
fish **el pescado**
flounder / plaice **la patija**
hake **la merluza**
herring **el arenque**
lobster **la langosta, el bogavante**
mussel **el mejillón**
octopus **el pulpo**
oyster **la ostra**

prawn **la gamba, [el camarón]**
prawns **las gambas, los langostinos**
salmon **el salmón**
sardine **la sardina**
scallop **la venera**
seafood **el marisco**
shell **el caparazón**
shellfish **el crustáceo, los mariscos**
shrimp **el camarón, el langostino**
snails **los caracoles**
sole **el lenguado**
squid **el calamar**
swordfish **el pez espada**
trout **la trucha**
tuna **el atún**
whitebait **el chanquete**

Is this fish fresh?	**¿Es fresco este pescado?**
I'd rather have tuna than crab.	**Prefiero comer atún que cangrejo.**
Would you prefer cod or sole?	**¿Prefiere usted bacalao o lenguado?**
"Shall we try the chicken?"	**— ¿Probamos el pollo?**
"I'd like a pork chop."	**— Me gustaría tomar una chuleta de cerdo.**
Can we both have steak, one rare and one well-done?	**¿Nos trae dos filetes de vaca, uno poco hecho y el otro muy hecho?**
I'll have a rare steak with fries / chips and salad, please.	**Quisiera un biftec poco hecho con patatas [papas] fritas y una ensalada, por favor.**
I want a tomato salad. Does it have garlic in it?	**Quisiera una ensalada de tomate. ¿Tiene ajo?**

Meat & meat products

bacon **el tocino, la panceta**
beef **la carne de vaca**
bolognese **boloñesa**
casserole **la cazuela, [la cacerola]**
chop **la chuleta**
cutlet **la chuleta**
ham **el jamón**
hamburger / beefburger **la hamburguesa**
hot dog **el perrito caliente**
kid **el cabrito**
kidney **los riñones**
lamb **el cordero**
liver **el hígado**
meat **la carne**
meatballs **las albóndigas**
minced meat **la carne picada**
mixed grill **la parrillada mixta**
mutton **la carne de cordero**
pâté **el paté**
pork **la carne de cerdo, el cerdo**

rabbit **el conejo**
salami **el salami, el salchichón**
sausage **la salchicha**
scallop **el escalope**
sirloin **el solomillo**
steak **el filete**
stew **el guiso, el estofado**
veal **la (carne de) ternera**

Poultry & game

capon **el capón**
chicken **el pollo**
  chicken breast **la pechuga de pollo**
duck **el pato**
goose **el ganso**
partridge **la perdiz**
pheasant **el faisán**
poultry **la carne de ave, el ave**
quail **la codorniz**
turkey **el pavo**
wild boar **el jabalí**
woodcock **la becada**

Traditional dishes

albóndigas spiced meatballs
almejas a la marinera clams in paprika sauce
calamares a la romana deep-fried squid
caldo gallego meat and vegetable broth
[chile con carne] stew of kidney beans, chili, and minced beef
chorizo spicy sausage made of pork, garlic, and paprika
conejo al ajillo rabbit with garlic
empanada gallega tenderloin of pork, onions, and chili peppers in a pie
empanadillas savory pasties stuffed with meat or fish

gambas a la plancha grilled prawns
menestra de pollo casserole of chicken and vegetables
paella valenciana saffron rice with chicken, shrimp, mussels, prawns, squid, peas, tomato, chili pepper, and garlic
riñones al jerez kidneys braised in sherry
sopa de mariscos seafood soup
sopa de pescado fish soup
[taco] cornmeal pancake stuffed with meat, chili pepper sauce, and mashed avocado

10c Vegetables, Fruit & Dessert

Vegetables

artichoke	**la alcachofa**
asparagus	**el espárrago**
avocado	**el aguacate**
baked beans	**las judías cocidas, [los frijoles cocidos]**
beans	**las judías, las habas**
beets	**la remolacha**
broccoli	**el brécol, [el brócoli]**
Brussels sprout	**la col de Bruselas**
cabbage	**la col, [el repollo]**
carrot	**la zanahoria**
cauliflower	**la coliflor**
celeriac	**el apio**
celery	**el apio**
chickpea	**el garbanzo**
corn / maize	**el maíz**
corn on the cob	**la mazorca**
cucumber	**el pepino, [el cohombro]**
eggplant / aubergine	**la berenjena**
endive / chicory	**la endivia**
French bean	**la judía enana, el frijol**
garlic	**el ajo**
gherkin	**el pepinillo**
green bean	**la alubia, la judía**
herb	**la hierba aromática**
leek	**el puerro**
lentil	**la lenteja**
lettuce	**la lechuga**
marrow	**el tuétano**
mushroom	**el champiñón**

onion	**la cebolla**
parsley	**el perejil**
parsnip	**la chirivía, la pastinaca**
pea	**el guisante, [la arveja]**
pepper (red / green)	**el pimiento (verde / rojo)**
potato	**la patata**
pumpkin	**la calabaza**
radish	**el rábano**
rice	**el arroz**
salad	**la ensalada**
spinach	**la espinaca**
sweetcorn	**el maíz dulce**
tomato	**el tomate**
turnip	**el nabo**
vegetable	**la verdura**
vegetable *(adj)*	**vegetal**
watercress	**el berro**
zucchini / courgette	**el calabacín**

Fruit

apple	**la manzana**
apricot	**el albaricoque**
banana	**el plátano**
berry	**la baya, el grano**
blackberry	**la mora, la zarzamora**
blackcurrant	**la grosella**
brazil nut	**la nuez del Brasil**
bunch of grapes	**el racimo de uvas**
cherry	**la cereza**
chestnut	**la castaña**
coconut	**el coco**
cranberry	**el arándano**

Traditional dishes

arroz con leche	rice pudding
bizcocho	sponge cake
crema catalana	caramel pudding
guacamole	mashed avocado
pastel de queso	cheesecake
[papusa]	pancake with cheese or bacon
tortilla de patatas	potato omelet

currant   la pasa de Corinto
date   el dátil
fig   el higo
fruit   la fruta
gooseberry   la grosella espinosa
grape   la uva
grapefuit   el pomelo
hazelnut   la avellana
kiwi fruit   el kiwi
lemon   el limón
lime   la lima
melon   el melón
nut   la nuez
olive   la aceituna
orange   la naranja
passion fruit   la fruta de la pasión, [el maracuyá]
peach   el melocotón
peanut   el cacahuete
pear   la pera
peel   la piel, la cáscara
I peel   pelo, quito la cáscara
peeled   pelado
piece of fruit   una fruta
pineapple   la piña
plum   la ciruela
pomegranate   la granada
prune   la ciruela seca
raisin   la pasa, [la uva pasa]
raspberry   la frambuesa
red currant   la grosella roja
rhubarb   el ruibarbo
seed   la pepita
stone   el hueso
strawberry   la fresa
sultana   la pasa

tangerine   la mandarina
walnut   la nuez

Dessert

biscuit / cookie   la galleta
cake   el pastel
caramel   el caramelo
chocolate   el chocolate
chocolates   los bombones
cream   la nata
crème caramel   el flan
custard   las natillas
dessert   el postre
flan   la tarta, [el flan]
flour   la harina
fresh fruit   la fruta fresca
fruit of the season   la fruta de la estación
fruit salad   la macedonia, [la ensalada de frutas]
Ice cream   el helado
mousse   la mousse
pancake   la hojuela, [el panqueque]
pastry   la pastita
pie   el pastel
pudding   el puding, el dulce, el pudín
sweet   dulce
tart   la tarta dulce
trifle   la trufa
vanilla   la vainilla
whipped cream   la nata batida
yogurt   el yogur

I'd rather have boiled potatoes than fries / chips. | **Prefiero las patatas [papas] cocidas a las patatas [papas] fritas.**

Two strawberry ice creams. Have you got any apple pie? | **Dos helados de fresa. ¿Tiene tarta de manzana?**

FOOD & DRINK

10d Cooking & Eating

Food preparation

I bake **cuezo al horno, horneo**
baked **al horno**
barbecue **la barbacoa**
I beat **bato**
beaten **batido**
I boil **hiervo**
boiled **hervido**
bone **el hueso, la espina**
boned **deshuesado, sin espinas**
  boned (fish) **sin espinas**
I bone **deshueso, quito las espinas**
I braise **braseo**
braised **braseado**
in breadcrumbs **empanado**
breast **la pechuga**
I carve **trincho**
I chop **corto en trozos, pico**
I clear the table **quito la mesa**
I cook **cocino**
cooking / cuisine **la cocina**
I cut **corto**
I dice **corto en cubitos**
dough **la masa, la pasta**
I dry **seco (los platos)**
egg **el huevo**
flour **la harina**
food preparation **la preparación de alimentos**
fried **frito**

I fry **frío**
I grate **rallo**
grated **rallado**
gravy **la salsa de carne**
I grill **aso (a la parrilla)**
grilled **asado (a la parrilla)**
ingredient **el ingrediente**
large **grande**
I marinate **pongo a marinar**
marinated **marinado**
medium **en su punto, término medio**
milk **la leche**
I mix **mezclo**
mixed **mezclado**
olive oil **el aceite de oliva**
pastry **la pasta**
  short(crust) pastry **la pasta quebradiza**
I peel **pelo**
peeled **pelado**
I pour **sirvo**
rare **poco hecho**
recipe **la receta**
roast **el asado**
I roast **aso al horno**
in sauce **en salsa**
I set / lay the table **pongo la mesa**
I sift **tamizo, cierno**
I slice **corto en rodajas**
sliced **en rodajas**

Chop two kilos of tomatoes and one kilo of peeled onions. Put into saucepan with 500 ml of malt vinegar. Add refined sugar and two teaspoons of salt.

Cook, stirring frequently for forty minutes until mixture thickens.

**Pique dos kilos de tomates y un kilo de cebollas peladas. Póngalos en una cacerola con 500 ml de vinagre de malta. Agregue azúcar refinada y dos cucharaditas de sal.
Cocínelo durante cuarenta minutos, revolviendo continuamente hasta que espese.**

I spread **extiendo**
stewed **estofado, guisado**
sunflower oil **el aceite de girasol**
I toast **tuesto**
toasted **tostado**
I wash up **friego, lavo**
I weigh **peso**
well-done **muy hecho, bien oooinado**
I whip **bato**
whipped **batido**
I whisk **bato (con batidora)**
whisked **batido (con batidora)**

Eating

additive **el aditivo**
I am hungry **tengo hambre**
I am thirsty **tengo sed**
appetite **el apetito**
appetizing **apetitoso**
bad **malo**
I bite **muerdo**
bitter **amargo**
calorie **la caloría**
   low calorie **bajo en calorías**
I chew **mastico**
cold **frío**
delicious **delicioso**
diet **el régimen, [la dieta]**
   I'm on a diet **sigo un régimen, [estoy a dieta]**
fatty / oily **graso**
fresh **fresco**

fresh(ly) *(adv)* **fresco**
healthy *(appetite)* **bueno**
   healthy *(food)* **sano**
I help myself **me sirvo**
hot **picante**
hunger **el hambre**
hungry **hambriento, con ganas de comer**
I like **me gusta**
mild **suave**
I offer **ofrezco**
I pass (salt) **paso**
piece **el trozo, el pedazo**
I pour **sirvo**
I provide **pongo, proporciono**
rancid *(cheese)* **rancio**
salty **salado**
I serve **sirvo**
sharp **ácido**
slice **la rebanada**
I smell **huelo**
soft **blando**
spicy **picante**
stale (bread) **duro**
still **no espumoso, sin gas**
strong **fuerte**
I swallow **trago**
tasty **sabroso**
thirst **la sed**
thirsty **sediento**
I try **pruebo**
vegan **vegetariano estricto**
vegetarian **vegetariano**

Pass the salt, please.	**Pase la sal, por favor.**
Just a small portion.	**Sólo una porción pequeña.**
Nothing more, thanks.	**Nada más, gracias.**

Health & Illness

11a Accidents & Emergencies

accident **el accidente**
ambulance **la ambulancia**
I attack **ataco**
break **la rotura, la ruptura, el rompimiento**
I break **rompo, me rompo**
I break my arm **me rompo el brazo**
breakage **la rotura, la ruptura, el rompimiento**
broken **roto**
I have broken my leg **me he roto la pierna**
bruise **la contusión, el cardenal, la magulladura, el moretón**
I bruise **contundo, magullo**
burn **la quemadura**
I burn **me quemo**
casualty **el herido, la víctima**
casualty department **la sección de accidentes**
I catch fire **me enciendo, prendo fuego**

I collide (with) **choco (con), colisiono (con)**
collision **la colisión, el choque**
I crash **choco, colisiono**
I crash (plane) **estrello (avión)**
crash **el choque, la colisión**
I crush **aplasto**
I cut (myself) **(me) corto**
I have cut my finger **me he cortado el dedo**
dead **muerto**
death **la muerte**
I die **muero**
emergency **la emergencia, urgencia**
emergency exit **la salida de emergencia / urgencia**
emergency services **las urgencias, los servicios de emergencia**
it explodes **estalla, explota, explosiona**

There has been an accident! My friend is injured.	**¡Ha habido un accidente! Mi amigo está herido.**
We need an ambulance quickly.	**Necesitamos una ambulancia, pronto!**
Call the fire brigade!	**¡Llama a los bomberos!**
I think I have broken my arm. It hurts a lot.	**Creo que tengo el brazo roto. Me duele mucho.**

explosion la explosión, el estallido
I extinguish apago, extingo
I fall caigo
fatal fatal, mortal
fine la multa
fire el fuego, el incendio
fire brigade el cuerpo de bomberos
fire engine el coche de bomberos
fire extinguisher el extintor
fireman el bombero
first aid los primeros auxilios
graze el roce, la abrasión, la rozadura
I graze raspo
I have an accident sufro un accidente
hospital el hospital
impact el impacto, el choque
incident el incidente
I injure hiero, hago daño a, lastimo, lesiono
injury la herida
injured herido
insurance el seguro, los seguros
I insure aseguro

I kill mato
killed matado, muerto
life belt el cinturón salvavidas
life jacket el chaleco salvavidas
oxygen el oxígeno
paramedic el paramédico
I recover recupero, me recobro
recovery la recuperación
I rescue rescato, salvo
rescue el rescate, el salvamento
rescue services los servicios de rescate
I run over atropello
I rush voy de prisa, me apresuro
safe salvo, seguro
safe and sound sano y salvo
safety belt el cinturón de seguridad
salvage el salvamento, la recuperación
I save rescato, salvo
seat belt el cinturón de seguridad
terrorist attack el ataque de terroristas
third party la tercera persona
witness el testigo

It was your fault, not mine.	Ha sido culpa tuya, no mía.
Are you a doctor?	¿Es usted médico?
Where's the nearest hospital?	¿Dónde está el hospital más cercano?

➤ MEDICAL TREATMENT 11c; HEALTH & HYGIENE 11d

ache   el dolor
alive   vivo
I am ill / sick   estoy enfermo
I am sick / vomit   vomito, devuelvo
he amputates   amputa
amputee   el amputado
amputation   la amputación
arthritis   la artritis
asthma   el asma (f)
black eye   el ojo amoratado
I bleed   desangro, sangro
blind   ciego
blind man / woman   el ciego, la ciega
blood   la sangre
breath   el aliento, la respiración
I breathe   respiro
breathless   falto de aliento, desalentado, jadeante
catarrh   el catarro
I catch cold   cojo frío, cojo un resfriado
cold   el resfriado, el catarro
constipated   estreñido
constipation   el estreñimiento
convalescence   la convalecencia
I am convalescing   convalezco
cough   la tos

I cough   toso
cripple   el lisiado, el mutilado
I cry   lloro
dead   muerto
deaf   sordo
deafness   la sordera
death   la muerte
depressed   deprimido
depression   la depresión, el abatimiento
diarrhea   la diarrea
I die   muero
diet   el régimen, la dieta
disabled   minusválido
disease   la enfermedad, el mal
dizziness   el mareo, el vértigo
dizzy   mareado
drug   la droga
drugged   drogado
drunk   borracho
dumb   mudo
earache   el dolor de oídos
I feel dizzy   me siento mareado
I feel ill / unwell   me siento enfermo
I feel (well)   me siento (bien)
fever   la fiebre
feverish   febril
flu   la gripe

I feel dizzy if I stand up.	Al levantarme me siento mareado.
I don't usually faint!	No suelo desmayarme.
I have been sick / vomited several times.	He vomitado varias veces.
I suffer from high blood pressure.	Padezco de hipertensión.
My children have diarrhea. I seem to be constipated.	Mis niños tienen la diarrea. Yo debo estar estreñido.

I get drunk **me emborracho**
I got better **me mejoré, me repuse, me restablecí**
I had an operation **me han operado**
I have a cold **tengo un resfriado**
I have a temperature **tengo fiebre**
headache **el dolor de cabeza**
health **la salud**
healthy **bien de salud**
heart attack **el ataque cardíaco**
high blood pressure **la hipertensión**
HIV positive **VIH positivo**
hurt **el dolor**
I hurt **me duele, tengo dolor de ...**
it hurts **me duele**
ill **enfermo**
illness **la enfermedad**
jaundice **la ictericia**
I live **vivo**
I look (ill) **parezco enfermo**
mental illness **la enfermedad mental**
mentally handicapped **minusválido mental**
mentally sick **enfermo de la mente**
migraine **la jaqueca**
mute **el mudo**
    mute *(adj)* **mudo**

pain **el dolor**
painful **doloroso**
pale **pálido**
paralysis **la parálisis**
paralyzed **paralizado**
physically handicapped **mutilado, minusválido**
recovery **el restablecimiento**
rheumatism **el reumatismo**
sick **enfermo**
I sneeze **estornudo**
sore throat **el dolor de garganta**
sting **la picadura, el escozor, la picazón**
it stings **me pica, me rasca**
stomach **el estómago**
stomachache **el dolor de estómago**
stomach upset **el trastorno estomacal**
I take drugs **tomo drogas, me drogo**
temperature **la fiebre**
tonsillitis **la amigdalitis**
toothache **el dolor de muelas**
I vomit **vomito, devuelvo**
what's wrong? **¿qué (te) pasa?**
I wound **hiero**
wounded **herido**

I don't know what is wrong with her.	**No sé qué tendrá.**
She seems to have a temperature.	**Parece tener fiebre.**
I have a sore throat and I have a migraine coming on.	**Tengo dolor de la garganta y me llega [me está empezando] una jaqueca.**

11c Medical Treatment

anesthetic / anaesthetic **el anestésico**
  I am under anesthetic **estoy anestesiado**
appointment **la cita**
bandage **la venda**
blood **la sangre**
blood test **el análisis sanguíneo / de la sangre**
blood pressure **la presión sanguínea**
capsule **la cápsula**
chemotherapy **la quimioterapia**
cure **la cura**
danger to life **el peligro mortal**
dangerous **peligroso**
death **la muerte**
I diet **estoy a régimen / [dieta]**
doctor (Dr.) **el médico**
dressing **el vendaje**
drop **la gota**
drug **la droga**
I examine **examino**
examination **el examen**
I fill **(re)lleno**
glasses **las gafas**

I have **tengo**
heating **la calefacción**
hospital **el hospital**
I improve **me restablezco, me repongo**
injection **la inyección**
insurance certificate **el certificado de seguro**
I look after **cuido de**
medical **médico**
medicine **la medicina**
midwife **la comadre, la comadrona, la partera**
nurse **la enfermera**
I nurse **cuido, atiendo**
office hours **las horas de consulta**
I operate **opero**
operation **la operación, la intervención quirúrgica**
pastille **la pastilla**
patient **el paciente, el enfermo**
pharmacist / chemist **el farmacéutico**
pharmacy **la farmacia**

Call a doctor! — **¡Llama a un médico!**

Is he a good doctor? Can he diagnose the symptoms and prescribe a cure? — **¿Es buen médico? ¿Puede diagnosticar los síntomas y recomendar una cura?**

He does not like injections. He has never had an X-ray. — **No le gustan las inyecciones. Nunca lo han radiografiado.**

Will I need an operation? I have my medical insurance. — **¿Necesitaré una operación? Tengo mi seguro de médico.**

physiotherapy   la fisioterapia
physiotherapist   el fisioterapeuta
pill   la píldora
plaster (of Paris)   el yeso mate
I prescribe   receto
prescription   la receta
radiotherapy   la radioterapia
receptionist   el / la recepcionista
service   el servicio
I set   encaso
spa resort   el balneario, la
   estación balnearia, la estación
   termal
specialist   el / la especialista
stitch   el punto de sutura
stitches   los puntos de sutura
sticking plaster   el esparadrapo
surgery   la cirugía
syringe   la jeringa, la jeringuilla
tablet   la tableta, el comprimido,
   la pastilla
therapeutic   terapéutico
therapy   la terapia, la terapéutica
therapist   el / la terapeuta
thermometer   el termómetro
I treat   trato, curo, atiendo
treatment   el tratamiento, la cura

ward   la sala, la crujía
wound   la herida
X-ray   el rayo x
I X-ray   radiografío

Dentist & optician

abscess   el flemón
contact lens   el lente de contacto
dentist   el dentista
denture   la dentadura
I extract   saco
eyeglass / spectacles case   el
   estuche para gafas
eyesight   la vista
farsighted / longsighted   présbite,
   hipermétrope
filling   el empaste
frame   la montura
glasses / spectacles   las gafas
lens   el lente
nearsighted / shortsighted   miope
optician   el óptico
sunglasses   las gafas do col
tinted   ahumado
I test / check   controlo
I have a toothache   tengo dolor de
   muelas

I have lost my tablets. I have to take them four times a day.	He perdido mis comprimidos [tabletas / pastillas]. Debo tomarlos [tomarlas] cuatro veces al día.
Can I have a prescription?	¿Me puede dar una receta?
He had an operation recently. He seems to be recovering.	Lo operaron recientemente. Parece que se está restableciendo.
We are so relieved — all the tests proved negative.	Estamos muy aliviados — todos los análisis salieron negativos.

11d Health & Hygiene

Physical state

ache **el dolor**
   aching *(adj)* **adolorido**
asleep **dormido**
awake **despierto**
blister **la ampolla**
boil **el divieso, el furúnculo**
bruise **la contusión, el cardenal,**
   la magulladura, el magullón,
   el moretón
comfort **la comodidad**
comfortable **cómodo, confortable**
discomfort **el malestar**
dizziness **el mareo, el vértigo**
dizzy **mareado**
drowsiness **la somnolencia**
drowsy **soñoliento**
I exercise **ejercito**
exercise bike **la bicicleta estática**
faint **mareado**
I faint **me desmayo, pierdo el**
   conocimiento
I feel **me siento**
fit **en buena forma, en buen**
   estado físico, sano, bien de
   salud
fitness **la buena salud, el (buen)**
   estado físico
graze **el roce, la abrasión, la**
   raspadura
I am hot / cold **tengo calor / frío**
hunger **el hambre** *(f)*
hungry **hambriento**
I am hungry **tengo hambre**
ill **enfermo**

I lie down **me acuesto**
I look **parezco**
queasy **mareado, bascoso**
I relax **me relajo**
I rest **descanso**
seasick **mareado**
sick **enfermo**
I sleep **duermo**
sleepy **soñoliento**
stamina **la resistencia, el aguante**
strange **extraño, curioso, raro**
thirst **la sed**
thirsty **sediento**
I am thirsty **tengo sed**
tired **cansado**
I am tired **tengo sueño, estoy**
   cansado
tiredness **el cansancio, la fatiga,**
   el sueño
uncomfortable **incómodo,**
   molesto
under the weather **indispuesto**
unwell **enfermo, indispuesto, de**
   mala salud
I wake up **me despierto**
well **bien de salud**
well-being **el bienestar**

Beauty & hygiene

bath **el baño**
beauty **la belleza**
beauty contest **el concurso de**
   belleza
beauty salon / parlor **el salón de**
   belleza

I need a shower. | **Necesito ducharme.**
I'd like a haircut, please. Don't cut it too short. | **Quiero un corte de pelo, por favor. No me lo corte demasiado.**

beauty queen **la reina de la belleza**
beauty treatment **el tratamiento de belleza**
body odor / odour **el olor a sudor**
I burp / belch **eructo**
I brush **cepillo**
brush **el cepillo**
I clean **limpio**
clean **limpio**
I clean my teeth **me limpio los dientes**
comb **el peine**
I comb my hair **me peino**
condom **el condón, el preservativo**
contraception **la contracepción, las medidas anticonceptivas**
contraceptive **el anticonceptivo**
I cut **corto, me corto ...**
dandruff **la caspa**
I defecate **defeco**
dirty **sucio**
diet *(usual food)* **la dieta**
I am on a diet **sigo un régimen**
electric razor **la afeitadora (eléctrica)**
facial **el tratamiento facial**
flannel **la manopla**
fleas **las pulgas**
hairbrush **el cepillo para el pelo**
haircut **el corte de pelo**
I get my hair cut **me hago cortar el pelo**
hairdo **el peinado**
healthy *(person)* **sano, con buena salud**
healthy *(diet, place)* **saludable**

laundry *(establishment)* **el lavadero, la lavandería**
laundry *(linen)* **la ropa sucia, la ropa por lavar**
louse / nit **el piojo**
I'm losing my hair **pierdo el pelo, me estoy quedando calvo**
manicure **la manicura, [el manicure]**
I menstruate **menstrúo**
menstruation **la menstruación**
nailbrush **el cepillo para las uñas**
period **el período, la regla**
period pains **los dolores de la regla**
razor **la afeitadora, la rasuradora, la maquinilla de afeitar**
sanitary **sanitario, higiénico**
sanitary napkin **el paño higiénico, la compresa (higiénica), [la toalla higiénica]**
scissors **las tijeras**
I shave **me afeito**
shower **la ducha**
smell *(bad)* **el olor**
I smell *(badly)* **huelo**
soap **el jabón**
I sweat **sudo**
sweat **el sudor**
I take a bath **me baño**
I take a shower **me ducho**
tampon **el tampón**
toothbrush **el cepillo de dientes**
toothpaste **la crema de dientes, la pasta dentífrica**
towel **la toalla**
I wash **me lavo**

A little more off the back and sides, please.
Un poco más por detrás y en los lados, por favor.

Please trim my mustache.
Córteme el bigote por favor.

Social Issues

12a Society

abnormal **anormal**
alternative **la alternativa**
amenity **la amenidad**
anonymous **anónimo**
attitude **la actitud**
available **disponible**
basic **básico**
basis **la base**
burden **la carga, el peso**
campaign **la campaña**
care **el cuidado**
cause **la causa**
change **el cambio**
circumstance **la circunstancia**
community **la comunidad**
compulsory **obligatorio**
contribution **la contribución**
cost **el precio, el coste, el costo**
I counsel **aconsejo, asesoro**
counseling **el asesoramiento, la asistencia**
criterion **el criterio**
debt **la deuda**
I am in debt **tengo deudas**
dependence **la dependencia**
dependent **dependiente**
depressed **deprimido, abatido**
depression **la depresión, la crisis**
deprived **privado de**
difficulty **la dificultad**

effect **el efecto**
effective **efectivo, eficiente**
fact **el hecho**
finance **las finanzas**
financial **financiero**
frustrated **frustrado**
frustration **la frustración**
guidance **la dirección, la orientación**
increase **el aumento**
inner city **el barrio céntrico de la ciudad**
institution **la institución**
loneliness **la soledad**
lonely **solitario**
long-term **a largo plazo**
measure **medida**
negative **negativo**
normal **normal, común**
policy **la política, los principios, los criterios**
positive **positivo**
power **el poder**
prestige **el prestigio**
problem **el problema, la cuestión**
protest movement **el movimiento de protesta**
I provide **proporciono, suministro**

There are immense social problems in the inner city.	**Existen enormes problemas sociales en los barrios céntricos de las ciudades.**
The unemployed often feel frustrated and lonely, as a result of unemployment.	**Los desempleados suelen sentirse frustrados y solitarios como consecuencia del paro.**

provision la provisión, el suministro, la estipulación, la disposición
psychological psicológico
quality of life la calidad de vida
question / issue la cuestión, el asunto
rate la tasa
responsibility la responsabilidad
responsible (ir-) (ir)responsable
result el resultado
role el papel
rural rural
scarcity la escasez
scheme el esquema
I am out of work no encuentro trabajo
secure (in-) (in)seguro
security (in-) la (in)seguridad
self-esteem la autoestima
short-term a corto plazo
situation la situación
social social
society la sociedad
stable (un-) (in)estable
stability (in-) la (in)estabilidad
statistics las estadísticas
status el estatus, la posición
stigma el estigma, la marca
stress el estrés, la fatiga
stressful estresante
structure la estructura, la configuración
superfluous superfluo
support el soporte, el apoyo, el sostén, la ayuda
urban urbano
value el valor

Some useful verbs

I adapt / conform me ajusto, me acomodo
it affects afecta
I can afford me puedo permitir
I alienate enajeno, traspaso
I break down fracaso
I campaign hago campaña
I care for me preocupo por
I cause causo
it changes cambia
I contribute contribuyo
I cope me arreglo, me las ingenio
I depend on dependo de
I deprive privo
I discourage desaliento
I dominate domino
I encourage aliento, animo
I help ayudo
I increase aumento
I lack carezco de
I look after cuido de
I need necesito
I neglect descuido, abandono
I owe debo
I protest protesto
I provide for proporciono, suministro
I put up with (me) aguanto
I rely on confío en, cuento con
I respect respeto
I share comparto
I solve resuelvo
I suffer from (disease) tengo
I support mantengo
I tackle hago frente a
I value valoro

Financial difficulties lead to loss of status and family problems.	Las dificultades económicas llevan a una pérdida de estatus y problemas familiares.
The quality of life suffers because of it.	Como consecuencia, se compromete la calidad de la vida.

ADDICTION & VIOLENCE 12d; PREJUDICE 12e

SOCIAL ISSUES

12b Poverty & Social Services

Social services

aid **la ayuda**
agency **la agencia, la oficina**
authority **las autoridades**
benefit **el beneficio**
I benefit **me beneficio**
charity **la caridad, la organización caritativa**
claim **la solicitud**
I claim **solicito**
claimant **el solicitante**
disability **la invalidez, la incapacidad**
disabled **el inválido, el minusválido**
I am eligible for **tengo derecho a, cumplo los requisitos para**
frail **débil, delicado**
frailty **la debilidad**
grant **la concesión, la beca**
handicap **la minusvalía, el obstáculo, la incapacidad**
handicapped **el minusválido, el incapacitado**
homeless shelter center **el centro de recepciones**
ill health **la mala salud**

income support **la pensión de subsistencia**
loan **el préstamo**
maintenance **el mantenimiento**
official **oficial**
Red Cross **la Cruz Roja**
refuge **el refugio**
refugee **el refugiado**
I register **me inscribo**
registration **la inscripción**
Salvation Army **el Ejército de Salvación**
service **el servicio**
social security **la seguridad social**
social services **los servicios sociales**
social worker **el asistente social**
support **la ayuda**
I support **ayudo**
welfare **el bienestar social**

Wealth & poverty

affluence **la prosperidad**
I beg **mendigo, pido**
beggar **el mendigo**
I am broke **no tengo un céntimo**

"What social services are available to those in need?"

"There is a homeless shelter. Many charities are active in this way. The physically handicapped can apply for help too. They are particularly vulnerable to unemployment."

— ¿Cuáles servicios sociales están a la disposición de los necesitados?
— Hay un centro de recepción para las personas sin hogar. Muchas sociedades benéficas son activas del mismo modo. Los minusválidos también pueden solicitar ayuda. Ellos son muy vulnerables en lo que se refiere al desempleo.

POVERTY & SOCIAL SERVICES 12B

debt **la deuda**
in debt **tengo deudas**
deprivation **la privación, la pérdida**
deprived **desventajado, desvalido**
destitute **el indigente, necesitado**
living standards **las condiciones de vida**
millionaire **el millonario**
need **la necesidad**
nutrition **la nutrición**
poor **pobre**
poverty **la pobreza, la miseria**
subsistence **la subsistencia**
tramp / vagrant **el vagabundo**
vulnerability **la vulnerabilidad**
vulnerable **vulnerable**
wealth **la riqueza**
I am well off **estoy acomodado**

Unemployment

I cut back (jobs) **recorto, reduzco**
I dismiss **despido**
dismissal **el despido**
dole **el subsidio de desempleo**
I give notice **aviso**
job **el empleo, el trabajo**
job center / employment center **la oficina de empleo**
job creation scheme **el programa de creación de empleo**
layoff / redundancy **el despido**
laid off / redundant **despedido**
long-term unemployed **el desempleado de larga duración**
I have lost my job **he perdido mi empleo**
part-time **la media jornada**
retraining **la recapacitación, el entrenamiento adicional**
I refuse a job **rechazo un empleo**
I resign **dimito, renuncio**
short-term work **la jornada reducida**
skill **la habilidad, la aptitud, la técnica, el oficio**
staffing **empleo de personal**
training program / scheme **el programa de formación**
unemployable **inútil para el trabajo**
unemployed **desempleado, parado**
unemployment **el paro, el desempleo**
unemployment benefit **el subsidio de paro / desempleo**
unemployment rate **la tasa de desempleo**
unskilled worker **trabajador no especializado**
vacancy **la vacante**

"How high is the level of unemployment?"
"In some areas it is about fifteen percent."
"Can people retrain or work part-time?"

"Yes, sometimes, and many retire early. Not everyone gets the unemployment benefits, as many have not worked for a long time."

— ¿Cuál es la tasa del desempleo?
— En algunas zonas llega al quince por ciento.
— La gente, puede recapacitarse o trabajar en horario de jornada reducida?
— Sí, a veces, y muchos se toman la jubilación anticipada. No todos reciben el subsidio del paro, pues muchos llevan mucho tiempo sin trabajar.

▶ PAY & CONDITIONS; JOB APPLICATION 14c

93

SOCIAL ISSUES

12c Housing & Homelessness

accommodation **la vivienda**
apartment / flat **el piso, el apartamento**
  apartment houses / block of flats **el bloque de pisos / apartamentos**
I build **construyo**
building **la construcción, el edificio**
  building land **los terrenos edificables / urbanizables**
  building plot **el solar para la construcción, [el lote]**
  building site **la obra**
camp **el campamento**
comfortable / homey **confortable, cómodo**
commune **la comuna**
dilapidated **desmoronado, ruinoso**
I demolish **demuelo**
demolition **la demolición**
it deteriorates **se deteriora, deteriora**

drab **monótono, triste**
I evict **desalojo, desahucio**
it falls down **está en ruinas**
furnished **amueblado**
homeless **sin hogar**
homelessness **la carencia de hogar**
hostel **el hostal**
house **la casa**
  detached house **el chalet**
  public housing **la casa protegida, la casa del ayuntamiento, [la vivienda estatal]**
  semidetached house **la casa adosada**
housing **la vivienda**
  builders' association **la sociedad constructora**
  housing shortage **la escasez de viviendas**
inner city **el barrio céntrico de la ciudad**

"Why do so many houses stand empty?
The houses deteriorate fast and squatters move in.

Aren't the town planners intending to demolish those houses?"

"Yes, but at the same time so many are homeless. They sleep in the open or squat."

"Is the municipality still building public housing?"

— ¿Por qué quedan vacías tantas casas?
Las casas se deterioran rápidamente, y luego las ocupan los squátters.

Y los urbanistas, ¿no tienen la intención de demoler estas casas?

— Sí, pero al mismo tiempo hay tantos sin hogar. Duermen al descubierto o ocupan las casas ilegalmente.

— Y el ayuntamiento [la alcaldía] ¿sigue construyendo viviendas protegidas?

landlord el dueño, el propietario (de la casa)

living conditions las condiciones de vida

I maintain mantengo

I modernize modernizo

mortgage la hipoteca, el préstamo hipotecario

mortgage rate el tipo de interés hipotecario

I move me mudo de casa

I occupy ocupo

overcrowded lleno de gente, atestado

overcrowding la superpoblación, la masificación

own propio

owner occupied ocupado por el dueño

public housing / social housing / council housing la vivienda protegida

I pull down demuelo, derribo

real estate / estate agent el agente de propiedad / de finca raíz

I redevelop reorganizo, reconstruyo

I renovate renuevo

I rent / let alquilo, arriendo

rent la renta, el alquiler

I repair reparo

repairs las reparaciones

shanty town el barrio de chabolas, [el arrabal]

shelter el refugio

slum la barriada, el barrio pobre

I sleep in the open duermo en la calle, estoy en la calle

slum clearance la demolición de barrios pobres

speculator el especulador

squalid miserable, escuálido

I squat ocupo sin derecho, usurpo la propiedad

squatter el ocupante sin derecho, el intruso, el usurpador

suburb el suburbio

it stands empty está vacío

tenant inquilino

town planning el planeamiento urbano

urban urbano

urban development el desarrollo urbano

unfurnished desamueblado

unfurnished rooms / digs las habitaciones sin muebles

wasteland la tierra baldía

"Yes, but not enough. Living conditions in the apartments / blocks of flats are extremely poor. They are overcrowded and the landlords no longer repair them."

Despite campaigns to help the homeless and unemployed, the situation remains serious.

It is impossible to find a furnished apartment / flat to rent. The area is fast becoming a slum.

— Sí, pero no bastan. Las condiciones de vida en los bloques de viviendas protegidas son malísimas. Están masificadas, y los propietarios ya no las reparan.

A pesar de las campañas para ayudar a los sin hogar y a los desempleados, la situación sigue siendo grave.

Es imposible encontrar un piso amueblado para alquilar. Este barrio se está convirtiendo rápidamente en un barrio bajo.

12d Addiction & Violence

abuse **el abuso**	effect **el efecto**
I abuse **abuso**	fatal **fatal, mortal**
act of violence **el acto de violencia**	fear **el temor, el miedo**
addict *(adj/ n)* **adicto**	I fear **temo, tengo miedo de**
addiction **la adicción**	force **la fuerza**
addictive **adictivo**	gang **la banda**
aggression **la agresión**	harass **hostigar, perseguir**
aggressive **agresivo**	hoodlum **el gamberro, el vándalo**
alcohol **el alcohol**	hostile **hostil**
alcoholic **el alcohólico**	hostility **la hostilidad**
alcoholism **el alcoholismo**	insult **el insulto**
anger **la rabia, el enfado**	I insult **insulto**
angry **enfadado**	intoxication **la intoxicación**
I attack **ataco**	legal (il-) **(i)legal**
attack **el ataque**	I legalize **legalizo**
I beat up **doy una paliza**	I mug **asalto, aporreo**
I bully **intimido**	mugger **el asaltante**
bully **la intimidación**	nervous **nervioso**
child abuse **el maltrato de los hijos**	nervousness **los nervios, el estado nervioso**
consumption **el consumo**	pimp **el chulo, el proxeneta**
dangerous **peligroso**	pornographic **pornográfico**
I drink **bebo**	pornography **la pornografía**
I get drunk **me emborracho**	prostitution **la prostitución**
drunk **borracho**	punk **el punki**
drunken driving **la conducción bajo los efectos del alcohol**	rape **la violación**
	he rapes **viola**
I dry out **me desalcoholizo**	rapist **el violador**

Violence and vandalism are common. Older people and women are sometimes afraid to go out alone.	**La violencia y el vandalismo son muy frecuentes. Los ancianos y las mujeres a veces tienen miedo de salir solos.**
Many young people have a drug problem. They start by sniffing solvents, or by taking soft drugs. Cannabis is the most common, and gives a feeling of intoxication. Then they go on to hard drugs.	**Muchos jóvenes tienen problemas con la toxicomanía. Empiezan inhalando disolventes o tomando drogas blandas. El cánabis es el más común, y da la sensación de intoxicación. Luego pasan a las drogas duras.**

rehabilitation **la rehabilitación**
I revert **revierto, reincido**
rocker **el rocker**
I seduce **seduzco, convenzo**
sexual harassment **el hostigamiento sexual**
skinhead **el cabeza rapada**
I smoke **fumo**
stimulant **el estimulante**
stimulation **la estimulación**
I terrorize **aterrorizo**
I threaten **amenazo**
thug **el gamberro, el desalmado**
vandal **el gamberro, el vándalo**
vandalism **el gamberrismo, el vandalismo**
victim **la víctima**
violent **violento**

Drugs

addicted to drugs **drogadicto**
AIDS **SIDA**
cannabis **el cánabis, la marijuana**
cocaine **la cocaína**
crack **el crack**
I deal **trafico**
drug **la droga**
drug scene **la escena de drogas, el barrio de drogas**

drug traffic **el tráfico de drogas, el narcotráfico**
I get infected **me infecto**
glue **el pegamento, el pegante**
hard drugs **las drogas duras**
hash **el hachís**
I have a fix **estoy enganchado, estoy drogado**
heroin **la heroína**
HIV positive **VIH positivo**
I inject **inyecto**
junkie **el yonqui, el drogadicto**
I kick (the habit) **me desintoxico**
LSD **LSD**
narcotic **el narcótico**
pusher **el camello, el traficante de drogas**
I sniff **esnifo, inhalo**
soft drugs **las drogas blandas**
solvent **el disolvente**
stimulant **el estimulante**
syringe **la jeringuilla**
I take drugs / a fix **tomo drogas, estoy enganchado**
tranquillizer **el tranquilizante**
withdrawal **la retirada, el desenganchamiento**

Junkies inject or smoke drugs.

Los toxicómanos se inyectan con las drogas o las fuman.

All drugs are dangerous, but injecting them brings risks of AIDS.

Todas las drogas son peligrosas, pero inyectarlas trae el peligro del SIDA.

The drug scene is troubling as so many people become dealers or turn to crime.

El mundo de las drogas es muy preocupante, pues muchas personas se hacen camellos [traficantes] o recurren a la criminalidad.

Withdrawal symptoms are very unpleasant.

El síndrome de la abstinencia es muy desagradable.

12e Prejudice

asylum seeker   **el solicitante de asilo político**
I call names   **insulto**
citizenship   **la ciudadanía**
country of origin   **el país de origen**
cultural   **cultural**
culture   **la cultura**
I discriminate   **discrimino**
discrimination   **la discriminación**
dual nationality   **la doble nacionalidad**
emigrant   **el emigrante**
emigration   **la emigración**
equal (un-)   **(des)igual**
equal opportunities   **las oportunidades iguales**
equal pay   **la paga igualitaria**
equal rights   **los derechos igualitarios**
equality (in-)   **la (des)igualdad**
ethnic   **étnico**
far right   **la extrema derecha**
fascism   **el fascismo**
fascist   **el fascista**
foreign   **el extranjero**
foreign worker   **el trabajador extranjero**

freedom   **la libertad**
freedom of speech   **la libertad de expresión**
ghetto   **el gueto**
human rights   **los derechos humanos**
I immigrate   **inmigro**
immigrant   **el inmigrante**
immigration   **la inmigración**
I integrate   **me integro**
integration   **la integración**
intolerance   **la intolerancia**
intolerant   **intolerante**
majority   **la mayoría**
minority   **la minoría**
mother tongue   **la lengua madre**
I persecute   **persigo**
persecution   **la persecución**
politically correct   **políticamente correcto**
prejudice   **el prejuicio**
prejudiced   **lleno de prejuicios**
rabid   **fanático**
race riot   **la manifestacíon racial**
racism   **el racismo**
racist   **el racista**
racist *(adj)*   **racista**

"Is racism a serious problem?"

— **¿Es un problema serio el racismo?**

"What about the ethnic minority population resident here?"

— **¿Y qué pasa con la minoría étnica que vive aquí?**

"Unfortunately they tend to get the worst jobs and to be paid less. They are more likely to be unemployed and can only afford cheap accommodation."

— **Desafortunadamente suelen obtener los peores empleos, y les pagan menos. Tienen más probabilidad de quedar desempleados, y sólo llegan a tener viviendas muy malas.**

refugee **el refugiado**
I repatriate **repatrio**
residence permit **el permiso de residencia**
right **el derecho**
  right to asylum **el derecho de asilo**
  right to residence **el derecho de residencia**
stereotypical **estereotípico**
tolerance **la tolerancia**
tolerant **tolerante**
I tolerate **tolero**
work permit **el permiso de trabajo**

sexuality

female **la mujer, la hembra**
feminine **femenino**
feminism **el feminismo**
feminist **la feminista**
gay **el homosexual, el marica**
gay club **el club para homosexuales**
gay movement **el movimiento homosexual**
heterosexual **el heterosexual**
  heterosexual *(adj)* **heterosexual**
homosexual **el homosexual**
  homosexual *(adj)* **homosexual**
homosexuality **la homosexualidad**
lesbian **la lesbiana**
  lesbian *(adj)* **lesbiana**
male **varón**
sexual **sexual**
sexuality **la sexualidad**
women's lib **la liberación de la mujer**
women's libber **el / la activista por la liberación de la mujer**
women's rights **los derechos de la mujer**

The law still discriminates against male homosexuals, although society is getting more tolerant.

La ley sigue discriminando a los homosexuales masculinos, aunque la sociedad se está haciendo más tolerante.

"Is there still antisemitism?"
"Unfortunately, although the situation has improved overall, there is still prejudice against the Jews."

— ¿Existe aún el antisemitismo?
— Por desgracia, aunque la situación ha mejorado, sigue habiendo prejuicio en contra de los judíos.

The feminist movement is still demanding equal rights for

El movimiento feminista sigue exigiendo derechos iguales para las mujeres.

Religion

13a Ideas & Doctrines

agnostic **el agnóstico**
Anglican **el anglicano**
apostle **el apóstol**
atheism **el ateísmo**
atheist **el ateo**
atheistic **ateístico**
authority **la autoridad**
belief **la creencia**
I believe (in) **creo (en)**
believer **el creyente**
Bible **la Biblia**
biblical **bíblico**
blessed **bendito**
Buddha **Buda**
Buddhism **el budismo**
Buddhist **el budista**
Calvinist **el calvinista**
he canonizes **canoniza**
cantor **el cantor**
Catholic **el católico**
charismatic **carismático**
charity **la caridad**
Christ **Cristo**
Christian **el cristiano**
Christianity **la cristianidad, el cristianismo**
church **la iglesia**
commentary **el comentario**
conscience **la conciencia**
conversion **la conversión**

covenant **la alianza, el pacto**
disciple **el discípulo**
divine **lo divino**
doctrine **la doctrina**
duty **el deber, la obligación**
ecumenism **el ecumenismo**
ethical **ético**
evil **el mal**
faith **la fe**
faithful **fiel**
I forgive **perdono**
forgiveness **el perdón**
free will **la libre voluntad**
fundamentalism **el fundamentalismo**
fundamentalist **el fundamentalista**
God **Dios**
god **el dios**
goddess **la diosa**
Gospel **el evangelio**
grace **la gracia**
heaven **el cielo, el paraíso**
Hebrew **el hebreo**
hell **el infierno**
heretical **herético**
Hindu **el hindú**
Hinduism **el hinduismo**
holiness **la santidad**
holy **santo, sagrado**
Holy Spirit **el espíritu santo**

The five pillars of Islam are belief in the One True God and his Prophet, prayer, fasting, giving alms, and pilgrimage to Mecca.

Los cinco pilares de la fe musulmana son la creencia en el Unico Dios Verdadero y en su Profeta, la oración, el ayuno, la limosna y el peregrinaje a Meca.

hope la esperanza
human humano
human being el ser humano
humanism el humanismo
humanity la humanidad
infallibility la infalibilidad
infallible infalible
Islam el islam
Islamic islámico
Jesus Jesús
Jew el judío
Jewish judío
Judaic judaico
Judaism judaísmo
Koran / Q'uran El Corán
Lord El Señor
merciful misericordioso
mercy la misericordia
Messiah El Mesías
Mohammed Mahoma
moral moral
morality la moralidad
Muslim musulmán
mystical místico
mysticism la mística, el
  misticismo
myth el mito
New Testament El Nuevo
  Testamento
nirvana la nirvana
Old Testament El Viejo
  Testamento
orthodox el ortodoxo
pagan el pagano, el infiel
parish la parroquia
Pentateuch el Pentateuco

prophet el profeta
Protestant el protestante
Protestantism el protestantismo
Quaker el cuáquero
redemption la redención, el
  perdón
religion la religión
sacred sagrado
saint el santo
Saint Peter San Pedro
he sanctifies santifica
Satan Satanás
he saves salva
scripture las escrituras *(pl)*
service el servicio religioso, la
  misa
Sikh sij
Sikhism sijismo
sin el pecado
sinful pecaminoso
sinner el pecador
soul el alma
spirit el espíritu
spiritual espiritual
spirituality la espiritualidad
Talmud el Talmud
Taoism el taoísmo
theological teológico
theology la teología
traditional tradicional
transcendental trascendental
Trinity la trinidad
true verdadero
truth la verdad
vision la visión
vocation la vocación

There is considerable disagreement about the ordination of women to the priesthood.

John Wesley said, "The world is my parish."

Hay un desacuerdo apreciable con respecto a la ordenación de las mujeres al sacerdocio.

John Wesley dijo, "El mundo es mi parroquia."

13b Faith & Practice

archbishop **el arzobispo**
baptism **el bautismo, el bautizo**
bar mitzvah **el bar-mitzah**
I bear witness to **testifico, doy testimonio**
bishop **el obispo**
bishopric / see **el obispado**
burial **el entierro**
cathedral **la catedral**
chapel **la capilla**
christening **el bautizo, el bautismo**
clergy **el clero**
clergyman **el clérigo**
communion **la comunión**
  Holy Communion **la santa comunión**
community **la comunidad**
I confess *(faith)* **soy**
I confess *(sins)* **confieso**
confession **la confesión**

confirmation **la confirmación**
congregation **la congregación**
  congregation *(of cardinals)* **la curia**
convent **el convento**
I convert *(others)* **convierto**
I convert *(self)* **me convierto**
Eucharist **La Eucaristía**
evangelical **evangélico**
evangelist **el evangelista**
I give alms **doy limosna**
I give thanks **doy gracias**
Imam **el Imam, el Imán**
intercession **la intercesión, la mediación**
laity **el laicado**
lay **seglar, profano**
layperson **el seglar, el laico**
the Lord's Supper **La Santa Cena**
Mass **La Misa**
I meditate **medito**

Bishops in the Church of England are not afraid to speak about social problems.

Los obispos de la Iglesia Anglicana no tienen miedo de hablar de los problemas sociales.

The sacrament of Holy Communion will be celebrated on Sunday at nine.

El Sacramento de la Sagrada Comunión se celebrará el domingo a las nueve.

The parish council meets regularly.

El Consejo Parroquial se reúne con regularidad.

Every Muslim is called to prayer five times a day.

A todos los musulmanes se les llama a rezar cinco veces al día.

During the holy month of Ramadan, Muslims fast from dawn to dusk. The month ends with the celebrations of the festival of Eid.

Durante el Mes Sagrado de Ramadán, los musulmanes ayunan desde el amanecer hasta el anochecer. El mes termina con las festividades de la fiesta de Eid.

meditation la meditación
minister el ministro de la iglesia
I minister to the parish soy el párroco, administro la parroquia
ministry el ministerio eclesiástico
mission la misión
missionary el misionario, el misionero
monastery el monasterio
monk el monje
mosque la mezquita
mullah mullah
nun la monja
parish la parroquia
parishioner el feligrés
pastor el pastor, el sacerdote
pastoral pastoral
pilgrimage el peregrinaje
Pope el Papa
I praise rezo, oro
I pray (for) rezo (por), pido (por)
prayer la oración

priest el sacerdote, el cura
rabbi el rabino
reformation la reformación, la reforma
I repent me arrepiento
repentance el arrepentimiento
repentant el arrepentido
I revere venero, reverencio
reverence la veneración, la reverencia
reverent reverente
rite el rito
ritual el ritual
sacrament el sacramento
synagogue la sinagoga
synod el sínodo
temple el templo
vow el voto
wedding la boda
witness el testigo
I witness testifico
worship la adoración
I worship adoro

Those who are called to the ministry must demonstrate their vocation before being accepted to theological colleges.

Los que tienen vocación por el sacerdocio tienen que manifestar su vocación antes de ser aceptados en los seminarios.

The Baptist tradition is very strong in the American south.

La tradición de la iglesia Bautista es muy fuerte en el sur de los Estados Unidos.

A few Muslim schoolgirls in France have come into conflict with the authorities because they chose to wear the veil in school.

Algunas colegialas musulmanas en Francia han entrado en conflicto con las autoridades por decidir llevar el velo en el colegio.

Religious fundamentalism can lead to fanaticism and intolerance in any religion.

En cualquier religión, el fundamentalismo religioso puede llevar al fanatismo y a la intolerancia.

Business & Economics

14a The Economics of Business

I administer **administro**
I agree (to do) **acepto (hacer)**
agreement **el acuerdo**
bureaucracy **la burocracia**
business **los negocios**
 a business **un negocio, un acuerdo negocial**
capacity *(industrial)* **la capacidad**
commerce **el comercio**
commercial **comercial**
company **la empresa, la compañía, la sociedad**
deal **el trato**
I deliver **suministro, envío**
demand **la demanda**
the product is in demand **el producto está en demanda, el producto tiene demanda**
development **el desarrollo**
I earn (a living) **(me) gano (la vida)**
I employ **empleo**
employment **el empleo**
executive **el ejecutivo**
I export **exporto**
exports **las exportaciones**
fall **la caída**
goods **los bienes**
it grows **crece**
I import **importo**

I increase **incremento, aumento**
increase **el incremento, el aumento**
industrial output **la producción industrial**
industry **la industria**
I invest **invierto**
investment **la inversión**
layoffs **los despidos**
living standards **el nivel de vida**
I manage **dirijo, gestiono, administro**
management **la dirección, la gestión, la administración**
multinational **la multinacional**
I negotiate **negocio**
negotiations **las negociaciones**
 face-to-face **cara a cara**
priority **la prioridad**
I produce **produzco**
producer **el productor**
production line **la línea de producción**
productivity **la productividad**
quality **la calidad**
I raise *(prices)* **subo, incremento**
raise / rise **el aumento**
 pay raise **el aumento salarial**
reliability **la fiabilidad**
services **los servicios**

Strikers blocked the port of Bilbao and all main roads to Barajas Airport.

Los huelguistas obstruyeron el puerto de Bilbao y todas las carreteras que llevan al Aeropuerto de Barajas.

Unemployment is rising to twelve percent.

El desempleo alcanza el doce por ciento.

I set *(priorities)* **establezco**
sick leave **la baja / licencia por enfermedad**
I sign *(contracts)* **firmo**
skilled labor / labour **el trabajo especializado**
workers' unrest **el descontento laboral**
social welfare **el bienestar social**
I strengthen **refuerzo**
supplier **el proveedor**
supply **el suministro**
tax **el impuesto**
I tax **cobro un impuesto**
unemployment **el desempleo**
unemployment benefit **el subsidio de desempleo**
unskilled labor / labour **el trabajo no especializado**
work ethic **la ética laboral, la ética del trabajo**
workforce **los trabajadores**
work week **la semana laboral**

Industrial / Labor dispute

I am on strike **estoy en huelga**
I am a strike breaker / blackleg **trabajo durante una huelga, soy esquirol**
I boycott **boicoteo**
I cross the picket line **cruzo la línea de piquetes**
demonstration **la manifestación**
dispute **la disputa**
industrial / labor dispute **la disputa laboral, el conflicto laboral**
industrial relations **las relaciones industriales**

I lock out **dejo en la calle, cierro la puerta**
lockout **quedarse en la calle**
minimum wage **el salario mínimo**
I picket **hago de piquete**
picket **el piquete**
productivity bonus **el bono de productividad, la prima de productividad**
I resume work **reanudo, vuelvo al trabajo**
settlement **el ajuste**
I slow down / go slow **desciendo el ritmo de trabajo**
stoppage **la suspensión, la huelga**
strike **la huelga**
unofficial strike **la huelga no autorizada**
I strike **hago huelga**
strike ballot **la votación de la huelga**
strikebreaker **el esquirol**
striker **el huelguista**
trade union **el sindicato**
trade unionist **el sindicalista**
unfair dismissal **el despido injustificado**
I unionize **me sindico, me sindicalizo**
unionized labor / labour **los trabajadores sindicados**
unrest **el descontento**
wage demand **la demanda salarial**
work by the book / to rule **la huelga de celo, el paro técnico**

The unions called for a reduction in the average hours of the workweek. **Los sindicatos exigieron una reducción en el promedio de horas semanales de trabajo.**

The President has agreed to meet union leaders for talks. **El Presidente ha consentido en entrevistarse con los líderes de los sindicatos.**

PAY & CONDITIONS 14c; FINANCE 14d; BANKING & THE ECONOMY 14e

BUSINESS & ECONOMICS

14b At Work

agenda **el orden del día**
  on the agenda **en el orden del día**
I am away on business **estoy en viaje de negocios**
business trip **el viaje de negocios**
canteen **la cantina, el bar**
career **la carrera, la trayectoria profesional**
I chair a meeting **presido una reunión**
I delegate **delego**
disciplinary proceedings **el procedimiento disciplinario**
free **gratis**
grant **la beca, la ayuda**
I grant (someone) **beco, concedo una ayuda**
job **el trabajo, el empleo**
manager **el gerente**
management functions **las funciones directivas**
I market **comercio (al por mayor)**
meeting **la reunión**
misconduct **la mala conducta**
occupation **la ocupación, la profesión**
I'm on sick leave / off work **no trabajo, estoy de baja**
post **el puesto de trabajo**
profession **la profesión**
professional **el profesional**
publicity **la publicidad**
I qualify **satísfago los requisitos**
I report to . . . **mi superior inmediato es ...**
I am responsible for **soy responsable de**
research **la investigación**
I sell **vendo**
semiskilled **semiespecializado**
I teach **enseño**
I toil **trabajo duro**
trade **el comercio**
training **el aprendizaje, el entrenamiento**

training course **el curso de aprendizaje, el curso de entrenamiento / capacitación**
I transfer **me traslado**
vacation / holiday **las vacaciones**
vocation **la vocación**
wage earner **el asalariado**
warning (verbal) **la amonestación verbal**
  written warning **la amonestación por escrito**
I work **trabajo**
work **el trabajo**
worker **el trabajador**
workforce **los trabajadores, la fuerza laboral**

In the office

business lunch **la comida de negocios**
business meeting **la reunión de negocios**
computer **el ordenador, [el computador]**
conference call **la convocatoria de la conferencia**
conference room **la sala de conferencias**
correcting fluid **el líquido corrector**
desk **la mesa, el mostrador**
I dictate **dicto**
dictating machine **el dictáfono**
electronic mail **el correo electrónico**
extension **la extensión**
fax **el fax**
fax machine **la máquina de fax**
I fax **mando un fax**
file **el archivo**
I file **archivo**
filing cabinet **el archivador**
intercom **el interfono**

open plan   la oficina de plan abierto
photocopier   la fotocopiadora
photocopy   la fotocopia
I photocopy   fotocopio
pigeonhole   el casillero
reception   la recepción
receptionist   el / la recepcionista
shorthand   la taquigrafía
swivel chair   la silla giratoria
telephone   el teléfono
typing pool   la sala de mecanógrafos
wastebasket   la papelera
word processor   el procesador de textos
workstation   el puesto de trabajo, la estación de trabajo

In the factory & on site

automation   la automatización
blue-collar worker   los trabajadores, los obreros
I build   construyo
bulldozer   la aplanadora
car / automobile industry   la industria automotriz / del automóvil
component   el componente, la pieza
concrete   el hormigón
construction industry   la industria de la construcción

crane   la grúa
forklift truck   la carreta elevadora
I forge   forjo
industry   la industria
heavy industry   la industria pesada
light industry   la industria ligera
I manufacture   fabrico
manufacturing   la fabricación
mass production   la producción en masa
mining   la minería
power industry   la industria eléctrica
precision tool   el instrumento de precisión
prefabricated   prefabricado
process   el proceso
I process   proceso
product   el producto
on the production line   en línea de producción
raw materials   las materias primas
robot   el robot
scaffolding   el andamio
shipbuilding   la construcción naval
steamroller   la apisonadora
steel smelting   la fundición del acero
textile industry   la industria textil

Employment patterns are shifting from the traditional model of regular permanent jobs for one employer to a wide range of professional services delivered as a freelancer to various employers.

La estructura del empleo está cambiando: en lugar del modelo tradicional de puestos regulares y permanentes con un solo patrón, está cambiando a una amplia gama de servicios profesionales prestados a varios patrones por trabajadores independientes.

➤ STATIONERY App. 22b; COMPUTERS 15d

BUSINESS & ECONOMICS

14c Pay & Conditions

apprentice **el aprendiz**
bonus **la prima**
I clock in / out **ficho la entrada / salida, marco tarjeta**
commission **la comisión**
  on commission **a comisión**
company car **el coche de la empresa**
contract **el contrato**
I am employed **tengo trabajo**
expenses **los gastos**
expense account **la cuenta de gastos**
flextime / flexi-time **la jornada flexible**
freelance **autónomo**
I work freelance **soy autónomo**
full-time **la jornada completa / a tiempo completo**
income **los ingresos** (pl)
overtime **las horas extraordinarias** (pl)
overworked **el recargado de trabajo**
part-time **la jornada a tiempo parcial, medio tiempo**
payday **el día de paga**
payslip **la hoja de sueldo**
pay raise / payrise **el incremento salarial, la subida de sueldo**
payroll **la nómina**
pension **la pensión**
perk **el gaje, los beneficios** (pl) **adicionales**
permanent **permanente, fijo**
I retire **me retiro, me jubilo**
retirement **el retiro**
salary **el salario, el sueldo**
self-employed **autónomo**
sexual harassment **el hostigamiento sexual**
shift **el turno**
  day shift **el turno de día, el turno diurno**
  night shift **el turno de noche, el turno nocturno**
temporary **temporal**
trial period **el período de prueba**
working hours **las horas laborales**
wages **el salario, el sueldo**

The conditions in this office are not good enough for your staff, Mr. Abril.

The place is cold, badly lit, and poorly ventilated. And you have far too many electrical appliances plugged into one socket. Unless you make considerable changes within three months, I shall be forced to close the office down. I shall come back next week to discuss your plans. Good-bye!

Las condiciones de trabajo en esta oficina no son bastante buenas para su personal, Señor Abril.
El lugar está frío, está mal iluminado, y mal ventilado. Y tienen ustedes un gran exceso de aparatos eléctricos conectados a un sólo enchufe. Si ustedes no introducen todos los cambios necesarios en un plazo de tres meses, me veré obligado a cerrar la oficina. Volveré la semana que viene para discutir con usted su plan de acción. ¡Adiós!

Job application

I advertise for a secretary **anuncio un puesto de secretaria**

advertisement **el anuncio de trabajo**

I apply for a job **solicito un trabajo**

classified ad(vertisement) **los anuncios por palabras, [los avisos clasificados]**

curriculum vitae / résumé **la hoja de vida**

discrimination **la discriminación**

racial discrimination **la discriminación racial**

sexual discrimination **la discriminación sexual**

employment agency **la agencia de trabajo**

interesting **interesante**

interview **la entrevista**

I interview **entrevisto**

job application **la solicitud de trabajo**

employment office **la oficina de empleo**

job description **la descripción del trabajo**

I find a job **encuentro un trabajo**

I have been laid off / made redundant **he sido despedido**

I look for **busco**

I promote (someone) **asciendo (a alguien)**

I am promoted **soy ascendido**

to create an opening *(vacancy)* **la creación (de un puesto)**

promotion **la promoción**

qualification **la titulación**

qualified **titulado, cualificado**

openings / situations vacant **los puestos vacantes**

I start work (for) **empiezo a trabajar (para)**

I take on *(employee)* **empleo**

vacancy **una vacante**

work experience **la experiencia laboral**

"Hello. May I speak to the personnel manager, please."

"Speaking. What can I do for you?"

"I saw your ad in the paper for a sales executive. Could you send me the job description and application forms? How many references are you asking for?"

"Two, including your present or last employer."

— Oiga. Quisiera hablar con el jefe de la administración del personal, por favor.
— Soy yo. ¿En qué puedo servirle?
— Vi su anuncio en el diario en el que se pedía un ejecutivo de ventas. ¿Podría usted mandarme la descripción del trabajo y las hojas de solicitud? ¿Cuántas referencias piden ustedes?
— Dos, incluyendo a su jefe actual o al último empleador que ha tenido.

BUSINESS & ECONOMICS

14d Finance & Industry

account   la cuenta
advance   el anticipo
   in advance   (por) adelantado
I advertise   anuncio
advertisement   el anuncio
advertising   la publicidad
advertising agency   la agencia de
   publicidad
audit   la auditoría
bill   la factura
board   la junta
bond   el bono
branch (of company)   la sucursal
budget   el presupuesto
capital   el capital
capital expenditure   los gastos de
   inversión
chamber of commerce   la cámara
   de comercio
collateral   la garantía
company   la empresa, la
   compañía, la sociedad
I consume (resources)   consumo
consumer goods   los bienes de
   consumo
consumer spending   los gastos de
   consumo
cost of living   el coste de la vida
costing   la estimación, la
   cotización
costs   los costes
credit   el crédito, el activo

debit   el debe, el pasivo
deflation   la deflación
economic   económico
economy   la economía
funds   los fondos
government spending   el gasto
   público
income   el ingreso, los
   ingresos
income tax   el impuesto sobre la
   renta
installment   el plazo
interest rate   el tipo de interés
I invest in   invierto en
investment   la inversión
invoice   la factura
labor / labour costs   los costos
   laborales
liability   la responsabilidad
manufacturing industry   la
   industria de fabricación
market   el mercado
market economy   la economía de
   mercado
marketing   la comercialización, el
   márketing
merchandise   la mercancía
national debt   la deuda nacional
I nationalize   nacionalizo
notice / advice note   el aviso
output   la producción, el
   rendimiento

Morales S.A. announced its
takeover bid for the Dani
supermarket chain.

The company informed
shareholders that this year's
operating profits will not match the
level seen last year.

**Morales S.A. anunció su oferta
pública de adquisición de la
cadena de supermercados Dani.**

**La compañía les informó a sus
accionistas que los beneficios
netos este año no alcanzarán el
valor de los del año pasado.**

---

pay **el pago**
price **el precio**
private sector **el sector privado**
I privatize **privatizo**
product **el producto**
production **la producción**
public sector **el sector público**
quota **la cuota**
real estate / realty **la propiedad inmobiliaria**
retail sales **las ventas al por menor**
retail trade **la venta al por menor**
salaries **los salarios**
sales tax **el impuesto sobre las ventas**
service sector **el sector de servicios**
share **la acción**
shares going up / down **la subida / bajada de las acciones**
share index **el índice de la bolsa**
statistics **las estadísticas**
stock exchange **la bolsa de valores**
I subsidize **subvenciono**
subsidy **el subsidio**
supply and demand **la oferta y la demanda**
supply costs **los costos de suministro**
I tax **cobro un impuesto**

tax **el impuesto**
tax increase **el incremento / la subida de los impuestos**
taxation **la imposición**
taxation level **el nivel de imposición**
turnover **la facturación**
VAT / value added tax **el IVA (impuesto sobre el valor añadido)**
viable **viable**
wages **el salario**

Financial personnel

accountant **el contable**
actuary **el actuario**
auditor **el auditor**
banker **el banquero**
    investment banker **el banquero (del banco) de inversiones**
    merchant banker **el banquero (del banco) comercial**
bank manager **el director del banco**
broker **el agente de negocios**
    insurance broker **el agente de seguros**
consumer **el consumidor**
investor **el inversionista**
speculator **el especulador**
stockbroker **el agente de bolsa**
trader *(Wall St.)* **el comerciante**

Spantax Air expressed cautious optimism and suggested that the worst recession in the history of the aviation industry is coming to an end.

News of the budget deficit caused panic in the stock exchange today.

**La compañía aérea Spantax hizo una declaración de optimismo prudente, e indicó que está terminando la peor recesión de la historia de la industria de la aviación.
La Bolsa fue presa del pánico hoy al recibir las noticias del déficit presupuestario.**

BUSINESS & ECONOMICS

14e Banking & the Economy

Banking & personal finance

account   la cuenta
automatic teller / cashpoint   el cajero automático
bank   el banco
bank loan   el préstamo bancario
I bank (money)   pongo dinero en el banco
bankcard / cashcard   la tarjeta de dinero, la tarjeta para el cajero automático
bankrupt   la bancarrota
cash   dinero efectivo, metálico
I cash a check / cheque   cobro un cheque, hago efectivo un cheque
cash register / cashdesk   la caja
I change   cambio
check / cheque   el cheque
credit card   la tarjeta de crédito
currency   la moneda, la divisa
deposit *(in a bank)*   el deposito, el ingreso
deposit *(returnable)*   el depósito retornable
down payment / deposit   el
desembolso inicial, la entrada
Eurocheque   el eurocheque
exchange rate   el tipo de cambio
I have a credit   tengo un crédito de, tengo un saldo positivo de
in deficit   en déficit
installment plan / hire purchase   la venta a plazos
in the red   descubierto, en números rojos
I lend   presto
loan   el préstamo
mortgage   la hipoteca, el crédito hipotecario
I mortgage   hipoteco, obtengo un crédito hipotecario
I open *(account)*   abro
overdraft   el descubierto, el sobregiro
repayment   el reembolso
I save   ahorro
savings   los ahorros
savings and loan association / building society association   la sociedad de crédito inmobiliario

---

"I'd like to open an account here."
"Certainly, sir. What sort of account do you need?"
"Just a normal checking account."

"Could you fill out this form with all your personal details?"

"Certainly. What overdraft privileges are available for students?"

"I need to check that for you."

—Quisiera abrir una cuenta aquí.
—Con mucho gusto, señor. ¿Qué tipo de cuenta necesita usted?
—Una cuenta corriente, nada más.
—Haga el favor de rellenar este formulario con todos sus detalles personales.
—De acuerdo. ¿Qué posibilidades de crédito al abierto tienen ustedes a disposición de los estudiantes?
—Tendré que verificarlo.

traveler's checks / travellers' cheques
los cheques de viaje
I withdraw **retiro**

Growth

amalgamation **la fusión**
appreciation **el incremento de valor**
assets **el activo, los bienes, el capital**
assurance **la garantía**
auction **la subasta**
boom **el boom, el auge**
competition **la competencia, la concurrencia**
economic miracle **el milagro económico**
efficiency **la eficacia**
material growth **el incremento de bienes**
merger **la fusión, el fusionamiento**
profit **el beneficio**
profitable **rentable, lucrativo**
progress **el progreso**
prosperity **la prosperidad**
prosperous **próspero, floreciente**

recovery **la recuperación**
takeover **la adquisición, la toma de control**
takeover bid **la oferta pública de adquisición de acciones**

Decline

bankrupt **la bancarrota**
credit squeeze **la restricción**
debt **la deuda**
it is declining **está en baja**
deficit **el déficit**
depreciation **la depreciación**
I dump **hago dúmping**
inflation **la inflación**
inflation rate **el índice de inflación**
loss **la pérdida**
slowdown **la ralentización de la economía**
slump **la recesión**
spending cuts **los recortes presupuestarios**
stagnant **estancado**
stagnation **el estancamiento de la economía**
zero-growth economy **la economía sin crecimiento**

"Did you hear about Borges & Sons?"
"No, what about them?"
"Unfortunately, they went bankrupt. They borrowed too heavily in order to introduce a new line that just didn't sell."

"And what was it?"
"A range of battery-powered toys that clearly couldn't compete with the videogames market."

— ¿Has oído las noticias acerca de Borges e Hijos?
— No. ¿Qué les pasa?
— Desafortunadamente, han quebrado. Tomaron demasiado dinero prestado para poder introducir un nuevo producto, que luego no se vendió.
— ¿Y qué fue?
— Fue una gama de juguetes a pila que, está claro, no pudo hacer competencia contra el mercado de los videojuegos.

15 Communicating with Others

15a Social Discourse

Meeting

I accept **acepto**
appointment **la cita**
at home **en casa**
ball **el baile**
banquet **el banquete**
I bump into *(someone)* **topo con**
I'm busy **estoy ocupado**
I celebrate **celebro**
celebration **la celebración**
club **el club**
I come and see **vengo a ver**
dance **el baile**
I dance **bailo**
date *(appointment)* **la cita, el compromiso**
diary / datebook **la agenda**
I drop in on *(someone)* **paso a ver**
I expect **espero**
I'm expecting . . . for dinner **espero a ... para cenar**
I'm free **estoy libre**
I greet **saludo**
guest **el invitado, el convidado, el huésped**
handshake **el apretón de manos**
I have fun **me divierto**
invitation **la invitación**
I invite **invito**
I join **me uno a, me reúno (con), me junto con**
  I join *(a society)* **me hago socio de, ingreso en**
I keep *(a date)* **cumplo**
meeting **la reunión**
I meet **encuentro, me reúno con**
member **el miembro**
party **la fiesta**
  I throw a party **doy una fiesta**
I pick up / fetch someone **busco a alguien**

reception **la recepción**
I see **veo**
I shake hands with **estrecho manos con**
social life **la vida social**
I socialize **socializo**
I take part **tomo parte**
I talk **hablo**
visit **la visita**
I visit **visito**

Greetings & congratulations

bow / curtsey (to someone) **la reverencia**
Cheers! **¡Salud!**
Come in! **¡Pase / Entre (usted)!**
I congratulate **felicito**
Congratulations! **¡Felicitaciones!, ¡Enhorabuena!, ¡Felicidades!**
Good afternoon / evening **Buenas tardes / noches**
Good morning **Buenos días**
Good night **Buenas noches**
I greet **recibo, saludo**
Happy Easter **Feliz Pascua**
Happy New Year **Feliz Año Nuevo**
Hello / Hallo **Hola**
Here's to . . . **¡Vaya por ... !, ¡Bebemos a la salud de ... ¡**
Merry / Happy Christmas **Feliz Navidad**
toast **el brindis**
I toast **brindo por**
Well done! **¡Bravo!, ¡Muy bien!**

Introduction

Bill, meet Jan. **Bill, te presento a Jane**
Doctor . . . **Doctor ...**
How do you do? **¿Cómo está usted?**

I introduce **le presento a**
I introduce myself **me presento**
introduction **la presentación**
I'd like you to meet . . . **Quiero presentarle a ...**
Madam **Señora**
May I introduce . . . ? **Quiero presentarle a ...**
Miss **Señorita**
Mr. **Señor**
Mrs. **Señora**
Pleased to meet you **¡Mucho gusto!, Encantado**
Professor . . . **Profesor ...**
sir **señor**
This is . . . **Este es ...**
I welcome **doy la bienvenida, acojo, recibo**

Pleasantries

I address *(someone)* **me dirijo a**
I address as "tú" **tuteo, trato de tú**
I address as "usted" **trato de usted**
Best regards from . . . **un saludo de**
Bless you! / Gesundheit! **¡Salud / ¡Jesús!**
I'm (very) fine, thank you **Estoy (muy) bien, gracias**
health **la salud**
I hope you get well soon **(Espero) que te mejores pronto**
How are you (keeping)? **¿Cómo está usted?**
How are you feeling? **¿Cómo te sientes?**
Much better, thank you **Mucho mejor, gracias**
the same to you *(polite)* **(Y) a usted, igualmente**
so-so **regular, ni bien ni mal**
To your (very good) health! **¡Salud!**

Thanking

Many thanks **Muchas gracias**
Nice / good of you to . . . **Es usted muy amable ...**

Not at all! / It's a pleasure **¡De nada!, ¡No hay de qué!**
I thank **agradezco**
Thanks! **¡Gracias!**
Thank you so much **Muchísimas gracias**
No, thank you! **¡No, gracias!**
I'm (very) grateful to you for . . . **Le estoy (muy) agradecido por ...**

Apologizing

I apologize **me disculpo, pido perdón**
I do apologize **le ruego me disculpe**
I beg your pardon **le ruego me perdone**
I excuse **perdono**
Excuse me **Discúlpeme**
Excuse me, please **¡Perdón!, ¡Por favor!, ¡Con (su) permiso!**
Forget it! **¡Olvídelo!, ¡No se preocupe!, ¡No importa!**
I forgive **perdono, disculpo**
it doesn't matter (at all / a bit) **no importa (nada), es igual**
Oh, dear! **¡Ay!, ¡Dios mío!**
I refuse **rehuso, rechazo**
I'm (so very) sorry that . . . **Siento (muchísimo) que ...**
What a shame / pity (that . . .) **¡Qué lástima (que ...)!**

Farewells

All the best! **¡Que tenga suerte!**
Good-bye! **¡Adiós!**
Good luck! **¡Que tenga suerte!**
I say good-bye **me despido**
Have a good time! **¡Que usted se divierta!, ¡Que lo pase bien!**
Have a safe trip / journey! **¡Buen viaje!**
See you later! / Cheerio! **¡Hasta luego!**
I will see you later / tomorrow **Nos veremos más tarde / mañana**
Sweet dreams! **¡Duerma usted bien!**

15b Comments & Interjections

Approval & disapproval

I quite agree! **¡estoy totalmente de acuerdo!**

agreement **el acuerdo**

approval **la aprobación**

I approve **apruebo**

Is this all right? **¿Vale?, ¿Está bien?**

Fine! **¡Estupendo!, ¡Magnífico!**

I'm glad / pleased (that . . .) **Me alegro (de que ...)**

Good! **¡Bueno!, ¡Muy bien!**

How nice! **¡Qué bien!**

You should(n't) have . . . **(No) debería haber ...**

Quiet! **¡Silencio!, ¡A callar!, ¡Cállate!, ¡Cállese!**

sh! **¡chitón!, ¡chist!**

tut-tut *(clicks)* **¡Vamos!, ¡Eso no!, ¡Qué horror!, ¡Pche!**

That's enough. **Basta (ya).**

That's just what I need. **Es precisamente lo que necesito.**

Permission & obligation

That's (quite) all right **(Eso) está (muy) bien**

allowed **permitido**

I allow **permito, dejo**

I am allowed to . . . **se me permite ...**

It is not allowed / permitted **No se permite**

Can I . . .? **¿Puedo ..., ¿Se puede ... ?**

I can(not) **(no) puedo**

You cannot (can't) **No puede(s)**

I have to **tengo que, debo**

May I . . . ? **¿Puedo ... ?**

I may (not) **(no) puedo**

I must (not) **(no) debo**

No **No**

Not now / here / tonight **Ahora / aquí / esta noche no**

I ought to . . . **debería ...**

you ought to . . . **deberías ...**

permission **el permiso**

permitted **permitido**

Please do! **Hágalo, por favor**

I'm (not) supposed to . . . **(no) debo ...**

Do you have time to . . .? **¿Tiene usted tiempo de ... ?**

I should **debería**

You should(n't) . . . **(No) deberías ...**

Surprise

Can that be . . . ? **¿Es posible (eso)?**

That cannot (can't) be **No puede ser**

Good grief! **¡IDios mío!**

Goodness! **¡IDios mío!**

Imagine / Fancy (that)! **¡Vaya!, ¡Fíjate!**

Is it possible that . . .? **¿Es posible que ... ?**

Just as I expected **Ya me lo figuraba.**

Oh really! **¡Eh!, ¡Ca!, ¡Qué cosas pasan!**

surprise **la sorpresa**

I surprise **sorprendo**

surprising **sorprendente**

Does that surprise you? **¿Le sorprende eso?**

So what? **¿(Pues) y qué?**

Well? **¿Y entonces?**

Wow! **¡Caramba!, ¡Caray!**

Hesitating

er . . . **pues, es decir, esto ...**

hesitation **la indecisión**

I hesitate **vacilo**

How shall I put it? **¿Cómo lo diría yo?**

Just a minute / moment! **Un minuto, momento, Un momentito**

Now let me think   **Déjame pensar, Veamos, Vamos a ver**
or rather . . .   **o bien ...**
that is to say . . .   **es decir ...**
That's not what I meant to say   **No es lo que quería decir**
thingamajig   **la cosa, el chisme**
What's his / her name?   **¿Cómo se llama (él / ella)?**

Listening & agreeing / disagreeing

I agree / don't agree (that) . . .   **(no) estoy de acuerdo que**
aha!   **¡ajá!**
Don't you agree (that)   **¿No crees que ?**
I believe so / not   **Creo que sí / no**
Certainly!   **¡Desde luego!, ¡Por supuesto!, ¡Por cierto!**
Certainly not!   **¡De ninguna manera!, ¡Ni hablar!**
correct   **correcto, exacto, justo**
I don't think so   **Creo que no**
Exactly!   **¡Exactamente!**
I find (that)   **encuentro (que)**
Indeed!   **¡Por cierto!, ¡En efecto!, ¡Claro que sí!, ¡Ya lo creo!**
Just so!   **¡Exactamente!, ¡Eso es!, ¡Perfectamente!, ¡Precisamente!**
never   **nunca, jamás**
No!   **¡No!**
Nonsense / Rubbish!   **¡Qué va! ¡Tonterías!, ¡Ni pensar!**
of course!   **¡claro!, ¡por supuesto!, ¡naturalmente!**
of course not!   **¡claro que no!**
Oh!   **¿De veras?**
Really?   **¿Verdad?, ¿De veras?**
right   **¡eso es!, ¡conforme!, ¡justo!, ¡bueno!**
That's not so   **No es así**
that's (not) right / true   **(no) es correcto, (no) es verdad**
that's right / correct   **es eso, eso es, es correcto**
I think so   **Creo que sí**

true   **verdad, verdadero**
you're wrong   **está usted equivocado**
that's wrong!   **es equivocado, es falso, no es correcto**
yes!   **¡Sí!**

Clarification & meaning

a kind / sort of . . .   **una especie de ... , algo así como ...**
Do you mean . . . ?   **¿Quiere usted decir?**
Did you say . . . ?   **¿Dijo usted que ... ?**
I explain   **explico**
How do you spell that, please?   **¿Cómo se escribe eso, por favor?**
I mean   **quiero decir**
I say   **digo**
Is that clear?   **¿Comprendido?, ¿Entendido?, ¿Está claro?**
it is spelled / you spell it . . .   **se escribe ...**
That's just what I had in mind   **Es exactamente lo que pensaba / buscaba**
That's not what I had in mind   **No es lo que yo había pensado**
What did you say?   **¿Qué dijo usted?**
What do you mean by . . . ?   **¿Qué quiere(s) decir con ... ?**
What I said was . . .   **Lo que dije fue que ...**
What is it in Spanish?   **¿Cómo es en español?**
Would you repeat that, please?   **Repite, por favor**
Would you speak more slowly, please?   **Hable (usted) más despacio, por favor**
Would you spell that, please?   **¿Quisiera usted deletrear eso, por favor?**
you know   **usted sabe**

COMMUNICATING WITH OTHERS

15c Mail/Post & Telephone

Mail/Post

abroad **el extranjero**
addressee **el destinatario, el consignatario**
airmail **el correo aéreo**
airmail letter **la carta por correo aéreo, el aerograma**
airmail paper **el papel para avión**
answer **la contestación, la respuesta**
collection **la recogida**
I correspond with **me escribo con**
correspondent **el corresponsal**
counter **el mostrador**
customs declaration **la declaración aduanera**
envelope **el sobre, la envoltura**
express delivery **la entrega urgente**
I finish (letter) **termino (la carta)**
first-class mail **el correo de primera clase**
general delivery **la lista de correos**
I get/receive **recibo**
I hand in **entrego**
letter **la carta**
letter/mail rate **la tarifa de cartas**
mail/post **el correo**
mailbox/letter-box **el buzón**
mailman/postman **el cartero**

money/postal order **el giro postal**
news **las noticias, las nuevas**
I note down **tomo apuntes**
notepaper **el papel para cartas, el papel para escribir**
package **el paquete, el bulto**
parcel **el paquete**
parcel rate **la tarifa de paquetes**
pen pal/pen-friend **el amigo por correspondencia**
I post **echo a correos, llevo a correos, echo al buzón**
post office **correos, la oficina de correos**
postage **los gastos de correo**
postcard **la (tarjeta) postal**
prepaid postage/freepost **correo libre de franqueo**
registered/recorded mail/**el correo certificado**
reply **la contestación, la respuesta**
sealed **sellado**
I send **mando, envío**
I send (greetings) **mando (un saludo/recuerdos)**
sender **el remitente**
stamp **el sello**
I write **escribo**
zip code/postcode **el código postal**

When does the mail/post arrive?	**¿A qué hora llega el cartero?**
I haven't heard from her in ages.	**Hace mucho tiempo que no tengo noticias suyas.**
Dear Sir,	**Muy señor mío:**
I am writing on behalf of my father, concerning. ...	**Le escribo de parte de mi padre, acerca de ...**
I look forward to hearing from you,	**Quedo a la espera de sus noticias,**
Yours sincerely, ...	**Le saluda atentamente, ...**

Telephone & telecommunications

booth **la cabina**
busy / engaged *(phone)* **está comunicando / ocupado**
button **el botón**
cell (mobile) phone **el celular, el móvil**
collect / reverse charge call **la llamada por cobro revertido**
conversation **la conversación**
dial **el disco**
electronic mail **el correo electrónico**
extension **la extensión, el supletorio, el interno**
extension number **el número de la extensión**
fax **el (tele)fax**
fax modem **el módem de fax**
local call **la llamada / conferencia local**
long-distance call **la conferencia interurbana**
operator **el / la telefonista**
out of order **no funciona**
phone booth / call-box **la cabina telefónica**
receiver **el auricular**
slot **la ranura**
subscriber **el abonado**
telecommunications links **los enlaces de telecomunicación**

telecommunications **las telecomunicaciones**
telegram **el telegrama**
telegraph **telégrafo**
telephone **el teléfono**
telephone directory **la guía telefónica**
telephone booth / kiosk **la cabina telefónica**
telephone / phone **el teléfono**
text message **el mensaje de texto**
I transmit **transmito**
unlisted / ex-directory **no figura en la guía**
word **la palabra**
wrong number **el número equivocado**
zero / nought **cero**

Telephoning

I call **llamo**
I connect with **comunico con**
I dial **marco**
I fax **mando por fax, faxeo**
I hang up **cuelgo**
I hold **estoy en espera**
I pick up **descuelgo**
I press **pulso, aprieto**
I put ... through (to) **me pongo con ..., (me) comunico con ...**
I speak to **hablo con**
I telephone / phone **llamo por / al teléfono, telefoneo**

Do you have change for the telephone?	¿Tiene usted moneda para el teléfono?
Can I dial / call direct?	¿Puedo marcar el número en directo?
Hello / Hallo! *(calling)*	¡Oíga(me), por favor!
Hello / Hallo! *(answering)*	¡Díga(me)!
Are you still there?	¿Aún está ahí?
Can you hear me?	¿Me oye usted?
Could you fax it to me?	¿Me lo puede mandar por fax, por favor?

15d Computers

Computer applications

adventure game **el videojuego de aventuras**
application **la aplicación**
artificial intelligence **la inteligencia artificial**
bar code **el código de barras**
bar code reader **el aparato lector de códigos de barras, la máquina lectora de códigos de barras**
browser **navegador**
calculator **la calculadora, la minicalculadora**
computer science / studies **la informática, las ciencias de la computación**
computerized **computerizado, informatizado**
desktop publishing / DTP **la autoedición**
electronic mail **el correo electrónico**
grammar checker **el corrector de gramática, el consultor de gramática**
information **la información**
information technology **la informática**
internet **la Internet**

optical reader **el lector óptico (de textos)**
simulation **la simulación**
simulator **el simulador**
spell check **el corrector ortográfico, el consultor de ortografía**
synthesizer **el sintetizador**
text **el texto**
thesaurus **el diccionario de sinónimos, la antología**
website **sitio Web**
word processor **el procesador de palabras, el procesador de textos**
word processing **el proceso de textos, el tratamiento de textos**

Word processing & operating

I abort **interrumpo (el programa), detengo prematuramente**
I access **entro**
I append **anexiono (al final)**
I apply boldface **pongo los caracteres en negrita**
I back up **hago una copia de apoyo**
I block (text) **agrupo**
I boot up **arranco, cebo, inicializo**
I browse **hojeo**

Is it possible to replace the central processing unit?	**¿Es posible reemplazar la unidad procesadora central?**
These computers are on a local area network.	**Estos ordenadores están conectados a una red de área local.**
I replied to your message yesterday.	**Ayer mismo te contesté el mensaje.**
How do you turn down the brightness?	**¿Cómo se baja el brillo?**
Can you repair this keyboard?	**¿Puede usted reparar este teclado?**

I cancel **anulo**

I click on **pulso el ratón**

I communicate **comunico**

I copy **copio**

I count **cuento**

I create **creo, abro (un archivo)**

I cut and paste **corto e inserto**

I debug **depuro, quito el duende de ...**

I delete **cancelo, borro**

I download **descargo**

I emulate **emulo**

I enter **introduzco, entro a**

I erase **borro**

I exit **salgo (del sistema)**

I export **exporto**

I file **ficho**

I format **formateo**

I forward **reenvío**

I handle (text) **trato (el texto)**

I import **importo**

I install **instalo**

I list **listo**

I log **apunto, anoto, registro**

I log off / out **salgo del sistema, finalizo la sesión, termino de operar**

I log on / in **entro al sistema, accedo, inicio la sesión**

I merge **fusiono**

I move **muevo**

I open (a file) **abro (un fichero), entro a un fichero**

I print **imprimo, grabo**

I print out **imprimo**

I (word) process **trato / manejo el texto**

I program(me) **programo**

I read **leo, estudio**

I receive **recibo**

I record **registro**

I remove **quito**

I replace **reemplazo, sustituyo**

I reply **contesto**

I retrieve **recupero, llamo**

I run **ejecuto**

I save **salvo, grabo guardo**

I search **busco**

I send a copy to **envío una copia a**

I send **envío, mando, emito**

I shift **quito**

I sort **ordeno**

I store **almaceno**

I switch off **quito, apago, desconecto**

I switch on **enciendo, pongo, conecto**

I tabulate **tabulo**

I type **tecleo**

I underline **subrayo**

I update **actualizo**

Don't show me your password!	**¡No me muestre su contraseña de acceso!**
I don't like the software package with this PC.	**No me gusta el paquete de programas que se ofrece con este ordenador personal.**
Is this spreadsheet easy to use?	**¿Esta hoja electrónica, es fácil de utilizar?**
You can always consult the pull-down menu.	**Siempre se puede consultar el menú desplegable.**
It has erased my file!	**¡Ha borrado mi fichero!**
This disk is corrupted.	**Este disco está degradado.**

16 Leisure & Sport

16a Leisure

activity **la actividad**	energetic **enérgico**
amateur **el amateur, el aficionado**	energy **la energía**
book **el libro**	enthusiasm **el entusiasmo**
boring **aburrido**	entrance **la entrada**
camera **la cámara**	entry fee **la tarifa de entrada**
I can **puedo**	excitement **la excitación**
card **la tarjeta**	exciting **excitante, divertido**
card game **el juego de cartas**	excursion **la excursión**
card table **la mesa de juego**	exit **la salida**
casino **el casino**	fair **la feria**
chess **el ajedrez**	fascinating **fascinante, encantador**
closed **cerrado**	
club **el club**	finished **terminado, finalizado**
I collect **colecciono**	free time **el tiempo libre**
coin **la moneda**	fun **la diversión**
collection **la colección**	I gamble **apuesto**
collectors' fair **la feria de colecciones**	I get in line/queue **hago cola**
	I go out **salgo**
connoisseur **el entendido, el conocedor**	guide **el guía**
	guided tour **el viaje con guía**
crossword puzzle **el crucigrama**	hobby/pastime **el hobby, la afición, el pasatiempo**
I decide **decido**	
discotheque **la discoteca**	interest **el interés, la afición**
do-it-yourself/DIY **hágalo usted mismo**	

"What is your favorite/favourite pastime?"
"Well, I used to go for a drive in the country every Sunday, but I have no time for hobbies nowadays. Sometimes I go fishing."

— ¿Cuál es tu pasatiempo favorito?
— Bueno, solía ir a conducir por el campo todos los domingos pero ahora no tengo tiempo para pasatiempos. Algunas veces voy a pescar.

I can meet you at the swimming pool or, if you prefer, at the gym.

Puedo encontrarme contigo [Podemos vernos] en la piscina, o si prefieres, en el gimnasio.

interesting **interesante**
I join **me uno**
leisure **el ocio**
I like (dis-) **(no) me gusta**
line / queue **la cola**
I listen to **escucho, oigo**
I look **miro, veo**
market **el mercado**
  antiques market **el mercado de antigüedades**
  flea market **el mercadillo, el mercado de la pulga**
I meet **veo a, quedo con, me reúno con**
meeting place **el punto de encuentro**
member **el miembro**
membership **la calidad de socio**
movie theater / cinema **el cine**
nightclub **el club nocturno**
open **abierto**
organization **la organización**
I organize **organizo**
photograph **la fotografía**
picnic **el picnic, la comida en el campo**
place **el lugar**
I play **juego**
pleasure **la satisfacción, el placer**
politics **la política**

I prefer **prefiero**
private **privado**
public **público**
I read **leo**
season **la estación**
season ticket **el billete de abono, [el tiquete de temporada]**
secluded **aislado**
slide **la diapositiva**
spectator **el espectador**
I start (doing) **comienzo, empiezo**
I stop (doing) **termino**
I stroll **paseo**
subscription **la suscripción**
television **la televisión, el televisor**
theater / theatre **el teatro**
ticket **el billete, la entrada, [el boleto, el tiquete]**
time **el tiempo**
tour **el viaje turístico, la excursión**
vacation / holiday **las vacaciones**
I visit **visito**
visit **la visita**
I walk **ando, camino**
I watch **observo, miro**
youth club **el club juvenil**
zoo **el zoo, el (jardín / parque) zoológico**

"What do you like doing on a rainy day?"
"Perhaps playing cards but not with my brother: he cheats!"

— **¿Qué te gusta hacer en un día lluvioso?**
— **Quizás, jugar a las cartas, pero no con mi hermano: ¡hace trampas!**

"Shall we take the children to the zoo?"
"Good idea. If we take Eve's children and their school friends as well, we can get a group discount."

— **¿Llevamos a los niños al zoológico?**
— **Buena idea. Si llevamos a los niños de Eva y a sus amigos del colegio también, nos harán un descuento de grupo.**

16b Sporting Activity

against **contra**	fall **la caída**
I aim **apunto**	I fall **me caigo**
archer **el arquero**	field **el campo**
athlete **el atleta**	finals **la final, las finales**
athletic **atlético**	fit **en forma**
ball **la pelota, el balón**	fitness **estar en forma**
bathtowel **la toalla de baño**	I get fit **me pongo en forma**
bet **la apuesta, la postura**	game **el juego**
boat **la barca, el bote**	goal **el gol**
I bowl **juego al boliche, juego a las bolas**	gym(nasium) **el gimnasio**
	hit **el golpe**
boxer **el boxeador**	I hit **golpeo**
captain **el capitán**	ice rink **la pista de patinaje**
I catch **cojo, recojo**	I ice skate **patino sobre hielo**
champion **el campeón**	injury **la herida, la lesión**
championship **el campeonato**	instructor **el instructor**
I climb **escalo**	I jog **troto, corro**
climber **el escalador**	jogger **el corredor**
coach **el entrenador**	jump **el salto**
cup *(trophy)* **la copa**	I jump **salto**
cycle **el ciclismo**	lawn **el césped**
I cycle **hago ciclismo**	league **la liga**
defeat **la derrota**	I lift weights **levanto pesas**
I dive **buceo**	locker / changing room **el vestuario**
I do *(sport)* **practico**	I lose **pierdo**
draw *(tie)* **el empate**	marathon **el maratón**
I draw *(tie)* **logro el empate**	match **el partido**
effort **el esfuerzo**	medal **la medalla**
endurance **la resistencia**	gold / silver / bronze **de oro / de plata / de bronce**
equipment **el equipo**	
I exercise **hago ejercicio**	

Without sponsorship, I won't be able to train using the best facilities. I cannot then compete at the highest level.	**Sin patrocinio no podré entrenar con las mejores instalaciones. Por lo mismo, no podré competir al nivel más alto.**
"Did you watch the match?" "No, I had to leave before the end. Who won?" "We lost 3 to 1."	**—¿Has visto el partido?** **—No, me tuve que ir antes del final. ¿Quién ganó?** **—Perdimos 3 a 1 (tres a uno).**

muscle   **el músculo**
Olympics Games (winter)   **los Juegos Olímpicos (de invierno)**
opponent   **el adversario**
pedal   **el pedal**
pentathlon   **el pentatlón**
physical   **físico**
I pitch   **lanzo**
pitcher   **el lanzador**
player   **el jugador**
I play   **juego**
point   **el punto**
professional *(adj)*   **profesional**
race   **la carrera**
I race   **participo en una carrera**
referee   **el árbitro**
rest   **el descanso**
result   **el resultado**
I ride   **monto a caballo**
riding school   **la escuela ecuestre**
I row   **remo**
run   **la carrera**
I run   **corro**
runner   **el corredor**
sail   **la vela**
I sail   **navego**
sailing school   **la escuela de náutica / navegación**
score   **el tanteo, el resultado, el puntaje**
I score *(a goal)*   **marco**
I shoot *(ball, puck)*   **chuto, tiro**
I shoot *(at a target)*   **tiro**
I shoot pool   **juego al billar**

show   **el espectáculo**
I ski   **esquío**
ski lift   **el remonte, la telesilla**
skier   **el esquiador**
sponsor   **el patrocinador**
sponsorship   **el patrocinio**
sport   **el deporte**
sports field   **el campo de deportes**
sprint   **el sprint**
stadium / ground   **el estadio, el terreno**
stamina   **el vigor, la resistencia**
strength   **la fuerza**
supporter   **el seguidor, el hincha**
I swim   **nado**
team   **el equipo**
team sport   **el deporte de equipos**
touchdown   **el tocado en tierra**
I throw   **lanzo**
tournament   **el torneo**
track   **la pista**
I train   **me entreno**
trainer   **el entrenador**
training   **el entrenamiento**
triumph   **el triunfo**
trophy   **el trofeo**
I am unfit   **no estoy en forma**
victory   **la victoria**
I win   **gano**
workout   **el entrenamiento, la preparación**
world championship   **el campeonato del mundo**
world cup   **la copa del mundo**

I still cannot understand how such a capable team could lose so disastrously after a brilliant season.
All sports commentators agree that they were particularly unlucky when the referee insisted on the penalty kick.

Todavía no puedo entender cómo un equipo tan bueno pudo perder tan desastrosamente tras una magnífica temporada.
Todos los comentaristas deportivos están de acuerdo en que tuvieron muy mala suerte cuando el árbitro insistió en la sanción.

LEISURE & SPORT

16c Sports & Equipment

Sports

aerobics **los ejercicios aeróbicos**
archery **el tiro con arco**
athletics **el atletismo**
badminton **el bádminton**
baseball **el béisbol**
basketball **el baloncesto**
bowling **la bolera, los bolos**
 tenpins / ten-pin bowling **el boliche**
boxing **el boxeo**
climbing **el montañismo, el alpinismo**
 free climbing **la escalada libre**
 rock climbing **la escalada en rocas**
crew **el equipo**
cricket **el cricket, el críquet**
cycling **el ciclismo**
decathlon **el decatlón**
diving **el buceo**
 deep water diving **el buceo en aguas profundas**
football **el fútbol norteamericano**
handball **el balonmano**
hockey **el hockey**
horse racing **las carreras de caballos**
horseback riding **montar a caballo**
ice hockey **el hockey sobre hielo**
ice skating **el patinaje sobre hielo**
jogging **el footing**

motor racing **el automovilismo, las carreras de coches**
paragliding **el planeador**
polo **el polo**
pool **el billar**
racing **las carreras**
riding **montar a caballo**
roller skating **el patinaje sobre ruedas**
rugby **el rugbi, el rugby**
sailing **la navegación**
skiing **el esquí**
 water skiing **el esquí acuático**
 cross-country skiing **el esquí nórdico**
 downhill skiing **el esquí alpino**
snooker **el snooker**
soccer **el fútbol**
swimming **la natación**
table tennis **el tenis de mesa, el pinpón, el ping-pong**
volleyball **el vóleibol**
water polo **el polo acuático**
weight training **el entrenamiento con pesas**
windsurfing **el windsurf**

Leisure wear & sport clothes

anorak **el anorak**
bathing suit **el traje de baño**
boots **las botas**
cycling shorts **los pantalones de ciclista**
dancing shoes **los zapatos de baile**

The most popular sports in North America are baseball, (American) football, basketball and (ice) hockey. In South America, soccer is the major passion.

Los deportes más populares en Norteamérica son el béisbol, el fútbol norteamericano, el baloncesto y el hockey sobre hielo. En Sudamérica la pasión es el fútbol.

SPORTS & EQUIPMENT 16c

gardening gloves **los guantes de jardinería**
leotard **el leotardo**
parka **la parka**
ski outfit / salopette **el mono de esquiar**
swimsuit **el bañador [el traje de baño] de mujer**
swimming trunks **el bañador [el traje de baño] de hombre**
rugby shirt **la camiseta de rugbi**
track suit **el chandal**
trainers **las zapatillas de deporte**
walking boots **las botas para andar**
waterproof jacket **el chaleco impermeable**
Wellington boots **las botas de agua**
wet suit **el traje de buceo**

Leisure & sport equipment

arrow **la flecha**
ball **la pelota, el balon**
bat **el bate, la maza, la paleta**
binoculars **los anteojos, los prismáticos**
bow **el arco**
boxing gloves **los guantes de boxeo**
camera **la cámara**
crash helmet **el casco**
equipment **el equipo, el material**
exercise bike **la bicicleta de ejercicio, la bicicleta estática**
fishing rod **la caña de pescar**

headphone **el auricular**
hi-fi **hi-fi, (de) alta fidelidad**
knapsack / rucksack **la mochila**
knitting needles **las agujas de hacer punto**
javelin **la javalina**
mountain bike **la bicicleta de montaña**
net **la red**
outrigger **el portarremos, el bote con portarremos exterior**
pruning shears / secateurs **las tijeras de podar, la podadora**
puck **el disco, el puck**
racket **la raqueta**
rifle **el rifle**
roller skates **los patines de ruedas**
rowing machine **el aparato de remo**
rowing boat **el bote de remo**
sailboat **el barco de vela**
sewing kit **el costurero**
skate **el patin**
skis **los esquis**
ski boots **las botas de esquí**
ski poles / sticks **los bastones de esquí**
spinning wheel **la rueca**
sports bag **la bolsa de deporte**
stick *(hockey)* **el palo**
surfboard **la tabla de surf**
weights **las pesas**
yacht **el yate**
zoom lens **el zoom**

In the final minutes, the goalkeeper made a spectacular save with his stick to flick the puck off the line and out of the goal.

En los últimos minutos, el portero impidió un gol de una manera espectacular con el palo quitando el puck de la línea y echándolo lejos de la portería.

17 The Arts

17a Appreciation & Criticism

abstract **abstracto**
abstruse **abstruso**
action **la acción**
aesthete **el esteta**
aesthetics **la estética**
I appreciate **aprecio**
appreciation **la apreciación**
art **el arte**
artist **el artista**
artistic **artístico**
atmosphere **la atmósfera**
atmospheric **atmosférico**
author **el autor**
award **el premio**
I analyze **analizo**
avant-garde *(adj)* **en vanguardia**
believable **creíble**
character **el personaje**
characterization **la caracterización**
characteristic **característico**
climax **el clímax, el punto culminante**
it closes **cierra**
comic **cómico**
commentary **el comentario**
conflict **el conflicto**
contemporary **contemporáneo**
contrast **el contraste**
it creates **crea**
creativity **la creatividad**
credible **creíble, verosímil**
critic **el crítico**
criticism **la crítica**
cultivated **cultivado**
culture **la cultura**
it deals with **trata de**
it describes **describe**
it develops **desarrolla**
development **el desarrollo**

device **la estratagema, el mecanismo**
dialogue **el diálogo**
disturbing **inquietante**
empathy **la empatía**
ending **el final, el fin**
it ends **finaliza, termina**
entertaining **divertido, entretenido**
entertainment **el divertimiento, el entretenimiento**
epic *(n)* **la épica**
event **el acontecimiento, el suceso, el evento**
eventful **memorable**
example **el ejemplo**
exciting **emocionante**
I explain **explico**
explanation **la explicación**
it explores **explora**
it expresses **expresa**
fake **falso**
fantastic **fantástico**
fantasy **la fantasía**
figure **la figura**
funny **gracioso, divertido**
image **la imagen**
imaginary **imaginario**
imagination **la imaginación**
inspiration **la inspiración**
inspired by **inspirado por**
intense **intenso**
intensity **la intensidad**
invention **la invención**
inventive **inventivo, imaginativo**
ironic **irónico**
irony **la ironía**
issue **la cuestión, el problema**
life **la vida**
long-winded **prolijo, extenso**

lyrical **lírico**
modern **moderno**
mood **el humor, la atmósfera**
moral **moral**
morality **la moralidad**
moving **conmovedor**
mystery **el misterio**
mysterious **misterioso**
mystical **místico**
nature **la naturaleza**
obscene **obsceno**
obscenity **la obscenidad**
obscure **oscuro, obstruso**
opinion **la opinión**
optimism **el optimismo**
optimistic **optimista**
parody **la parodia**
passion **la pasión**
passionate **apasionado**
pessimism **el pesimismo**
pessimistic **pesimístico**
it portrays **representa, describe**
portrayal **la representación, el retrato**
precious **valioso, precioso**
protagonist **el protagonista**
I read **leo**
reader **el lector**

realistic **realista**
reference **la referencia**
I reflect **reflejo**
reflection **la reflexión, el pensamiento**
relationship **la relación, la conexión**
review **la revisión, el análisis**
sad **triste**
satire **la sátira**
it satirizes **satiriza**
satirical **satírico**
style **el estilo**
  in the style of **al estilo de**
stylish **con estilo, elegante**
subject **el tema, el contenido**
technique **la técnica**
tension **la tensión**
theme **el tema**
tone **el tono**
tragedy **la tragedia**
tragic **trágico**
true **verdadero, auténtico**
vivid **vívido**
viewpoint **el punto de vista**
witty **ingenioso**
work of art **la obra de arte**

Artistic styles & periods

Art Nouveau **el art nouveau**
Aztec **azteca**
baroque **barroco**
classical period **el período clásico**
Enlightenment **el Siglo de las luces**
existentialist **existencialista**
expressionist **expresionista**
futuristic **futurístico**
Georgian **georgiano**
Gothic **gótico**
Greek **griego**
medieval **medieval**
naturalistic **naturalístico**

Norman **normando**
Persian **persa**
poetic **poético**
postmodernist **pos-modernista**
realism **el realismo**
Renaissance **el Renacimiento**
rococo **rococó**
Romanesque **románico**
romantic **romántico**
structuralist **estructuralista**
surrealist **surrealista**
symbolist **simbolista**
twentieth century **el siglo veinte**
Victorian period **el período victoriano**

THE ARTS

17b Art & Architecture

antique   **antiguo**
antiquity   **la antigüedad**
architect   **el arquitecto**
art   **el arte**
artifact   **el artefacto**
artist   **el artista**
art student   **el estudiante de arte**
auction sale   **la subasta**
auctioneer   **el subastador**
balance   **el equilibrio**
baroque   **barroco**
beam   **la viga**
bronze   **el bronce**
brush   **el pincel**
I build   **construyo**
building   **la construcción, el edificio**
bust   **el busto**
caricature   **la caricatura**
I carve   **esculpo, tallo**
I cast   **fundo**
ceramics   **la cerámica**
charcoal   **el carbón, el carboncillo**
chisel   **el cincel**
chiseled   **cincelado**
classical   **clásico**
clay   **la arcilla**
collage   **el collage**
decorated   **decorado**
decoration   **la decoración**
decorative arts   **las artes decorativas**
I design   **diseño**
design   **el diseño**

dimension   **las medidas, la dimensión**
I draw   **dibujo**
drawing   **el dibujo**
easel   **el caballete**
elevation   **la elevación**
enamel   **el esmalte**
I engrave   **grabo**
engraving   **el grabado**
I etch   **grabo al aguafuerte**
etching   **el aguafuerte**
exhibition   **la exposición**
figure   **la figura**
figurine   **la figurilla**
filigree   **la filigrana**
fine arts   **las bellas artes**
flamboyant   **rimbombante, llamativo**
form   **la forma**
freehand   **hecho a pulso**
fresco   **el fresco**
frieze   **el friso**
genre   **el género**
graphic arts   **las artes gráficas**
gravity   **la gravedad**
holograph   **el ológrafo, el olograma**
interior   **interior, interno**
intricate   **intrincado**
ironwork   **el herraje**
landscape   **el paisaje**
landscape gardener   **el arquitecto de jardines**

We have a very good view of the cupola from this terrace. Look, in the foreground you can see the monastery, which dates back from 1679 and which is such a good example of religious architecture, and in the background the medieval towers are still visible.

La vista de la cúpula desde esta terraza es muy buena. Mira, al fondo puedes ver el monasterio que fue construido en 1679 y es un buen ejemplo de la arquitectura religiosa, y detrás pueden verse todavía las torres medievales.

landscape painter el paisajista
large-scale works las obras a
   gran escala
later works las últimas obras
light la luz
   light (adj) luminoso
lithography la litografía
luminosity la luminosidad
luminous luminoso
masterpiece la obra maestra
metal el metal
miniature la miniatura
model el modelo
monochrome monocromo, de un
   solo color
moorish árabe
mosaic el mosaico
museum el museo
oil painting la pintura al óleo
ornate ornado, florido
I paint pinto, dibujo
paint la pintura
painting el cuadro, la pintura
pastel el pastel
portrait el retrato
potter el ceramista
pottery la cerámica
it represents representa
representation la representación
reproduction la reproducción
restoration la restauración
I restore restauro
restored restaurado
restorer el restaurador

school la escuela
I sculpt esculpo
sculptor el escultor
sculpture la escultura
seascape el paisaje marino, la
   marina
shadow la sombra
shape la forma
I shape doy forma, moldeo
sketch / roughcast el boceto,
   el esbozo
I sketch hago un boceto
sketching el dibujo, el boceto
stained glass la vidriera
statuary el estatuario
statue la estatua
still life el bodegón, la naturaleza
   muerta
I stipple punteo
studio el estudio
style el estilo
surrealism el surrealismo
tapestry el tapiz
tempera la témpera, la pintura al
   temple
town planning el urbanismo
traditional tradicional
translucent translúcido
transparent transparente
visual arts las artes visuales
watercolor / -colour la acuarela
wood la madera
wood carving la talla de madera
woodcut la incisión

I have just been to the exhibition at the Royal Academy, which has already attracted thousands of visitors. There is the most wonderful collection of drawings and sculptures of the Italian artist. Two of the paintings have been very skillfully restored.

Acabo de visitar una exposición en la Real Academia que ya ha atraído a miles de visitantes. Tiene la mejor colección de dibujos y esculturas del artista italiano. Dos de los dibujos han sido muy bien restaurados.

THE ARTS

17c Literature

autograph   **el autógrafo**
book   **el libro**
bookstore / shop   **la librería**
bookseller   **el librero**
character   **el personaje**
   main character   **el personaje
   principal, el protagonista**
   secondary character   **el
   personaje secundario**
comic   **cómico**
dialogue / dialog   **el diálogo**
fictional   **ficticio**
hardback   **la cubierta dura**
I imagine   **imagino**
imagination   **la imaginación**
inspiration   **la inspiración**
inspired by   **inspirado por**
it introduces   **introduce**
introduction   **la introducción**
I leaf through   **hojeo**
librarian   **el bibliotecario**
library   **la biblioteca**
   public library   **la biblioteca
   pública**
   reference library   **la biblioteca
   de consulta**

literal(ly)   **literal(mente)**
map   **el mapa**
myth   **el mito**
mythology   **la mitología**
it narrates   **narra**
narrative   **la narrativa**
narrator   **el narrador**
note   **la nota**
page   **la página**
paperback   **la cubierta rústica**
paragraph   **el párrafo**
poem   **el poema**
poetic   **poético**
poetry   **la poesía**
punctuation   **la puntuación**
quote   **la cita**
I quote   **cito**
I read   **leo**
I recount   **cuento, refiero**
rhyme   **la rima**
it is set in   **está situado en**
table   **la tabla**
text   **el texto**
title   **el título**
verse   **el verso**

"What are you reading at the moment?"

— **¿Qué lees ahora?**

"A spine-chilling story with a tragic conclusion.
It is set in contemporary Buenos Aires."

— **Una historia escalofriante con un final trágico.
Está situado [Tiene lugar] en el Buenos Aires actual.**

It is a vivid account of life in the thirties. The writer explores the theme of lost innocence.

Es un retrato vivo de la vida de los años treinta. El escritor explora el tema de la inocencia perdida.

Types of books

adventure story **la historia de aventuras**
atlas **el átlas**
autobiography **la autobiografía**
biography **la biografía**
children's literature **la literatura infantil**
comic novel **la novela cómica**
cookbook **el libro de cocina**
detective story **la novela policíaca**
diary **el diario**
dictionary **el diccionario**
  bilingual **el diccionario bilingüe**
  monolingual **el diccionario monolingüe**
encyclopedia **la enciclopedia**
epic poem **el poema épico**
essay **el ensayo**
table **la fábula**
fairy tale **el cuento de hadas**
feminist novel **la novela feminista**
fiction **la ficción, la narrativa**
Greek tragedy **la tragedia griega**
horror story **la historia / el cuento de terror**

letters **las cartas**
manual **el manual**
memoirs **las memorias**
modern play **la obra teatral moderna**
mystery play **la obra teatral de misterio**
nonfiction **la literatura no novelesca**
novel **la novela**
picaresque novel **la novela picaresca**
poetry **la poesía**
reference book **el libro de consulta**
restoration comedy **la comedia de la restauración**
satirical poem **el poema satírico**
science fiction story **la historia de ciencia ficción**
short story **el cuento, la historia corta**
spy story **la historia de espionaje**
teenage fiction **la literatura juvenil**
travel book **el libro de viajes**
war novel **la novela de guerra**

A collection of modern foreign fiction. | **Una colección de narrativa extranjera actual.**

My novel deals with changes in nineteenth century Spanish rural society. | **Mi novela trata de los cambios de la vida rural española en el siglo diecinueve.**

It opens with a lyrical description of the valley. It ends with the last entry in the hero's diary. | **Comienza con una descripción lírica del valle. Termina con lo último que el héroe escribió en su diario.**

THE ARTS

acoustics la acústica
agent el agente
album el álbum
amplifier el amplificador
audience el público, la audiencia
audition la audición
auditorium el auditorio
ballet el balet
bandleader el director de la banda
baton la batuta
brass band la banda, la charanga
cassette tape la cinta de casete
cassette deck el casete
chamber music la música de cámara
choir el coro
choral la coral
chorale coral
choreography la coreografía
chorister el corista
chorus el coro, el estribillo
compact disc / disk el compact disc, el disco compacto
competition el concurso
compilation la recopilación
I compose compongo
composer el compositor
composition la composición
concert el concierto
concert hall la sala de conciertos
I conduct dirijo
conductor el director de orquesta
dance la danza

I dance danzo
dancer el danzarín
dance music la música de danza
discotheque la discoteca
disc jockey el disc jockey
drummer el batería
ensemble el conjunto, la agrupación
euphony la eufonía
folk music la música folk, la música popular
gig la actuación
group el grupo
harmony la armonía
harmonic la armónica
hit (song) la canción de éxito
hit / chart parade la lista de éxitos
I hum canturreo
instrument el instrumento
instrumental music la música instrumental
instrumentalist el instrumentalista
I interpret interpreto
interpretation la interpretación
jazz el jazz
judge / adjudicator el juez del concurso
jukebox la máquina de música
key la clave
lesson la lección
I listen to escucho, oigo
listening la audición
microphone el micrófono

"There is a concert at the students' union."
"What is the name of the band?"
"I don't know. Their lyrics are quite good but the music is dreadful."

Rehearsals will be held in the cathedral on Friday evening

— Hay un concierto en el Sindicato de Estudiantes.
— ¿Cómo se llama el grupo?
— No lo sé. La letra es bastante buena pero la música es malísima.

Los ensayos se harán el viernes por la tarde en la catedral.

---

music   la música
musically   musicalmente
musician   el músico
musicologist   el musicólogo
note   la nota
orchestra   la orquesta
orchestration   la orquestación
it is performed   es tocado, es
   representado
performance   la representación
performed by   representado por,
   ejecutado por
performer   el ejecutor
pianist   el pianista
piano   el piano
piece   la pieza musical
I play   toco
player   el músico
portable   portátil
I practice / practise   practico
promotional video   el vídeo
   promocional
I put on a record   pongo un disco
recital   el recital
record   el disco, la grabación
I record   grabo
recording   la grabación
recording studio   el estudio de
   grabación
refrain   el estribillo
I rehearse   ensayo
rehearsal   el ensayo
repertoire   el repertorio
rhythm   el ritmo

rhythmic   rítmico
rock   el rock
show   el espectáculo
I sing   canto
singer   el cantante
solo   el solo
soloist   el solista
song   la canción
songwriter   el autor de canciones
string   la cuerda
string orchestra   la orquesta de
   instrumentos de cuerda
symphony   la sinfonía
tape   la cinta
tour   la gira
   on tour   de gira
tune   el tono
   in tune   entonado, [afinado]
   out of tune   desentonado,
   [desafinado]
I tune   entono
tuner (of instruments)   afinador de
   instrumentos
tuning fork   el diapasón
violin maker   el fabricante de
   violines
vocal music   la música vocal
voice   la voz
I whistle   silbo
whistling   el silbido
wind band   la orquesta de
   instrumentos de viento
wind instruments   los
   instrumentos de viento

"Do you play an instrument?"
"I play the viola."
"I never learned to play an
instrument but I have just bought
an electric guitar."

The conductor was greeted by a
standing ovation.

— ¿Tocas algún instrumento?
— Toco la viola.
— Nunca he aprendido a tocar un
instrumento pero acabo de
comprar una guitarra eléctrica.

El público aplaudió en pie al
director.

THE ARTS

act **la actuación**
I act **actúo**
acting school **la escuela de teatro**
actor **el actor**
actress **la actriz**
I applaud **aplaudo**
applause **el aplauso**
audience **el público**
auditorium **el auditorio**
I book **reservo**
box **el palco**
box office **la taquilla**
cabaret **el cabaret, el**
espectáculo de variedades
camera **la cámara**
camera crew **los operadores de**
cámara
cameraman **el cámara, el**
camarógrafo
cartoons **los dibujos animados**
choreographer **el coreógrafo**
circle **la galería**
circus **el circo**
I clap **aplaudo**
clapping **el aplauso**
coatroom / cloakroom **el**
guardarropa
comedian **el comediante, el actor**
cómico
comedienne **la comediante, la**

actriz cómica
curtain **el telón**
I design **diseño**
designer **el diseñador**
I direct **dirijo**
director **el director**
drama **el drama**
dress rehearsal **el ensayo general**
dubbed **doblado**
dubbing **el doblaje**
effect **el efecto**
expectation **la expectación**
farce **la farsa**
farcical **farsesco, absurdo**
first night **el estreno**
floor show **el espectáculo de**
variedades / de cabaret
flop **el fracaso**
gaffer **el lluminista**
intermission **el intervalo, el**
descanso
interval **el descanso**
lights **las luces, los focos**
in the limelight **en candelero**
lobby **el pasillo, el vestíbulo**
location work **los exteriores, el**
rodaje fuera del estudio
I make a movie / film **hago una**
película
masterpiece **la obra maestra**

It does not transfer well to the
screen.

No se transfiere bien a la
pantalla.

Foreign films are usually dubbed,
but some film clubs show them
in the original language.

Las películas extranjeras
generalmente se doblan, pero
algunos clubs de cine las dan
en el idioma original.

Stuntpersons have been used for
the most dangerous scenes.

Se han usado dobles para las
escenas más peligrosas.

matinée la función de tarde
melodrama el melodrama
mime el mimo
movie / film la película
movie / cinema buff el cinéfilo
movie / film maker el cineasta
movie / film producer el productor de cine
movie / film star la estrella de cine
movies / cinema el cine
music hall la sala de fiestas
offstage entre bastidores
opening night el estreno
ovation la ovación
pantomime la pantomima
performance la actuación, la ejecución
photography la fotografía
play la obra de teatro
I play actúo
playwright el dramaturgo
premiere el estreno
I produce produzco
producer el productor
production la producción
public el público
retrospective la retrospectiva
role el papel
row la fila
scene la escena
scenery el escenario
screen la pantalla
screen test la prueba de proyección, la toma

screening la proyección
script el guión
scriptwriter el guionista
seat la butaca
sequel la continuación, el desenlace
sequence la secuencia
it is shot está filmado
I show *(a movie / film)* muestro
sold-out vendido
sound track la banda sonora
special effects los efectos especiales
stage *(theater / theatre)* el escenario, la escena
stage *(movies / cinema)* el escenario, el decorado
stage directions la acotación
stage effects los efectos escenográficos, los efectos teatrales
stage fright el miedo al público
stalls las butacas
stuntperson el doble que realiza las escenas peligrosas
trailer el tráiler, el avance
understudy *(theater / theatre)* el suplente
understudy *(movies / cinema)* el doble
usherette la acomodadora
walk-on part el papel de figurante
I zoom capto, doy un golpe de zoom

Sci-fi films were popular in the sixties.	**Las películas de ciencia-ficción eran populares en los años sesenta.**
I want to see the latest production of her three-act play. All the critics will be there.	**Quiero ver la última producción de su obra de teatro en tres actos. Toda la crítica acudirá.**
He is playing one of the most demanding roles of his career.	**Está jugando uno de los papeles más difíciles de su carrera.**

The Media

18a General Terms

admission **la admisión**	detailed **detallado**
I admit **admito**	it discriminates **discrimina**
I analyze **analizo**	disaster **el desastre**
analysis **el análisis**	disinformation **la desinformación**
I appeal to **apelo a, recurro a**	educational **educativo**
I argue **discuto**	I entertain **divierto, entretengo**
argument **el argumento**	ethical **ético**
attitude **la actitud**	event **el suceso, el**
biased **parcial**	**acontecimiento**
campaign **la campaña**	example **el ejemplo**
censorship **la censura**	expectations **las expectativas**
cogent **lógico, convincente,**	I exploit **exploto**
fuerte	fallacious **engañoso, falaz**
comment **el comentario**	fallacy **la falacia, el engaño**
conspiracy **la conspiración**	freedom **la libertad**
criticism **la crítica**	full / detailed **detallado, extenso**
critique **la crítica**	gullible **crédulo, simplón**
cultural **cultural**	hidden **escondido, oculto**
culture **la cultura**	homophobic **homofóbico**
cultured **culto**	ignorance **la ignorancia**
current events **los sucesos de**	I ignore **ignoro, desconozco**
actualidad	influential **influyente, prestigioso**
declaration **la declaración**	information **la información**
it declares **declara**	informative **informativo**

During the recent elections it was difficult to find an example of unbiased reporting.	**Durante las elecciones recientes fue difícil encontrar un ejemplo de información objetiva en los medios de comunicación.**

interview la entrevista
it intrudes se entromete, obstruye
intrusion la intrusión, la intromisión
intrusive intruso
issue (problem) el problema, el asunto, la cuestión
I keep up with (news) estoy al día con
libel la difamación, la calumnia
libellous difamante, calumnioso
likely probable
it is likely es probable
local interest news las noticias de interés local
(mass) media los medios (masa) de comunicación
material el material
meddling entrometido
news las noticias
news item la noticia, el asunto
partisan partidario
persuasive persuasivo
prejudice el prejuicio
political político
politics la política
press la prensa
privacy la intimidad, la privacidad
privacy law la legislación para la protección de la intimidad

problem el problema
review el análisis de las noticias
I review analizo
scoop la exclusiva, la primicia informativa
sensational sensacional
sensationalism el sensacionalismo
sexism el sexismo
sexist sexista
silence el silencio
silent silencioso
social social
society la sociedad
specious especioso
summary el sumario
summary (adj) sumario
it takes place tiene lugar
trust la confianza
I trust confío
trustworthy fiable
truth la verdad
truthful verdadero
unbiased objetivo
untrustworthy no fiable
up-to-date actualizado
violent violento, agresivo
violence la violencia
weekly semanal

I am a freelance journalist specializing in investigative journalism.

Soy periodista independiente, especializado en periodismo investigativo.

In recent years many war correspondents have lost their lives while reporting from the front or have been taken as hostages.

En años recientes, muchos corresponsales de guerra han perdido la vida informando desde el frente o han sido hecho [tomados como] rehenes.

➤ ADVERTISING 18d

THE MEDIA

advice column / problem page **el consultorio**

advice for the lovelorn / agony aunt **el columnista del consultorio sentimental**

article **el artículo**

back page **la última página**

barons **los magnates de la prensa**

broadsheet **el periódico sábana / de gran formato**

cartoon **el tebeo, la caricatura**

chief editor **el jefe de edición**

circulation **la circulación**

color / colour supplement **el suplemento en color**

column **la columna**

comic **el cómic, el tebeo**

correction **la corrección**

correspondent **el corresponsal**

foreign correspondent **el corresponsal extranjero**

crossword puzzle **el crucigrama**

daily newspaper **el diario**

I edit **edito, redacto**

edition **la edición, la tirada**

editor **el editor, el redactor, el director**

editorial **editorial**

forgotten **olvidado**

front page **la primera página, la portada**

glossy magazine **la revista de lujo**

gutter press **la prensa basura, la prensa amarilla, la prensa sensacionalista**

headline **el titular**

heading **el título, el encabezamiento**

illustration **la ilustración**

it is published **está publicado**

journalist **el periodista**

layout **la distribución, la diagramación**

leader **el editorial, el artículo de fondo**

local paper **el periódico local**

magazine **la revista**

monthly **la revista mensual**

national newspaper **el periódico nacional**

newsagent **la tienda de prensa**

newspaper **el periódico**

newsstand **el kiosco de prensa, el quiosco de prensa**

page **la página**

pamphlet **el panfleto**

periodical **la revista / la publicación periódica**

power **el poder**

powerful **poderoso**

press agency **la agencia de prensa**

press conference **la conferencia de prensa**

European current affairs are not always reported in the American press, though all quality papers have foreign correspondents in all the European capitals.

Las noticias de actualidad europea no siempre aparecen en la prensa americana, a pesar de que todos los periódicos de calidad tienen corresponsales en todas las capitales europeas.

The gutter press has a surprisingly high readership.

La prensa sensacionalista tiene una sorpendente cantidad de lectores.

I print **imprimo**
print **la impresión**
print room **la sala de impresión**
I publish **publico**
publisher **el dueño de la casa editorial**
publishing company **la casa editora, la editorial**
quality press **la prensa de calidad**
reader **el lector**
I report **informo**
report **el reportaje**
reporter **el reportero**

short news item **las noticias breves, las breves**
small ad **los anuncios por palabras**
special correspondent **el corresponsal especial**
special issue **la edición especial**
sports page **la página de deportes**
I subscribe to **me suscribo a**
subscription **la suscripción**
tabloid **la prensa sensacionalista**
type(face) **el tipo de letra, el formato de la letra**
weekly **el semanario**

Newspaper sections

Advice column / Problem page **consultorio**
Announcements **anuncios**
Arts **arte**
Economy **economía**
Editorial **artículo de fondo**
Entertainment **ocio**
Finance **finanzas**
Food and Drink **gastronomía**
Games **pasatiempos**
Gossip column **la columna rosa**
Horoscope **horóscopo**

International news **noticias internacionales**
Letters to the editor **cartas al director**
National / Home news **noticias nacionales**
Obituary **necrológicas, obituario**
Property **propiedad, inmobiliaria**
Sport **deportes**
Travel **viajes**
Women **mujer**

Media barons have dominated the press in many western countries.

Los magnates de la prensa han dominado la prensa en muchos paises occidentales.

When is the color / colour supplement published?

¿Cuándo se publica el suplemento en color?

What a scoop! I guess the circulation of the paper has increased significantly in the last two weeks.

¡Qué primicia! Supongo que la circulación del periódico ha subido mucho en las dos últimas semanas.

➤ PUBLISHING App. 17c

THE MEDIA

aerial **la antena**
anchorman **el presentador**
anchorwoman **la presentadora**
announcer **el presentador, el locutor**
audience **el público, la audiencia**
boob tube / goggle box **la caja boba, la caja tonta**
I broadcast **emito**
broadcasting station **la emisora**
cable TV **la televisión por cable**
cameraman **el cámara, el camarógrafo**
channel **el canal**
commercial **el anuncio de televisión**
couch potato **el haragán del sofá**
dubbed **doblado**
earphones **los auriculares, [los audífonos]**
episode **el episodio**
high frequency **la alta frecuencia**
interactive **interactivo**
listener **el oyente**
live broadcast **la emisión en directo**
live coverage / commentary **el reportaje en directo**
loudspeaker **el altavoz**
low frequency **la baja frecuencia**
microphone **el micrófono**
newsreader **el locutor**
personal stereo **el walkman®**
production studio **el estudio de producción**
program(me) **el programa**
radio **la radio**
on radio **en la radio**
I record **grabo**
recording **la grabación**
remote control **el mando a distancia, el control remoto**
I repeat **repito**
repeat **repetir**
satellite dish **la antena parabólica**
satellite TV **la televisión por satélite**
screen **la pantalla**
I show **presento, muestro**
signal **la señal**

"What! Still glued to the set? You have been watching the box all evening! You have become a real couch potato!"

— ¡Que! ¿Todavía pegado a la televisión? Has estado viendo la caja boba toda la tarde. Te has convertido en un verdadero haragán de la televisión.

"I'm just going to record this movie / film then I'll join you. Have you got any blank videocassettes?"

— Voy a grabar esta película y entonces voy contigo. ¿Tienes alguna cinta de video en blanco?

Until recently most television commercials portrayed women in exclusively traditional roles.

Hasta hace muy poco tiempo, en los anuncios de televisión las mujeres aparecían exclusivamente en papeles tradicionales.

station **la estación**
subtitles **los subtítulos**
I switch off **apago**
I switch on **enciendo**
teletext **el teletexto**
television **la televisión**
   on television **en televisión**
I transmit **retransmito**
TV / telly **la tele**
TV set **el aparato de televisión**

TV studio **el estudio de televisión**
video clip **el videoclip**
videogame **el videojuego**
video library **la videoteca**
video recorder **el aparato de vídeo**
viewer **el teleespectador, el televidente**
I watch **veo**

TV & radio program(me)s

cartoons **los dibujos animados**
children's program(me) **el programa infantil**
comedy **la comedia**
current affairs **la actualidad**
drama **el drama**
documentary **el documental**
education programs **los programas educativos**
feature movie / film **el largometraje**
light entertainment **el programa de variedades**

news **las noticias**
quiz program(me)s **los programas concurso**
regional news **las noticias regionales**
soap **la telenovela**
school broadcasting **la emisión escolar**
science program(me) **el programa científico**
sports program(me) **el programa deportivo**
weather forecast **el pronóstico del tiempo**

Was the Pink Floyd concert broadcast live from Venice?

There should be a program / programme on student grants on this channel, but perhaps the children would prefer watching the cartoons. Where is the TV guide?

During the summer the traffic bulletin is broadcast every hour in four languages for the benefit of foreign visitors.

¿El concierto de Pink Floyd se emitió en directo desde Venecia?

Debería haber un programa sobre becas para estudiantes en este canal, pero quizás los niños preferirían ver los dibujos animados. ¿Dónde está el programa [la programación] de la televisión?

Durante el verano el boletín de información del tráfico se emite cada hora en cuatro idiomas como servicio a los visitantes extranjeros.

THE MEDIA

18d Advertising

I advertise **anuncio**
advertisment **el anuncio**
advertising **la publicidad**
advertising industry **la industria de la publicidad**
appeal **el atractivo**
it appeals to **atrae, tiene atractivo para**
billboard **la cartelera, la valla publicitaria**
brand **la marca**
brochure **el folleto**
campaign **la campaña publicitaria**
catalog(ue) **el catálogo**
it catches the eye **se mete por los ojos**
commercial **el anuncio comercial**
competition *(rival)* **la competencia**
competition *(game)* **el concurso**
consumer **el consumidor**
consumer society **la sociedad de consumo**
copywriter **el escritor de material publicitario**
I covet **codicio, deseo**

it creates a need **crea una necesidad**
demand **la demanda**
disposable income **la renta disponible**
distributor **el distribuidor, el concesionario**
ethical **ético**
goods **los bienes**
hidden persuasion **la persuasión oculta**
image **la imagen**
junk mail **la propaganda de buzón**
I launch **lanzo**
lifestyle **el estilo de vida**
market **el mercado**
down-market **inferior, la sección popular del mercado**
up-market **superior, la sección superior del mercado**
market research **el análisis de mercados**
materialism **el materialismo**
model **el modelo**

"Do you think that TV ads are more effective than ads in newspapers?"

"National television reaches many more potential consumers but is extremely expensive."

This image will reach about a million potential consumers.

This has been his least successful campaign: next time we will use another agency or perhaps a freelance copywriter.

— **¿Piensas que los anuncios de la televisión sean más eficaces que los anuncios de los periódicos?**
— **La televisión nacional llega a muchos más consumidores potenciales, pero es muy cara.**

Esta imagen llegará a un millón de consumidores potenciales.

Esta ha sido su campaña de menos éxito; la próxima vez usaremos otra agencia, o quizás un periodista independiente.

I motivate **motivo**
need **la necesidad**
persuasion **la persuasión**
poster **el póster, el afiche**
product **el producto**
I promote **promociono**
promotion **la promoción**
publicity **la publicidad**
I publicize **doy publicidad a, anuncio**
public relations **las relaciones públicas**
purchasing power **el poder adquisitivo**
radio advertisements **los**

anuncios de la radio
it sells **vende**
slogan **el eslogan, el lema**
status symbol **el símbolo del estatus**
stunt **el truco publicitario**
I target **mi objetivo es, me dirijo a**
target group **el grupo objeto**
I tempt **tiento**
trend **la tendencia**
trendy **muy al día**
truthful **verdadero**
TV advertisements **los anuncios de televisión**
unethical **no ético**

Small ads

accommodation **el alojamiento**
appointments **citas**
births **natalicios, nacimientos**
courses and conferences **cursos y conferencias**
deaths **necrológicas, obituario**
engagements **compromisos**
exchange **divisa**
exhibitions **exposiciones**

for sale **se vende**
health **salud**
lonely hearts **encuentros**
marriages **bodas**
personal services **servicios personales**
property **propiedad inmobiliaria**
travel **viajes**
vacations / holidays **vacaciones**
wanted **se quiere, se requiere**

The buildings are covered in ugly publicity billboards.

Los edificios están cubiertos con vallas publicitarias feas.

This publicity can be offensive to some ethnic groups.

Esta publicidad puede ser ofensiva para algunos grupos étnicos.

SPECIAL OFFER! For one week only! Buy two and get one free! Plus twenty percent discount on your next purchase!

¡OFERTA ESPECIAL! ¡Durante una semana nada más! ¡Compre dos y le regalamos uno! ¡Más veinte por ciento de descuento en su próxima compra!

Travel

19a General Terms

I accelerate / speed up **acelero**	distance **la distancia**
accident **el accidente**	documents **los documentos**
adult **el adulto**	driver *(car)* **el conductor**
announcement **el anuncio**	early **temprano, pronto**
arrival **la llegada**	emergency **la emergencia, la**
I arrive (at) **llego (a)**	**urgencia**
assistance **la ayuda, la asistencia**	emergency call **la llamada de**
I ask for assistance **pido ayuda**	**emergencia / urgencia**
bag **la bolsa**	emergency stop **la parada de**
baggage **el equipaje**	**emergencia**
baggage checkroom / left-luggage	en route **en ruta**
office **la consigna**	entrance **la entrada**
I book **reservo**	exit **la salida**
booking office **la oficina de**	extra charge **el recargo, el**
reservas	**suplemento**
briefcase **el maletín**	fare **la tarifa**
business trip **el viaje de negocios**	fare reduction **la reducción de**
I buy a ticket **compro un billete**	**tarifa**
I call at **paso (por), hago escala**	reduced fare **la tarifa reducida**
en	fast **rápido, veloz**
I cancel **cancelo**	I fill out a form **relleno un**
I carry **llevo**	**formulario**
I catch **cojo**	free **gratis**
I check *(tickets)* **confirmo**	from **de**
child **el niño, la niña**	information **la información**
class **la clase**	information office **la oficina de**
I confirm **confirmo**	**información**
connection **el transbordo**	I inquire **pregunto, pido**
I cross **cruzo**	**información**
delay **el retraso**	inquiry **la pregunta, la consulta**
I am delayed **tengo retraso, voy**	insurance **el seguro**
con retraso, [estoy retrasado]	help **la ayuda, el socorro**
I depart **salgo**	helpful **útil**
departure **la salida**	late **tarde**
destination **el destino**	I leave *(place)* **salgo**
direct **directo**	I leave *(person / object)* **dejo**
direction **la dirección**	I leave at **salgo a**
disabled **el inválido**	lost **perdido**

lost and found / lost property office
la oficina de objetos perdidos
loudspeaker **el altavoz, el**
altoparlante
luggage / baggage **el equipaje**
message **el mensaje, el recado,**
la nota
I miss **pierdo**
money **el dinero**
nonsmoker **no-fumador**
notice **el aviso**
nuisance **la molestia**
occupied **ocupado**
on board **a bordo**
on time **a tiempo**
one-way / single ticket **el billete de**
ida
I pack **hago la maleta**
passenger **el pasajero**
porter **el mozo**
porter (hotel) **el portero, el**
conserje
perfect timing **el horario perfecto**
reduction **el descuento, la rebaja**
rescue **el rescate**
reservation **la reserva**
I reserve **reservo**
restroom / toilet **el servicio**
I return **vuelvo**
return **la vuelta**
round-trip / return ticket **el billete de**
ida y vuelta
safe **seguro**
safety **la seguridad**
seat **el asiento**
seatbelt **el cinturón de seguridad**
I set off **salgo**
signal **la señal**
slow **lento**
I slow down **reduzco la velocidad**
smoking **fumar**
speed **la velocidad**
staff **el personal**
I start from **salgo de**

stop **la parada**
I stop **paro**
on strike **de huelga**
I take (bus, train) **cojo**
ticket **el billete**
ticket desk **la ventanilla de**
billetes, el despacho de
billetes, la taquilla
ticket office **la oficina de billetes,**
la taquilla
timetable **el horario**
I travel **viajo**
travel **el viaje**
travel agent **el agente de**
viajes
travel agency **la agencia de**
viajes
travel documents **los**
documentos
travel information **la**
información de viajes
travel pass **el pase de viaje, el**
pasaporte
travel sickness (car) **el mareo**
traveler **el viajero, el pasajero**
tunnel **el túnel**
turn **el giro, la vuelta**
I turn **giro**
I unpack **deshago la maleta**
useless **inútil**
valid **válido**
via / through **a través, pasa por**
visitor **el visitante**
warning **el aviso**
way in **la entrada**
way out **la salida**
weekdays **los días de la semana**
weekend **el fin de semana**
Welcome! **¡Bienvenido!**
welcoming **acogedor**
window **la ventana**
window seat **el asiento al lado de**
la ventana

19b Going Abroad & Travel by Boat

Going abroad

I cross (the English Channel) **atravieso / cruzo (el canal de la Mancha)**

currency **la moneda**

currency exchange office **la oficina de cambio de moneda**

customs **la aduana**

customs control **el control de aduanas**

customs officer **el oficial de aduana**

customs regulations **la legislación / el reglamento de aduanas**

declaration **la declaración**

I declare **declaro**

duty **el derecho, el impuesto**

duty-free goods **los productos libres de impuestos**

duty-free shop **la tienda de productos libres de impuestos**

English Channel **la Mancha** Channel Tunnel **el túnel de la Mancha**

exchange rate **la tasa de cambio**

expired **caducado, vencido**

foreign currency **la moneda extranjera**

frontier **la frontera**

I go through customs **paso la aduana**

I go through passport control **paso el control de pasaportes**

immigration office **la oficina de inmigración**

immigration rule **el reglamento de inmigración**

passport **el pasaporte**

I pay duty on **pago el impuesto de**

smuggler **el contrabandista**

smuggling **el contrabando**

visa **la visa**

Travel by boat

boat **el barco**

bridge **el puente**

cabin **el camarote**

calm sea **el mar calmado, el mar en calma**

"Here are my documents. My final destination is Santiago."
"Thank you. Have a nice trip!"

— **Aquí están mis documentos. Mi destino final es Santiago.**
— **Gracias. Buen viaje.**

"I have nothing to declare. This is for my personal use."

— **No tengo nada que declarar. Esto es para mi uso personal.**

"What! All forty bottles of whisky and one hundred cartons of cigarettes?"

— **¡Qué! ¿Cuarenta botellas de whisky y cien cajas de cigarillos?**

For your comfort and safety, please fasten your seatbelts.

Por su comodidad y seguridad, por favor, abróchense los cinturones de seguridad.

captain el capitán, el comandante
coast la costa
crew la tripulación
crossing la travesía
cruise el crucero
deck la cubierta
  lower deck la cubierta inferior
  upper deck la cubierta superior
deck chair la butaca de cubierta
I disembark desembarco
disembarkation el desembarco
dock el muelle
I embark embarco
embarkation card la tarjeta de embarque
ferry el ferry
I go on board entro a bordo
harbor / harbour el puerto
lifeboat el bote de salvamento
lifejacket el chaleco salvavidas
lounge la sala
ocean el océano
offshore el mar abierto, la alta mar
on board a bordo

overboard por la borda
port (a) babor
port (of call) el puerto (de escala)
quay el muelle
reclining seat el asiento reclinable
sea el mar
  calm sea el mar en calma
  choppy sea el mar picado / agitado
  heavy sea el mar grueso
  stormy sea el mar borrascoso
seaman el marino, el marinero
seasickness el mareo
ship el buque
shipping forecast el pronóstico del mar
shipyard el astillero
smooth en calma
starboard (a) estribor
storm la tormenta
tide la marea
waves las olas
wind el viento
windy ventoso
yachting la navegación en yate, el deporte de la vela

From which quay does the ship leave?

"Do you have any remedy against seasickness?
"Yes, I have some pills in my cabin. Meet me on C deck in ten minutes."
"Thanks, but I don't think I'll survive that long."

Is passport control carried out on board?

¿De qué muelle sale el barco?

— ¿Tiene algo para el mareo?

— Sí, tengo pastillas en mi camarote. Lo veo en la cubierta C dentro de diez minutos.
— Gracias, pero no creo que sobreviva tanto tiempo.

¿Se controlan los pasaportes a bordo?
[¿El control de pasaportes se lleva a cabo a bordo?]

19c Travel by Road

access   **el acceso**
I allow   **permito**
automatic   **automático**
I back up / reverse   **doy marcha atrás**
bicycle / bike   **la bicicleta**
black ice   **el hielo invisible en la carretera**
bottleneck   **el embotellamiento**
breathalyzer   **el respirador para la prueba de alcoholemia, el alcoholímetro**
breathalyzing test   **la prueba de alcoholemia**
breakdown   **la avería**
breakdown service   **el servicio de avería**
I breakdown   **tengo avería**
broken   **roto**
bus   **el autobús, [la guagua]**
bus fare   **la tarifa del autobús**
bus stop   **la parada del autobús**
car   **el coche, [el carro]**
car parts   **las piezas del coche**
car rental / hire   **el alquiler de coches**
car wash   **el lavado de coches, el autolavado**
caution   **la prudencia**
caution (legal)   **la amonestación**
I change gear   **cambio de marcha**
chauffeur   **el chófer**
check   **el control**
I collide   **me estrello, choco**
collision   **la colisión, el choque**
company car   **el coche / [el carro] de la empresa**
competent   **competente**
conductor (bus)   **el cobrador**
I cross   **cruzo, atravieso**
dangerous   **peligroso**
detour / diversion   **la desviación**
diesel   **el diesel**

I do thirty miles per hour   **voy a treinta millas por hora**
I drive   **conduzco**
drive / driving   **la conducción**
driver   **el conductor**
driver's license / driving licence   **el carné / carnet de conducir**
driving instructor   **el profesor de conducir**
driving lesson   **la lección de conducir**
driving school   **la autoescuela, [la escuela de conducción]**
driving test   **el examen de conducir**
drunken driving   **la conducción bajo los efectos del alcohol**
engine trouble   **el problema del motor**
I fasten (seatbelt)   **me ajusto**
I fill up   **lleno**
filling station   **la gasolinera, la estación de servicio / de gas, [la bomba]**
fine   **la multa**
I fix / repair   **arreglo**
flat / puncture   **el pinchazo**
forbidden   **prohibido**
for rent / hire   **en / para alquiler**
garage   **el garaje**
gear   **la marcha**
  in gear   **en marcha**
  in first gear   **en primera (marcha)**
  in neutral   **en punto muerto, [en neutro]**
  in reverse   **en marcha atrás, en reversa**
I get in the car   **me monto en el coche, subo al coche**
I get in lane   **me meto en el carril**
I get out   **salgo**

highway **la carretera**
highway police **la policía de carreteras**
I hitchhike **hago autoestop**
hitchhiker **el autoestopista**
hitchhiking **el autoestop**
I honk / sound the horn **toco la bocina, [pito]**
I am insured **estoy asegurado**
insurance **el seguro**
insurance policy **la póliza del seguro**
jack **el gato**
it is jammed **está bloqueado**
I keep my distance **guardo mi distancia**
key ring **el llavero**
keys **las llaves**
kilometer **el kilómetro**
line of cars **la fila de coches**
logbook **los documentos del coche**
make of car **la marca de coches**
mechanics **la mecánica**
mechanical **mecánico**
motel **el motel**
motor caravan **la caravana**
auto show **la exposición de coches / de automóviles**
one-way only **la dirección única, [una sola vía]**
I overtake / pass **adelanto, doblo**
overtaking / passing **el adelantamiento, el paso**
I park **aparco, estaciono, [parqueo]**
parking **el aparcamiento**
parking ban **la prohibición de aparcar**
parking lot / car park **el aparcamiento de coches, el estacionamiento, el párking, [el parqueadero]**
multistoried / multistorey **de muchos pisos**

parking meter **el contador de aparcamiento / [parqueadero]**
parking ticket **el ticket / la multa de aparcamiento / estacionamiento**
I pass **paso**
passenger **el pasajero**
pedestrian **el peatón**
gasoline / petrol **la gasolina**
leaded **con plomo**
regular / two-star **normal**
super / four star **súper**
unleaded / lead-free **sin plomo**
picnic area **la zona de picnic**
police **la policía**
policeman **el policía**
policewoman **la mujer policía**
police station **la comisaría / [estación] de policía**
position **la posición**
private car **el coche particular**
public transportation **el transporte público**
ramp **la rampa**
registration papers **los papeles de inscripción**
I rent / hire **alquilo**
rental / hired car **el coche alquilado**
rental charge **el precio de alquiler**
repair **la reparación**
I repair **reparo**
I reverse **doy marcha atrás, doy reversa**
(in) reverse **(en) marcha atrás, (en) reversa**
right of way **la preferencia**
road **la carretera**
road accident **el accidente de carretera**
road block **el bloqueamiento de la carretera**
road hog **el loco del volante**
road map **el mapa de carreteras**
road sign **la señal de tráfico**
road works **las obras de la carretera**

TRAVEL

route **la ruta**
I run over **atropello**
rush hour **la hora de punta, [la hora pico]**
safety / traffic-free zone **la zona libre de tráfico, la zona peatonal**
seatbelt **el cinturón de seguridad**
self-service **el autoservicio**
service **el servicio**
service area **el área de servicio**
I set off **salgo**
signal **la señal**
signpost **el poste de señales, el poste indicador**
slippery **resbaladizo**
slow **lento**
I slow down **reduzco la velocidad**
speed **la velocidad**
I speed up **acelero**
speed limit **el límite de velocidad**
I start *(engine)* **enciendo**
student / learner driver **el conductor novato**
I switch off / on **apago / enciendo**
taxi / cab **el taxi**
taxi / cab driver **el taxista**
taxi stand / rank **la parada de taxis**
I test **compruebo**
toll **el peaje**

I tow away **quito remolcando, retiro a remolque**
city plan **el plano de la ciudad**
city traffic **el tráfico urbano**
traffic **el tráfico, la circulación**
traffic code **el código de la circulación**
traffic jam **el atasco de tráfico, [el trancón]**
traffic light **el semáforo**
traffic news **el informe del tráfico**
traffic police **la policía de tráfico**
traffic violation / offence **el incumplimiento de las normas de tráfico**
trailer / caravan **la caravana**
trailer truck / lorry **el camión articulado / a remolque**
trip **el viaje**
truck / lorry **el camión [el carro]**
truck / lorry driver **el conductor de camiones, el camionero**
I turn left **giro a la izquierda**
I turn right **giro a la derecha**
I turn off at **giro a**
I turn off *(engine)* **apago**
underground **subterráneo**
used / second-hand car **el coche de segunda mano**
U-turn **el giro en U**

I have a flat / punctured tire, and the lights are not working. Could you also have a look at the clutch?

Tengo una rueda pinchada y las luces no funcionan. ¿Puede echarle un vistazo al embrague también?

Fill it up with unleaded, please.

Lleno. Gasolina sin plomo, por favor.

I had to stop on the road shoulder. Thankfully, emergency phones are found on all highways / expressways.

Tuve que parar en el arcén de la autopista. Afortunadamente, hay teléfonos de emergencia en todas las autopistas.

This new model has very low gas / petrol consumption. It also has excellent handling around corners.

Este nuevo modelo consume muy poca gasolina. También se maneja muy bien en las curvas.

vehicle **el vehículo**
vehicle inspection / MOT **la ITV (Inspección Técnica de Vehículos)**
I wait **espero**
warning **el aviso**
witness **el testigo**
I yield / give way **doy paso**

Roads

access / slip road **el carril de acceso**
alley **el callejón**
avenue **la avenida**
beltway / ring road **la carretera de circunvalación**
bridge **el puente**
built–up area **la zona edificada, la zona urbanizada**
bump **el badén, el bache**
bypass **la carretera de circunvalación**
closed *(road)* **cerrada**
corner **la esquina**
crossing **el cruce**
crossroad **el cruce de carreteras**
cul-de-sac **la calle sin salida**
curve / bend **la curva**
highway / expressway **la autopista**
    entry **la entrada, el acceso**

exit **la salida**
junction **el cruce**
inside lane **el carril interior**
intersection **el cruce, la intersección**
junction **el cruce**
lane **el carril**
level crossing **el paso a nivel**
main street **la calle principal**
median divider / central reservation **la mediana**
one-way street **la calle de dirección única**
outside lane **el carril exterior**
pedestrian crossing **el cruce de peatones**
pedestrian island **la isleta de peatones**
road **la carretera**
road / hard shoulder **el arcén**
roundabout **la rotonda**
side road / lay-by **el apartadero**
side street **la calle lateral**
sidewalk / pavement **el pavimento**
square **la plaza**
street **la calle**
underground passage **el pasaje subterráneo**
white / yellow line **la raya blanca / amarilla**

Because of black ice on the roads, there is a risk of collision: so keep your distance.

There has been a serious accident on highway / expressway A1 between junction 7 and 8. A truck traveling towards Madrid has crashed against the divider. Three vehicles are involved, and one of the drivers is seriously injured. I have put on the hazard lights. Send an ambulance immediately.

Debido al hielo invisible en la carretera, hay riesgo de choque: así que guarda la distancia.

Ha habido un accidente grave en la autopista A1 entre los cruces 7 (siete) y 8 (ocho). Un camión viajando a Madrid ha chocado contra la barrera central. Tres vehículos han sufrido y uno de los conductores está gravemente herido. He encendido la luz de emergencia. Mande una ambulancia inmediatamente.

▶ PARTS OF THE CAR App. 19c; ROAD SIGNS App. 19c; ACCIDENTS 11a

19d Travel by Air

aircraft **la nave aérea**
airplane / aeroplane **el avión**
airline **la aerolínea**
airline counter **la ventana de la línea aérea**
air travel **el viaje de avión**
airport **el aeropuerto**
I am airsick **estoy mareado**
baggage **el equipaje**
body search **el registro personal, la requisa**
I board a plane **subo a bordo de un avión**
boarding card **la tarjeta de embarque**
business class **la clase de ejecutivo**
by air **por avión**
cabin **la cabina**
canceled flight **el vuelo cancelado**
carousel **la cinta de equipaje**
charter flight **el vuelo chárter**
I check in **facturo**
check-in operations **las operaciones de facturación**

control tower **la torre de control**
copilot **el copiloto**
crew **la tripulación**
desk **la ventana**
direct flight **el vuelo directo**
domestic flight **el vuelo interior / interno**
during landing **durante el aterrizaje**
during takeoff **durante el despegue**
during the flight **durante el vuelo**
duty-free goods **los productos libres de impuestos**
economy class **la clase económica**
emergency exit **la salida de emergencia**
emergency landing **el aterrizaje de emergencia**
excess baggage **el exceso de equipaje**
I fasten **ajusto**
flight **el vuelo**

Can I make a connection to Zaragoza? Do I have to change flights?

¿Puedo hacer un transbordo para Zaragoza? ¿Tengo que cambiar el vuelo?

"I have some excess luggage."
"Have you packed your luggage yourself?"

—Tengo exceso de equipaje.
—¿Ha hecho su equipaje usted mismo?

There is some turbulence in the Andes.
The expected landing time is now 11:40, local time.

Hay algunas turbulencias en los Andes.
La hora de aterrizaje está prevista para las 11.40, hora local.

flight attendant **el asistente de vuelo**
I fly **vuelo**
I fly at a height of **vuelo a una altura de**
flying **la aviación**
fuselage **el fuselaje**
gate **la puerta**
instructions **las instrucciones**
hand luggage **el equipaje de mano**
headphones **los auriculares**
highjacker **el secuestrador (aéreo)**
immigrant **el inmigrante**
immigration **la inmigración**
immigration rules **las normas de inmigración**
I land **aterrizo**
landing **el aterrizaje**
landing lights **las luces de aterrizaje**
lifejacket **el chaleco de salvavidas**
no-smoking sign **la señal de no fumar**
nonstop **sin parada**

on board **a bordo**
parachute **el paracaídas**
passenger **el pasajero**
passengers' lounge **la sala de pasajeros**
passport control **el control de pasaportes**
pilot **el piloto**
plane **el avión**
refreshments **los refrescos**
runway **la pista de aterrizaje**
security measures **las medidas de seguridad**
security staff **el personal de seguridad**
steward **el auxiliar de vuelo**
stewardess / air hostess **la azafata**
I take off **despego**
take-off **el despegue**
terminal **el terminal**
tray **la bandeja**
turbulence **la turbulencia**
view **la vista, el panorama**
window **la ventana, la ventanilla**
window seat **el asiento junto a la ventana**

"Will Mr. / Ms. Bosé traveling on flight IB 131 to Alicante please contact the information desk immediately."
"Where do I check in for flight IB 131?"

—El señor / la señora Bosé viajando en el vuelo IB 131 para Alicante, por favor preséntense en el mostrador de información.
—¿Dónde facturo para el vuelo IB 131?

This is the last call for passengers traveling on flight IB 881 to Buenos Aires.

Última llamada para los pasajeros del vuelo IB 881 para Buenos Aires.

How long is the delay?

¿Cuánto dura el retraso?

My luggage has not yet been unloaded.

Mi equipaje no ha sido descargado todavía.

What is the flight number?

¿Cuál es el número del vuelo?

TRAVEL

19e Travel by Rail

announcement   **el anuncio**
barrier   **la barrera**
buffet   **el menú**
club / buffet car   **el vagón-cafetería, el coche-comedor**
coach   **el vagón**
compartment   **el compartimiento**
connection   **la conexión, el transbordo**
dining car   **el vagón restaurante**
exemption   **la exención**
fare   **la tarifa**
inspector   **el inspector, el revisor**
I lean out   **me asomo**
level crossing   **el paso a nivel**
luggage rack   **la reja de equipaje, la baca**
menu / buffet   **el menú**
I miss   **pierdo**
nonrefundable   **sin devolución**

(non)smoking car   **el compartimiento de (no) fumadores**
occupied   **ocupado**
on time   **a tiempo**
platform   **el andén, [la plataforma]**
porter   **el portero**
I punch (ticket)   **perforo**
railroad / railway   **la red ferroviaria**
elevated railway   **el ferrocarril elevado**
ramp   **la rampa**
reduction   **el descuento**
reservation   **la reserva**
reserved   **reservado**
sleeper   **el coche cama**
smokers   **fumadores**
speed   **la velocidad**
stairs   **las escaleras**
stationmaster   **el jefe de estación**
stop   **la parada**

A special announcement:
On Sundays and holidays
the service to Valencia does not
operate, and on weekdays after nine
in the morning fares are subject to
supplementary charges.
In addition, reservations are
required for seats in the
nonsmoking cars on the
Gijón service. We apologize for
any inconvenience.

Un anuncio especial:
Los domingos y festivos no sale
el servicio para Valencia y en
los días laborales después de
las nueve de la mañana las
tarifas están sujetas a cargos
suplementarios. Además, se
necesitan reservas para los
compartimientos para
no fumadores en el servicio para
Gijón. Pedimos disculpas por
los inconvenientes.

The 11:45 to Lima is now leaving
from platform 10.

El tren de las 11.45 (las doce
menos cuarto) para Lima
sale del andén 10.

The subway / underground is closed
until seven in the morning.

El metro está cerrado hasta las
siete de la mañana.

subway / underground **el metro**
supplement **el suplemento**
taxi stand / rank **la parada de taxis**
ticket **el billete, [el tiquete, el boleto]**
  first class **de primera clase**
  group **de grupo**
  one-way / single **de ida**
  round-trip / return **de ida y vuelta**
  second class **de segunda clase**
ticket collector **el revisor de billetes, [el controlador de boletos]**
ticket office **la oficina / el despacho de billetes, la taquilla**
timetable **el horario**
  summer timetable **el horario de verano**
  winter timetable **el horario de invierno**

timetable changes **los cambios de horario**
track **la vía**
traveler **el viajero**
train **el tren**
  direct train **el tren directo**
  express train **el tren expreso, el rápido**
  Intercity train **el tren interurbano / de largo recorrido**
  local train **el tren local**
  night train **el tren nocturno**
train / rail station **la estación de tren**
train / rail tracks **el raíl, la vía, la carrilera**
trolley **el tranvía**
user **el usuario**
I wait **espero**
waiting room **la sala de espera**
warning **el aviso**
window **la ventana**

Where do I have to change?

¿Dónde tengo que cambiar?

When is the first train?

¿Cuándo es el primer tren?

Excuse me, this a nonsmoking compartment.

—Perdone, éste es un compartimiento para no fumadores.

Is this the Intercity to Barcelona?

¿Es este el servicio de largo recorrido para Barcelona?

There are no facilities for disabled travelers on this train.

No hay servicios para pasajeros inválidos en este tren.

This is a public announcement for all passengers travelling to Seville. We are sorry to announce that this service is subject to delays. There will also be a platform change.

Anuncio para los pasajeros viajando a Sevilla. Sentimos anunciar que este servicio tiene retraso. También se hará un cambio de andén [plataforma].

Vacation / Holidays

20a General Terms

abroad   **el extranjero**
accommodation   **la vivienda, la estancia, el alojamiento**
alone   **solo**
area   **el área, la zona**
arrival   **la llegada**
available   **disponible**
beach   **la playa**
camera   **la cámara**
city map / town plan   **el mapa de la ciudad**
clean   **limpio**
climate   **el clima**
closed   **cerrado**
clothes   **la ropa**
cold   **frío**
comfort   **el confort, la comodidad**
comfortable   **confortable, cómodo**
congested   **congestionado, lleno**
cost   **el costo, el precio**
country   **el país**
countryside   **el campo**
dirty   **sucio**
disadvantage   **la desventaja**
disorganized   **desorganizado**
exchange   **el cambio**
fire   **el fuego**
folding chair   **la silla plegable**
folding table   **la mesa plegable**
food   **la comida**
free   **gratis**
full / full-up   **lleno, completo**
I go   **voy**
group   **el grupo**
group travel   **el viaje en grupo**
guide   **el guía**
guidebook   **la guía**
guided tour   **el viaje con guía**
guided walk   **la visita con guía**
land   **el país, la tierra**

landscape   **el paisaje**
journey   **el viaje**
knapsack / rucksack   **la mochila**
mild *(climate)*   **templado**
money   **el dinero**
open   **abierto**
organization   **la organización**
I organize   **organizo**
organized   **organizado**
plan *(town)*   **el plano**
I plan   **planeo**
portable   **portátil**
I return *(to a place)*   **vuelvo**
sea   **el mar**
seascape   **el paisaje marino**
seaside resort   **punto de veraneo en la playa, el lugar de veraneo**
show   **el espectáculo**
I show   **muestro, demuestro, exhibo**
sight   **la vista**
I spend time   **paso tiempo**
stay   **la estancia**
I stay   **estoy en**
sun   **el sol**
sunny   **soleado**
I sunbathe   **tomo el sol**
I tan / get brown   **me bronceo**
tour   **la gira, el viaje, la excursión**
tourism   **el turismo**
tourist   **el turista**
tourist menu   **el menú turístico**
tourist office   **la oficina de turismo**
town   **la ciudad, el pueblo**
travel   **el viaje**
I travel   **viajo**
travel adaptor   **el adaptador de viaje**
trip   **el viaje**
I understand   **entiendo**

I unpack **deshago la maleta**
vacation / holiday **las vacaciones**
visit **la visita**
I visit **visito**
visiting hours **las horas de visita**
visitors **los visitantes**
welcome **la bienvenida**
worth seeing **visita recomendada**

Holiday activities

beach vacation / holiday
  vacaciones en la playa
boating vacation / holiday **las**
  vacaciones en barco
bus trip **las vacaciones**
  en autobús
camping **el camping**
canoeing **el viaje en canoa**
car trip / motoring holiday **las**
  vacaciones en coche / [carro]
cruise **el crucero**
cycling **el ciclismo**

fishing **la pesca**
fruit picking **la recolección de**
  fruta
home exchange **el intercambio**
  de casas
hunting **la caza**
mountain climbing **el**
  montañismo, la escalada de
  una montaña
rock climbing **la escalada en**
  rocas
sailing **la navegación**
shopping **las compras**
sightseeing **el excursionismo**
skiing **el esquí**
study vacation / holiday **las**
  vacaciones de estudio
sunbathing **el baño de sol**
volunteer work **el trabajo**
  voluntario
walking **caminar, andar**
wine tasting **la cata de vinos**

Dear all at work,

Having a wonderful vacation. The
weather is hot (I have a great tan),
the campsite is clean, and the local
food is excellent.

The kids are having a great time
too, enjoying the water sports,
building sandcastles, and making
lots of friends.

I'm not looking forward to coming
home!
Best wishes, María.

Mis queridos colegas

**Me estoy divirtiendo en estas
vacaciones. Hace calor (estoy
muy bronceada), el camping está
limpio, y la comida regional es
excelente.**

**Los chicos están pasándolo
bien también, disfrutando de las
actividades acuáticas, haciendo
castillos de arena, y haciendo
muchos amigos.**

¡ No tengo ganas de volver!

Un afectuoso saludo de María.

➤ TRAVEL 19; HOBBIES 16a; ON THE BEACH App. 20a; WEATHER 24d

20b Accommodations & Hotel

Accommodations

apartment **el apartamento**
bed and breakfast **la pensión**
campsite **el camping, la zona de camping**
efficiency unit / self-catering **el piso con cocina propia**
farm **la granja**
full board **la pensión completa**
half board **la media pensión**
home exchange **el intercambio de casas**
hotel **el hotel**
mobile home **la caravana**
inn **la posada, la fonda, el mesón**
trailer / caravan **la caravana**
villa **la villa**
youth hostel **el albergue juvenil**

Booking & payment

affordable **asequible, razonable**
all-included **todo incluido**
bill **la cuenta**
I book / reserve **reservo**
brochure **el folleto**
I cash **hago efectivo, cobro**
cheap **barato**
check / cheque **el cheque**
cost **el costo, el coste**
credit **el crédito**
credit card **la tarjeta de crédito**
economical **económico**
Eurocheque **el eurocheque**
excluding **excluido**
exclusive **exclusivo**

expensive **caro**
extra charge **el suplemento, el recargo**
evening meal **la cena**
fee **el precio**
I fill in **relleno, lleno**
form **el impreso, el formulario**
free **gratis**
inclusive **completo, que incluye**
I pay **pago**
payment **el pago**
pricelist **la lista de precios**
receipt **el recibo**
reduction **el descuento, la rebaja**
refund **la devolución, el reembolso**
reservation **la reserva**
I reserve **reservo**
sales tax / VAT **el IVA**
I sign **firmo**
signature **la firma**
traveler's check / traveller's cheque **el cheque de viaje / viajero**

Hotel

adjoining / en-suite bathroom **el baño adjunto**
air-conditioning **el aire acondicionado**
amenities **los servicios**
balcony **el balcón**
bath **el baño**
bed **la cama**
bedding / bed linen **la ropa de cama**
bedspread **el cubrecama, el cobertor, la colcha**

I'd like to reserve a double room with a double bed and a bath for three days from March 5th.

We are checking out now. I shall collect the luggage at ten thirty.

Do not disturb.

Quisiera reservar una habitación doble con baño por tres días desde el cinco de marzo.

Ahora pagamos. Recogeré el equipaje a las diez y media.

No molestar.

bed and breakfast **la pensión (desayuno incluido)**

billiard room / pool hall **la sala de billar**

board **la pensión**
full board **pensión completa**
half board **media pensión**

breakfast **el desayuno**

broken **roto, estropeado**

business meeting **la reunión de negocios**

call **la llamada**

I check in / out **facturo / me retiro**

coathanger **la percha, el perchero**

comfortable **cómodo, confortable**

I complain **me quejo, reclamo**

complaint **la queja, el reclamo**

conference **la conferencia**

conference facilities **el salón de conferencias**

damage **el daño, el perjuicio**

dining room **el comedor**

early morning call **la llamada por la mañana temprano**

elevator / lift **el ascensor**

facilities **los servicios**

fire exit **la salida de incendios**

fire extinguisher **el extintor de fuego, el extinguidor**

guest **el huésped**

hairdresser **el peluquero**

hairdryer **el secador de pelo**

heating **la calefacción**

hotel **el hotel**

key **la llave**

laundry **la lavandería**

laundry service **el servicio de lavandería**

meal **la comida**

night porter **el portero de noche**

noisy **ruidoso**

nuisance **la molestia**

overnight / weekend bag **el maletín de fin de semana**

pants / trouser press **la prensa de pantalón**

parking space **el espacio para aparcar**

plug **el enchufe**

porter **el portero**

privacy **privacidad, intimidad**

private toilet **el wáter particular, el baño privado**

reception **la recepción**

receptionist **el recepcionista**

room **la habitación**
double room **la habitación doble**
family room **la habitación familiar**
twin bedded room **la habitación con camas gemelas**

room service **el servicio a la habitación**

shower **la ducha**

showercap **el gorro de ducha**

stay **la estancia**

I stay **estoy en, me alojo en**

view **la vista**

water **el agua**

I'd like to complain. The hot water tap does not work, and the elevator is out of order. There is only one coathanger in the wardrobe, and I asked for a room with a view.

Press the button.

Quiero hacer un reclamo. Ni el grifo de agua caliente ni el ascensor funcionan. Sólo hay una percha en el armario, y había pedido una habitación con vista.

Apriete el botón.

▶ ROOMS 8a; FURNITURE & FURNISHINGS 8c; EATING OUT 10a

20c Camping & Self-Service / -Catering

air bed **el colchón inflable**

antihistamine cream **la crema antihistamínica**

ants **las hormigas**

barbecue **la barbacoa**

battery **la pila**

I camp **acampo**

camp bed **la cama de camping**

camper **el campista**

camping **el camping**

camping equipment / gear **el equipo de camping**

camping gas **el camping gas**

campsite **el camping**

can / tin opener **el abrelatas**

connected **conectado**

cooking facilities **la posibilidad de cocinar**

disconnected **desconectado**

drinking water **el agua potable**

extension cord **la extensión**

flashlight / torch **la interna, la antorcha**

forbidden **prohibido**

fun **la diversión**

gas cylinder **la bombona de gas**

gas stove / cooker **la cocina de gas**

ground-sheet **la tela impermeable**

guy rope **el viento de la tienda**

laundromat / launderette **la lavandería**

I make friends **hago amigos**

medicine kit **el botiquín**

mosquito bite **la picadura de mosquito**

mosquito net **la red contra los mosquitos, el mosquitero**

mosquitos **los mosquitos**

pan **la sartén, el cazo, la cacerola, la cazuela**

peg **la estaca**

I pitch / put up my tent **pongo mi tienda de campaña**

registration **la inscripción**

services **los servicios**

sheet **la sábana**

showers / washing facilities **las duchas**

site **el emplazamiento, el sitio**

sleeping bag **el saco de dormir**

"Where shall we put up the tent?" — **¿Dónde ponemos la tienda de campaña?**

"Away from the main block." — **Lejos del bloque principal.**

"I'll pitch it in the shade." — **La montaré a la sombra.**

"No, it is a bit damp there. This is better here, and there are no mosquitos." — **No, está un poco húmedo allí. Está mejor aquí, y no hay mosquitos.**

"Where's the flashlight / torch? It's not in the tent." — **¿Dónde está la linterna? No está en la tienda de campaña.**

"It was in the knapsack / rucksack just now." — **Justo ahora estaba en la mochila.**

"Keep your voice down, please, we are trying to sleep!" — **Baja la voz por favor, estamos tratando de dormir.**

Do you have a few spare pegs? **¿Tienes algunas estacas que me podrías dejar?**

---

space **el espacio**

I take down (tent) **quito (la tienda de campaña)**

tent **la tienda de campaña**

toilet **el servicio, el baño**

trailer / caravan **la caravana**

trashcan / dustbin **el bote / la caneca de la basura**

uncomfortable **incómodo, poco confortable**

vehicles **los vehículos**

water filter **el filtro de agua**

Self-service / -catering

agency **la agencia**

agreement **el acuerdo**

amenities **las facilidades**

apartment **el apartamento**

I clean **limpio**

I cook **cocino**

damaged **dañado, estropeado**

damages **los daños, los perjuicios**

dangerous **peligroso**

electricity **la electricidad**

equipment **el equipo**

farm **la granja**

maid **la criada**

meter **el contador**

owner **el dueño, el propietario**

rent **el alquiler, la renta**

I rent **alquilo, arriendo**

I rent out **doy en alquiler**

repair **la reparación**

I repair **reparo**

I return *(give back)* **devuelvo**

ruined **en ruinas, estropeado, dañado**

self-service **el autoservicio**

set of keys **el juego de llaves**

I share **comparto**

shutters **las contraventanas**

smelly **oloroso, que huele**

spare keys **las llaves de repuesto**

water supply **el suministro de agua**

well **el pozo**

well-kept **bien guardado**

I'm making a packed lunch.

Estoy preparando un almuerzo empaquetado.

The apartment is close to the town center / centre, just a few kilometers / kilometres from the nearest stores / shops and convenient for the swimming pool.

El apartamento está cerca del centro de la ciudad, a sólo unos kilómetros de las tiendas más cercanas, y cerca de la piscina.

You will find the electric meter under the stairs.

El contador de electricidad está debajo de las escaleras.

There are no blankets, the stove / cooker doesn't work, and there is a frog in the bathroom.

No hay mantas, no funciona el horno, y hay una rana en el baño.

Is there no more water?
Beware of the dog!

¿No queda agua?
¡Perro peligroso!

Language

21a General Terms

accuracy **la exactitud**
accurate **exacto**
I adapt **adapto**
I adopt **adopto**
advanced **avanzado**
aptitude **la aptitud**
artificial language **el lenguaje artificial**
based on **basado en**
bilingual **bilingüe**
bilingualism **el bilingüismo**
borrowing **el préstamo**
branch **la rama**
classical languages **las lenguas clásicas**
it derives from **se deriva de, viene de**
development **el desarrollo**
difficult **la dificultad**
easy **fácil**
error **el error**
foreign language **el idioma extranjero**
I forget **olvido, me olvido de**
grammar **la gramática**
grammatical **gramático**

I improve **mejoro**
influence **la influencia**
known **conocido**
language **el idioma, la lengua**
language course **el curso de idiomas**
language family **la familia de idiomas**
language school **la escuela de idiomas**
language skills **las habilidades para los idiomas**
Latin **el latín**
I learn **aprendo**
learning **el aprendizaje**
level **el nivel**
linguistics **la lingüística**
link **el nexo**
living **vivo**
major languages **los idiomas principales**
it means **significa, quiere decir**
I mime **represento con gestos**
minor languages **los idiomas secundarios**
mistake **el error**

Minor languages may disappear; however, thanks to the oral tradition in some communities, some have been preserved.

Los idiomas secundarios podrían desaparecer, sin embargo gracias a la tradición oral en algunas comunidades, algunos se han preservado.

modern languages **las lenguas modernas**
monolingual **monolingüe**
mother tongue **la lengua madre, la lengua materna**
mutation **la mutación, el cambio**
name **el nombre**
nation **la nación**
national **nacional**
native **el nativo**
natural **natural**
official **oficial**
offshoot **el ramal**
origin **el origen**
phenomenon **el fenómeno**
I practice / practise **practico**
preserved **preservado**
question **la pregunta**
register **el registro**
self-assessment **la autoevaluación**
separate **separarado, independiente**
sign language **el lenguaje de señas**
survival **la supervivencia**
it survives **sobrevive**
I teach **enseño**
teacher **el profesor**
teaching **la enseñanza**
test **la prueba, el examen**

I test **evalúo, corrijo un examen, ensayo**
I translate **traduzco**
translation **la traducción**
I understand **entiendo, comprendo**
unknown **desconocido**
widely **ampliamente**
witticism **la agudeza**

Words & vocabulary

antonym **el antónimo**
colloquial **familiar**
consonant **la consonante**
dictionary **el diccionario**
expression **la expresión**
idiom **la expresión idiomática**
idiomatic **idiomático**
jargon **la jerga**
lexicographer **el lexicógrafo**
lexicon **el léxico**
phrase **la frase, la oración**
phrase book **el libro de frases**
sentence **la frase, la oración**
slang **el argot**
syllable **la sílaba**
synonym **el sinónimo**
vocabulary **el vocabulario**
vowel **la vocal**
word **la palabra**
wordplay **el juego de palabras**

I am not very good at languages, but my sister is a gifted linguist.

No soy muy bueno para los idiomas, pero mi hermana es dotada para las lenguas.

She learned French and Italian in school, then she traveled extensively and picked up Bulgarian and Urdu while working as a volunteer.

Aprendió francés e italiano en el colegio, y ha viajado mucho y aprendió un poco de búlgaro y de urdú mientras trabajaba como voluntaria.

LANGUAGE

21b Using Language

Speaking & listening

accent **el acento**
   regional accent **el acento regional**
articulate **elocuente**
I articulate **articulo**
clear **claro**
I communicate **comunico**
conversation **la conversación**
I converse **converso, hablo**
dialect **el dialecto**
diction **la dicción**
I express myself **me expreso**
fluent **la fluidez, la soltura, la facilidad**
fluently **con fluidez, con soltura, con facilidad**
I interpret **interpreto**
interpreter **el intéprete**
intonation **la entonación**
lisp **el ceceo**
I lisp **ceceo**
I listen **escucho, oigo**
listener **el oyente**
listening **la audición**
listening skills **las habilidades para audición**

I mispronounce **pronuncio mal**
mispronunciation **el error de pronunciación**
oral(ly) **oral(mente), verbal(mente)**
I pronounce **pronuncio**
pronunciation **la pronunciación**
rhythm **el ritmo**
sound **el sonido**
I sound **sueno**
I speak **hablo**
speaker **el hablante**
speaking **el habla**
speaking skills **las habilidades para hablar, las habilidades verbales**
speech **el discurso**
speed **la velocidad**
spoken **hablado**
spoken language **el lenguaje hablado**
stress **la entonación**
stressed (un-) **(in)acentuado**
I stutter / stammer **tartamudeo, balbuceo**
unpronounceable **impronunciable**
verbally **verbalmente**

"I have no difficulty in reading Spanish, but I don't understand it when people speak very fast or with a strong regional accent."

—No tengo dificultad para leer el español, pero no lo entiendo cuando la gente habla muy rápido o con un acento regional fuerte.

"Do you practice Spanish with a native speaker?"
"No, I prefer to attend a class."

—¿Practicas español con un nativo?
—No, prefiero ir a clase.

Don't worry about spelling mistakes for the moment.

No te preocupes por los errores de ortografía de momento.

Writing & reading

accent **el acento**
   acute accent **el acento agudo**
   tilde **la tilde**
alphabet **el alfabeto**
alphabetically **alfabéticamente**
in bold **en negrita, en negrilla**
Braille **el Braille**
character **el carácter**
code **el código**
I correspond (with) **estoy en correspondencia (con)**
correspondence **la correspondencia**
I decipher **descifro**
graphic **gráfico**
handwriting **la escritura a mano, la letra**
ideogram(me) / ideograph **el ideograma**
illiterate **analfabeto**
italic **en bastardilla**
I italicize **pongo en bastardilla**
letter *(alphabet)* **la letra**
literate **alfabetizado, que sabe leer y escribir**
literature **la literatura**
note **la nota**

paragraph **el párrafo**
philology **la filología**
philologist **el filólogo**
pictograph **el pictograma**
I print **imprimo**
I read **leo**
reading **la lectura**
reading skills **las habilidades para la lectura**
I rewrite **escribo de nuevo**
scribble **los garabatos**
I scribble **garrapateo, hago garabatos**
sign **el signo**
I sign **firmo**
signature **la firma**
I spell **deletreo**
spelling **la ortografía**
text **el texto**
I transcribe **transcribo**
transcription **la transcripción**
I underline **subrayo**
I write **escribo**
writing **la escritura**
writing skills **las habilidades para la escritura**
written language **el lenguaje escrito**

Which languages have a Slavic alphabet?

¿Qué idiomas tienen un alfabeto eslavo?

Portuguese spoken here.

Aquí se habla portugués.

Do you have any previous knowledge of Russian?

¿Tienes algún conocimiento previo de ruso?

"Which is the easiest language to learn for an English speaker?"

—¿Cuál es el idioma más fácil de aprender para un hablante de inglés?

"Spanish, of course!"

—¡El español, por supuesto!

▶ LANGUAGES, LANGUAGE FAMILIES App. 21a

Education

22a General Terms

achievement **el éxito, el logro**

admission **la admisión**

   I am admitted to school **estoy admitido en el colegio**

absent **ausente**

age group **el grupo etario, [el grupo de la misma edad]**

I am away **estoy ausente**

aptitude **la aptitud, la facilidad**

I analyze **analizo, estudio**

answer **la respuesta**

I answer (someone) **respondo, contesto (a alguien)**

   I answer (a question) **respondo (a una pregunta)**

I ask **pregunto**

I attend (a school) **voy (al colegio)**

board of education **la delegación, el consejo local de educación**

boring **aburrido**

career **la carrera, la profesión**

career counseling **el asesoramiento sobre la profesión**

caretaker **el cuidador, el bedel, el vigilante, el conserje**

I catch up **me pongo al día**

chapter **el capítulo**

cheat **el tramposo, el petardista**

class **la clase**

class council **la reunión de delegados de clase**

class representative **el delegado de la clase**

class teacher **el profesor**

class trip **el viaje escolar, el viaje con la clase**

club **el club, el grupo**

I complete **completo**

comprehension **la comprensión**

compulsory schooling **el colegio obligatorio**

computer **el ordenador, [el computador]**

concept **el concepto**

I copy(out) **copio**

copy **la copia**

course **el curso**

deputy head **el subdirector**

detention **la detención**

   I am in detention **estoy castigado**

difficult **difícil**

discuss **la discusión**

easy **fácil**

education **la educación**

educational system **el sistema educativo**

I encourage **aliento, doy ánimo**

essay **la redacción, el ensayo**

example **el ejemplo**

excellent **excelente**

extracurricular / out of school activity **la actividad fuera del colegio**

favorite / favourite **el favorito**

favorite / favourite subject **la asignatura favorita**

I forget **olvido**

governing body **la junta directiva**

holidays **las vacaciones**

homework **la tarea, los deberes**

instruction **la instrucción, la enseñanza**

interesting **interesante**

I learn **aprendo**

I leave **salgo, dejo**

lesson **la lección, la clase**

   lesson (chapter) **la lección**

   lessons **las lecciones**

I listen **escucho, oigo**
I look at **miro, considero**
I misunderstand **entiendo mal, no entiendo bien, malinterpreto**
mixed ability group **el grupo de alumnos con capacidades diversas**
modular **modular**
module **el módulo**
occupational career education **la guía vocacional / profesional**
occupational education teacher **el profesor encargado del asesoramiento profesional de los alumnos**
oral **oral**
outdoor **exterior**
parents' evening **la tarde de reunión de los padres**
pastoral care **la tutoría**
I play truant **hago rabona, hago novillos, me ausento**
I praise **alabo**
principal **principal**
principal / headteacher **el director**
project **el proyecto**
punctual **puntual**
I punctuate **escribo los signos de puntuación**
I punish **castigo**
punishment **el castigo**
pupil **el alumno**
qualification **el título, los requisitos**
I qualify **saco un título, lleno los requisitos**
question **la pregunta**
I question **pregunto**
question mark **el signo de interrogación**
I read **leo**
reading **la lectura**
I repeat a year **repito un curso**
report **las notas, el certificado escolar**
research **la investigación**
I research **investigo**

resource center / centre **el centro de servicios escolares / de recursos**
scheme of work **el esquema de trabajo, el plan de trabajo**
school administration **la administración**
school book **el libro escolar**
school council **el consejo escolar**
schoolfriend / pal **el amigo del colegio**
set **el grupo**
school sets **los grupos, las clases**
skill **la habilidad**
specialist teacher **el profesor especializado**
spelling **la ortografía**
staff **el personal**
I stay in **me quedo en casa**
I stay down *(year)* **repito curso**
strict **estricto**
I study **estudio**
sum **la suma**
I summarize **resumo, sumarizo**
I cram / swot **empollo**
task **el deber, la tarea**
I teach **enseño**
teacher **el profesor, el maestro**
teaching **la enseñanza**
term / semester **el semestre**
I train **preparo, entreno**
training **la preparación**
I translate **traduzco**
translation **la traducción**
tutor **el tutor**
I understand **entiendo, comprendo**
understanding **el entendimiento, la comprensión**
unit (of work) **la unidad de trabajo**
I work **trabajo, estudio**
I work hard **estudio mucho**
work experience **la experiencia laboral**
I write **escribo**
written (work) **escrito**

EDUCATION

2b School

athletic field   **el campo de deportes**
blackboard   **la pizarra**
blackout   **el bloqueo**
book   **el libro**
break   **el recreo**
briefcase   **la maleta del colegio, el maletín**
canteen   **el bar del colegio, la cantina del colegio**
cassette (audio / video)   **la cinta**
cassette recorder   **la grabadora**
classroom   **la clase**
computer   **el ordenador, [la computadora]**
desk   **el pupitre**
dormitory   **el dormitorio**
gym(nasium)   **el gimnasio**
headphone   **el auricular, [el audífono]**
interactive TV   **la televisión interactiva**
laboratory   **el laboratorio**
(language) laboratory   **el laboratorio (de idiomas)**
library   **la biblioteca**
lunchtime   **el descanso para comer, la hora de almuerzo**
note   **la nota**
office   **la oficina**
playground   **el patio de juego**
radio   **la radio**
ruler   **la regla**

slide   **la diapositiva**
satellite TV   **la television por satélite**
schoolhall   **la sala**
schoolbag / bookbag / satchel   **la maleta del colegio**
sports center   **el polideportivo**
staffroom   **el cuarto de profesores**
studio   **el estudio**
timetable   **el horario**
video   **el vídeo**
   video *(adj)*   **de vídeo**
video camera   **la cámara de vídeo**
video cassette   **la cinta de vídeo**
video recorder   **el aparato de vídeo**
workshop   **el taller**

Type of school

boarding school   **el internado**
boarder   **el interno**
comprehensive school   **el colegio de enseñanza secundaria**
day school   **el colegio (que no es internado)**
further education   **la formación profesional, la educación media**
grammar school   **la escuela pública elemental**
high school   **el colegio de segunda enseñanza, el instituto**

"At what age do children start school?"
"They have to go to school when they are six years old."

Our son already goes to kindergarten and is looking forward to school.

—¿ A qué edad empiezan los niños la escuela?
—Tienen que ir a la escuela a la edad de seis años.

Nuestro hijo ya va al jardín de infancia, y tiene ganas de ir a la escuela.

70   ENERAL EDUCATIONAL TERMS 22a

nursery school **el colegio infantil, la guardería**
playgroup **el grupo de juego**
primary **primario**
primary / elementary school **el colegio de enseñanza primaria**
school **el colegio, la escuela**
school type **el tipo de colegio**
of school age **en edad escolar**
secondary **secundario**
secondary school / junior high school **el colegio de enseñanza secundaria**
secondary school / senior high school **el colegio de enseñanza secundaria**
senior year / sixth form **el último curso de la enseñanza secundaria**
special school **el colegio especial**
technical school **el colegio técnico**

Classroom commands

Answer the question! **¡Contesta la pregunta!**
Be careful! **¡Ten cuidado!**
Be quiet! **¡Cállate!**
Be quick! **¡Sé rápido!**
Bring me your workbook! **¡Tráeme tu cuaderno!**
Clean the blackboard! **¡Limpia la pizarra!**
Close the door! **¡Cierra la puerta!**
Come here! **¡Ven aquí!**

Come in! **¡Entra!**
Copy these sentences! **¡Copia estas frases!**
Do your homework! **¡Haz la tarea!**
Don't talk / chatter! **¡No charles!**
Fill in the boxes! **¡Rellena los cuadrados!**
Go out! **¡Salte fuera!, ¡Fuera!**
Learn by heart! **¡Aprende de memoria!**
Listen carefully! **¡Escucha con atención!, ¡Escucha atentamente!**
Make less noise! **¡No hagas tanto ruido!**
Open the window! **¡Abre la ventana!**
Pay attention! **¡Atiende!**
Read the text! **¡Lee el texto!**
Show me your book! **¡Enséñame tu libro!**
Sit down! **¡Siéntate!**
Stand up! **¡Levántate!**
Take notes! **¡Toma apuntes!, ¡Coge apuntes!**
Work in pairs! **¡Trabajad en parejas!**
Work in groups! **¡Trabajad en grupos!**
Write it down! **¡Escribe esto!**
Write out in rough / draft! **¡Escribe en sucio!, ¡Escribe en borrador!**
Write out neatly / in neat! **¡Escribe con buena letra!, ¡Escribe claramente!**

Our daughter goes to elementary / primary school. She reads to her teacher every day and can read well now.

Nuestra hija va a la escuela primaria. Lee a su maestra todos los días y ya sabe leer bien.

"Do you move up a class every year?"
"No, last year I had to repeat the year."

—¿Subes una clase todos los años [un grado cada año]?
—No, el año pasado tuve que repetir el curso.

EDUCATION

22c School Subjects & Examinations

Subjects

arithmetic **la aritmética**
art **el arte**
biology **la biología**
business studies **los estudios empresariales / de negocios**
chemistry **la química**
commerce **el comercio**
compulsory subject **la asignatura obligatoria**
computer studies **la informática**
design technology **la tecnología de diseño**
economics **la economía**
English **el inglés**
foreign language **el idioma extranjero**
geography **la geografía**
gymnastics **la gimnasia**
history **la historia**
home economics **la economía doméstica**
information technology **la informática**
Italian **el italiano**
Latin **el latín**
law **el derecho**

main subject **la asignatura principal**
mathematics **las matemáticas**
metalwork **el trabajo con metal**
minor / subsidiary subject **la asignatura secundaria**
music **la música**
occupational / careers education **la formación profesional**
option(al subject) **la asignatura optativa**
philosophy **la filosofía**
physical education **la educación física**
physics **la física**
religious education **la educación religiosa**
science **la ciencia, las ciencias**
sex education **la educación sexual**
social studies **los estudios sociales**
sociology **la sociología**
Spanish **el español**
sport **el deporte**
  type of sport **el tipo de deporte**
subject **la asignatura**

"Which school do you go to?"
"I go to the high school. I enjoy it a lot. There are lots of clubs and activities."
"Which is your favorite subject?"
"I like math / maths, but prefer physics."
My favorite / favourite subject is physical education.
I don't like history, it is so boring.

I'm good at English, since I did an exchange.
I work very hard at it.

— **¿A qué escuela vas?**
— **Voy al instituto. Me gusta mucho. Hay muchos clubs y actividades.**
— **¿Qué asignatura prefieres?**
— **Me gustan las matemáticas, pero prefiero la física.**
Mi asignatura preferida es la educación física.
No me gusta la historia, es tan aburrida.
Estoy fuerte en inglés, desde que hice un intercambio.
Trabajo mucho en inglés.

---

technical drawing   el dibujo
   técnico
technology   la tecnología
textiles   los estudios textiles
woodwork   el trabajo con madera

Examinations

I assess   evalúo, corrijo
assessment   la evaluación
certificate   el certificado
degree   el grado
diploma   el diploma, el título
dissertation   el proyecto de fin de
   carrera, [la tesis]
distinction   la matrícula de honor
doctorate   el doctorado
examination   el examen
   external   externo, exterior
   final   final
grade / mark   la nota
I grade   califico, doy nota a
grading / mark system   el sistema
   de notas
graduate (in engineering)   el
   licenciado (en ingeniería)
listening comprehension   la
   comprensión de escucha
mark   la nota

masters degree   el título de
   máster
merit   el mérito
oral   oral
point   el punto
post-graduate course   el curso de
   post-licenciado, [el curso de
   posgrado]
reading comprehension   la
   comprensión de textos
I pass (an exam)   apruebo
I sit for / take an exam   me
   presento a un examen
I test   examino
test   el examen, el test, la prueba
thesis   la tesis
trainee   el aprendiz, el estudiante
written test   el examen escrito

Grades / Marks

very good   sobresaliente
good   notable
satisfactory   bien,
   satisfactorio
pass   aprobado
poor   insuficiente
very poor   muy deficiente

Here are your grades!
Well done! Isabel, you have done
excellent work.
Teodoro, you will need to work
harder. Your spelling is very poor.

Anna, this is very satisfactory, but
please improve your handwriting.
Your work is so sloppy.

Next month we are having another
test. It will count towards your final
grade.

¡Aquí tenéis vuestras notas!
¡Bravo! Isabel, tu trabajo es
sobresaliente.
Teodoro, tendrás que trabajar
más. Tu ortografía es muy
deficiente.
Ana, esto es muy satisfactorio,
pero haz lo que puedas para
mejorar tu escritura. Tu trabajo
es tan descuidado.
El mes que viene haremos otra
prueba / evaluación. Se incluirá
en vuestra nota final.

EDUCATION

22d Further & Higher Education

adult **de adultos**
adult education **la educación de adultos**
alumnus **el graduado**
apprentice **el aprendiz**
apprenticeship **el aprendizaje**
chair *(university)* **la cátedra**
college **el colegio universitario**
    college of further education **el colegio de formación profesional**
course of study **el curso**
diploma **el diploma, el título**
faculty **el profesorado**
further education **la formación profesional**
graduate **licenciado**
in-service training **el cursillo de formación de profesorado**
lecture **la clase, la conferencia**
lecture hall **el aula, el salón de conferencias**

lecturer **el profesor universitario**
masters degree **el título de máster**
part-time education **la educación a tiempo parcial / de medio tiempo**
polytechnic **el politécnico**
practical **la clase práctica**
principal **el director**
professor **el profesor universitario, el catedrático**
quota *(for university entry)* **el cupo**
research **la investigación**
residence hall / hall of residence **la residencia de estudiantes**
retraining **la reeducación, la recapacitación**
I retrain **hago un curso de reeducación**
scholarship *(grant)* **la beca, la ayuda escolar**
seminar **el seminario**
student **el / la estudiante**

We have increased the number of universities and are aiming for a broader provision.

Hemos aumentado el número de universidades, y aspiramos a conseguir una provisión más amplia.

The technical colleges now belong to the university sector and we now speak of a comprehensive university.

Los colegios técnicos ya pertenecen al sector universitario, y ahora nos referimos a una universidad abierta.

The length of course is four years (eight semesters).

La duración del curso es de cuatro años (ocho semestres).

Financial support is of the greatest importance. Many students get a state grant.

El apoyo económico es muy importante. Muchos estudiantes reciben una beca del estado.

Many students apply for places, but they cannot all be admitted.

Muchos estudiantes solicitan puestos, pero no se les puede admitir a todos.

GENERAL TERMS 22a; EXAMINATIONS 22c; SCHOOL SUBJECTS 22c

student council   la junta de delegados de clase
student grant   la beca de estudios
student union   el sindicato de estudiantes, la asociación de estudiantes
teacher-training college   la escuela de magisterio
technical college   el colegio técnico
university / college   la universidad
university admission qualification   el certificado de selectividad, [el exámen de clasificación]

Faculties & departments

accounting / accountancy   la contabilidad
architecture   la arquitectura
business management   la organización de negocios
catering   la hostelería
classics   los clásicos
civil engineering   la ingeniería civil
commerce   el comercio
construction   la construcción
education   la educación

electronics   la electrónica
electrical engineering   la ingeniería eléctrica
economics   las ciencias económicas
engineering   la ingeniería
environmental sciences   las ciencias del medioambiente
history of art   la historia del arte
hotel management   la dirección hotelera
languages   los idiomas
law   el derecho
literature   la literatura
mechanical engineering   la ingeniería mecánica
medicine   la medicina
pharmacy   la farmacia
nuclear science   la ciencia nuclear
office skills   el secretariado
philosophy   la filosofía
psychology   la psicología
sociology   la sociología
theology   la teología
tourism   el turismo

There is now an entrance restriction.	Ahora la entrada tiene restricciones.
College admission depends on SAT scores.	El derecho a un puesto universitario depende de las notas obtenidas en los exámenes de SAT.
They require particularly high grades / marks for medicine.	Se exigen notas especialmente altas para poder estudiar medicina.
Our results are always outstanding.	Nuestros resultados siempre son sobresalientes.
Many students want job / vocational qualifications.	Muchos estudiantes quieren sacar títulos profesionales.
They can easily transfer between courses.	Pueden cambiar fácilmente los cursos.

Science: The Changing World

23a Scientific Study & Life Sciences

Scientific study

academic paper **el artículo académico, [la ponencia]**
I analyze **analizo**
analysis **el análisis**
authentic **auténtico**
Bunsen burner **el mechero Bunsen**
I challenge **desafío**
I check **compruebo, reviso**
classification **la clasificación**
I classify **clasifico**
control **el control**
I discover **descubro**
discovery **el descubrimiento**
(electron) microscope **el microscopio (electrónico)**
experiment **el experimento**
I experiment **experimento**
flask **el frasco, el matraz**
hypothesis **la hipótesis**
I identify **identifico**
I investigate **investigo**
I invent **invento**

invention **el invento**
laboratory **el laboratorio**
material **el material**
I measure **mido**
measurement **la medición**
I observe **observo**
origin **el origen**
pipette **la pipeta**
process **el proceso**
research **la investigación**
I research **investigo**
result **el resultado**
I solve *(problem)* **resuelvo**
test **la prueba**
I test **compruebo**
test tube **el tubo de ensayo**
theory **la teoría**
I transfer **transfiero**

Biology

bacteria **la bacteria**
botanical **botánico**
I breathe **respiro**
cell **la célula**

The researcher took a sample, mounted it on a slide, and put it under the microscope for examination.	**La investigadora tomó una muestra, la fijó en una platina y la puso debajo del microscopio para examinarla.**
All the results from the experiments support her hypothesis.	**Todos los resultados de los experimentos apoyan su hipótesis.**

chlorophyll la clorofila
it circulates circula
decay la decadencia
decline el descenso, la
  disminución
it declines desciende
it excretes excreta
excretion la excreción
it feeds alimenta
food chain el ciclo alimenticio, la
  cadena alimenticia
gene el gen, el gene
genetic genético
genetic disorder la alteración
  genética
it grows crece
growth el crecimiento
habitat el hábitat
it inherits hereda
membrane la membrana
it mutates se transforma, cambia
nucleus el núcleo
organic orgánico
organism el organismo
photosynthesis la fotosíntesis
population la población
it reproduces se reproduce
respiration la respiración
sensitivity la sensibilidad
survival la sobrevivencia
it survives sobrevive
virus el virus

Medical science & research

DNA el ADN
donor el donante
embryo el embrión
embryo research la investigación
  embrionaria
ethical consideration la
  consideración ética
experiments on animals los
  experimentos con animales
hereditary illness la enfermedad
  hereditaria
IVF (in vitro fertilization) FIV (la
  fertilización / fecundación
  In vitro)
I justify justifico
microorganism el
  microorganismo
organ transplant el transplante de
  órgano
pacemaker el marcapasos
I permit permito
plastic / cosmetic surgery la
  cirugía plástica
recipient el recipiente
I reject *(organ)* rechazo
risk el riesgo
I risk me arriesgo
survival rate la tasa de
  sobrevivencia
test-tube baby el niño probeta
transplant el transplante
X ray el rayo X

A girl of seventeen was today given a new heart in a transplant operation that lasted ten hours.

Research on human embryo tissue is likely to remain highly controversial.

A una chica de diecisiete le dieron hoy un nuevo corazón, en una operación de transplante que duró diez horas.

Los trabajos de investigación sobre los tejidos de embrión humano probablemente serán siempre una cuestión muy controvertida.

SCIENCE: THE CHANGING WORLD

23b Physical Sciences

Chemistry

acid **el ácido**
air **el aire**
alkali **el álcali**
alkaline **alcalino**
I analyze **analizo**
I calculate **calculo**
chemical **químico**
compound **el componente**
composition **la composición**
it dissolves (in water) **se disuelve (en agua)**
element **el elemento**
emulsion **la emulsión**
equation **la ecuación**
gas **el gas**
inorganic **inorgánico**
insoluble **insoluble**
liquid **el líquido**
 liquid *(adj)* **líquido**
litmus paper **el papel de tornasol**
matter **la materia**
metal **el metal**
natural gas **el gas natural**
opaque **opaco**
it oxidizes **oxida**
periodic table **la tabla periódica**
physical **físico**
pure **puro**
it reacts **reacciona**
reaction **la reacción**
salt **la sal**
solid **el sólido**
 solid *(adj)* **sólido**
soluble **soluble**
solution **la solución**
stable **estable**
substance **la sustancia**
transparent **transparente**

Physics & mechanics

it accelerates **acelera**
acceleration **la aceleración**
acoustics **la acústica**
artificial **artificial**
automatic **automático**
ball bearing **de bolas**
boiling point **el punto de ebullición**
circuit **el circuito**
cog **el diente, la rueda dentada**
conservation **la conservación, la preservación**
density **la densidad**
dial **la esfera, el dial**
distance **la distancia**
energy **la energía**
it expands **se expande**
fiber / fibre **la fibra**
force **la fuerza**
it freezes **se congela**
formula **la fórmula**
freezing point **el punto de congelación**
friction **la fricción, el rozamiento**
gauge *(measuring)* **el calibrador, el indicador**
gear **el engranaje**
gravity **la gravedad**
I heat **caliento**
heat **el calor**
heat loss **la pérdida de calor**
laser **el láser**
laser beam **el rayo láser**
lever **la palanca**
light **la luz**
light beam **el rayo de luz, el haz de luz**
lubricant **el lubricante**

Water has a boiling point of one hundred degrees centigrade.

El agua tiene un punto de ebullición de cien grados centígrados.

machinery la maquinaria, el mecanismo
magnetism el magnetismo
magneto la magneto
mass la masa, el peso
mechanics la mecánica
mechanical mecánico
mechanism el mecanismo
metallurgy la metalurgia
microwave la microonda
mineral el mineral
missile el misil
model el modelo
motion el movimiento
observation la observación
I operate (machinery) manejo
operational operacional
optics la óptica
pressure la presión
property la propiedad
proportional proporcional
ray el rayo
reflection la reflexión
refraction la refracción
relativity la relatividad
resistance la resistencia
resistant resistente
robot el robot, el autómata
I sort clasifico
sound el sonido
speed la velocidad
structure la estructura
synthetic sintético
temperature la temperatura
theory la teoría
time el tiempo
transmission la transmisión
turbine la turbina
vapor / vapour el vapor
it vibrates vibra
vibration la vibración

wave la onda
long waves las ondas largas
medium / short waves las ondas medías / cortas
wavelength la longitud de onda
it works funciona

Electricity

battery (large) la batería
battery (small) la pila
charge la carga
I charge the battery cargo la batería
current la corriente
electrical eléctrico
electricity la electricidad
electrode el electrodo
electron el electrón
electronic electrónico
electronics la electrónica
positive positivo
negative negativo
voltage el voltaje

Nuclear physics

atom el átomo
atomic atómico
it emits emite
fission la fisión, la escisión
fusion la fusión
molecular molecular
molecule la molécula
neutron el neutrón
nuclear nuclear
nuclear energy la energía nuclear
nucleus el núcleo
particle la partícula
proton el protón
quantum theory la teoría cuántica
radiation la radiación
reactor el reactor

What's the voltage of this equipment?

¿Cuál es el voltaje de este aparato?

23c The Earth & Space

Geology & minerals

bauxite **la bauxita**
carbon dating **la prueba del carbono**
chalk **la creta**
chalky **cretoso**
clay **la arcilla**
diamond **el diamante**
I excavate **excavo**
exploration **la exploración**
geologist **el geólogo**
geology **la geología**
gemstone **la gema**
granite **el granito**
graphite **el grafito**
layer **la capa**
lime **la cal**
limestone **la piedra caliza**
loam **la marga**
marble **el mármol**
mine **la mina**
I mine **trabajo en la mina**
ore **la mena, el mineral**
quartz **el cuarzo**
quarry **la cantera**
raw materials **las materias primas**
sand **la arena**
sandstone **la piedra arenisca**
sediment **el sedimento**
silica **la sílice**
slate **la pizarra**
soil **la tierra, el suelo**
stalactite **la estalactita**
stalagmite **la estalagmita**

Energy & fuels

atomic energy **la energía atómica**
coal **el carbón**
concentration **la concentración**
coolant **el refrigerante**
energy **la energía**
energy conservation **la conservación de energía**
energy consumption **el consumo de energía**
energy needs **las necesidades energéticas**
energy saving **el ahorro de energía**
energy source **la fuente de energía**
fossil fuels **el combustible fósil**
fuel **el carburante, el combustible**
fuel consumption **el consumo de combustible**
it generates **genera, produce**
geothermal energy **la energía geotérmica**
hydroelectric dam **la presa hidroeléctrica**
hydroelectric power **la fuerza hidroeléctrica**
natural gas **el gas natural**
nuclear energy **la energía nuclear**
nuclear power station **la central nuclear**
nuclear reactor **el reactor nuclear**
oil **el petróleo**
oil production **la producción de petróleo**
oil-producing countries **los países productores de petróleo**
ozone layer **la capa de ozono**
petroleum **el petróleo**
solar cell **la célula solar**
solar energy **la energía solar**
I strike oil **descubro un yacimiento de petróleo**
thermal energy **la energía térmica**
wave power **la energía de las ondas**
tidal power station **la planta colectora de energía de las mareas**
wind energy / power **la energía eólica**

Space

asteroid   el asteroide
big bang theory   la teoría del big-
 bang
black hole   el agujero negro
eclipse   el eclipse
it eclipses   eclipsa
galactic   galáctico
galaxy   la galaxia
gravitational pull   la fuerza de
 atracción planetaria, la fuerza
 de gravedad
the heavens   los cielos
light-year   el año luz
meteorite   el meteorito
moon   la luna
 full moon   la luna llena
 new moon   la luna nueva
nova   la nova
orbit   la órbita
planet   el planeta
shooting star   la estrella fugaz
solar system   el sistema solar
solstice   el solsticio
space   el espacio
star   la estrella
sun   el sol
sunspot   la mancha solar
universe   el universo

Space research & travel

antenna   la antena
astrologer   el astrólogo
astronomer   el astrónomo
astronaut   el astronauta
cosmonaut   el cosmonauta
dish antenna   la antena
 parabólica

I launch   lanzo
launch pad   la plataforma de
 lanzamiento
lunar module   el módulo lunar
moonbuggy   el vehículo lunar
moonwalk   el paseo sobre la
 superficie lunar
observatory   el observatorio
orbit   la órbita
planetarium   el planetario
it reenters   vuelve a entrar,
 reentra
relativity   la relatividad
rocket   el cohete
rocket fuel   el combustible del
 cohete
satellite   el satélite
 communications   de
  comunicaciones
 spy   espía
 weather   meteorológico
sky lab   el laboratorio
 espacial
space flight   el vuelo espacial
space probe   la prueba espacial
space shuttle   el transbordador
 espacial
space walk   el paseo espacial
spacecraft   la nave espacial
spacesuit   el traje de
 astronauta
stratosphere   la estratosfera
telescope   el telescopio
time warp   el salto en
 el tiempo
touchdown on land   el aterrizaje
 on sea   el amerizaje
 on moon   el alunizaje
zodiac   el zodíaco

By studying the light received from stars many millions of light years away, scientists hope to discover the origins of the universe.

Los científicos esperan descubrir el orígen del universo por medio de sus estudios de la luz que nos llega de estrellas que están a muchos millones de años luz.

24 The Environment: The Natural World

24a Geography

archipelago **el archipiélago**
area **el área, la zona**
bank (river) **la ribera (del río)**
bay **la bahía**
beach **la playa**
bog **el pantano, la ciénaga**
bottom **el fondo**
canyon **el cañón**
clean **limpio**
cliff **el acantilado, el precipicio**
coast **la costa**
coastline **el litoral**
continent **el continente**
copse / coppice **el soto, el bosquecillo**
country **el país**
   in the country **en el campo**
countryside **el campo**
creek **la cala, el riachuelo, la ensenada**
dangerous **peligroso**
deep **profundo**
delta **el delta**
desert **el desierto**
dirty **sucio**
dune **la duna**
earth tremor **el temblor de tierra**
earthquake **el terremoto**
equator **el ecuador**
equatorial **ecuatorial**
eruption **la erupción**
it erupts **erupciona**
escarpment **la escarpa**
estuary **el estuario**
field **el campo**
fjord **el fiordo**
flat **plano, llano**
it flows **fluye, discurre**
foothills **las estribaciones**
forest **el bosque**

friendly **no perjudicial**
geographical **geográfico**
geography **la geografía**
geyser **el géiser**
globe **el globo terráqueo, la esfera terrestre**
gradient **la pendiente, la inclinación**
hemisphere **el hemisferio**
high **alto**
hill **la colina**
incline / slope **la inclinación, la pendiente**
it is situated **está situado**
island **la isla**
jungle **la jungla**
lake **el lago**
land **la tierra**
it is located **está situado, se localiza en**
location **la situación, la localización**
map **el mapa**
marsh **el pantano, la ciénaga, la marisma**
meridian **el meridiano**
mountain **la montaña**
mountain range **la cordillera**
national **nacional**
national park **el parque nacional**
nature **la naturaleza**
nice / pleasant **agradable**
ocean **el océano**
ocean floor **el fondo del mar**
peaceful **tranquilo, silencioso**
peak **el pico, la cumbre**
peninsula **la península**
plateau **la meseta, el altiplano**
pole **el polo**
province **la provincia**

reef el arrecife
region la región
regional regional
ridge la cresta, la sierra
river el río
riverbed el lecho del río
rockpool la charca entre rocas
sand la arena
scenery el escenario, la vista
sea el mar
seaside el borde del mar
shore la orilla del mar
spring la fuente, el manantial
steep escarpado, empinado
steppe la estepa
stream el arroyo, la corriente
summit la cima, la cumbre
tall alto, elevado
territory el territorio
top la cima, la cumbre
tropics los trópicos
tundra la tundra
unfriendly perjudicial
valley el valle
volcano el volcán
water el agua (f)
  freshwater el agua dulce /
  limpia
  saltwater el agua salada
  seawater el agua de mar
waterfall la catarata, el salto
wood la madera, el bosque

woodland el bosque, la región
  boscosa
zenith el zénit
zone la zona

Man-made features

aqueduct el acueducto
bridge el puente
canal el canal
capital (city) la capital
city la ciudad
country road la carretera
  secundaria, el camino
dam la presa, la represa, el
  dique
embankment el terraplén
factory la fábrica
farm la granja
farmland las tierras de labranza
hamlet la aldea, el caserío
harbor / harbour el puerto
industry la industria
marina el puerto deportivo
oasis el oasis
reclaimed land la tierra ganada al
  mar
reservoir el pantano, el embalse
town la ciudad, el pueblo
track el camino, la pista
village la aldea, el pueblo
well el pozo, el manantial

The area was marshy and unsuitable for development.

The village is situated in a valley about five kilometers / kilometres north of a small provincial Chilean town.

The inhabitants of the small towns at the foot of Everest were among the poorest people in the world before 1950.

La zona no era apta para el desarrollo por ser pantanosa.

El pueblo está situado en un valle a unos cinco kilómetros al norte de una pequeña ciudad provincial chilena.

Los habitantes de los pequeños pueblos al pie del Everest figuraban entre la gente más pobre del mundo antes de 1950.

FARMING & GARDENING 24c; WEATHER 24d; POLLUTION 24e

24b The Animal World

Animals

animal	**el animal**
it barks	**ladra**
it bites	**muerde**
it bounds	**salta hacia delante**
it breeds	**cría**
burrow	**la madriguera**
cage	**la jaula**
carnivore	**el carnívoro**
cat	**el gato**
it crawls	**anda a gatas**
den	**la guarida, la madriguera**
dog	**el perro**
I feed	**doy de comer, alimento**
it feeds	**alimenta**
food	**la comida, el alimento**
gerbil	**el gerbo**
goldfish	**el pez de colores**
guinea pig	**el conejo de Indias, el curí**
habitat	**el hábitat**
hamster	**el hámster**
herbivore	**el herbívoro**
it hibernates	**hiberna**
it howls	**aúlla**
hutch / hut	**la conejera**
I keep a cat	**tengo un gato**
kitten	**el gatito**
lair	**el cubil, la guarida**
it leaps	**salta**
litter	**la camada**

mammal	**el mamífero**
it meows	**hace miau**
mouse	**el ratón**
omnivore	**el omnívoro**
pack	**la manada, la jauría**
parakeet / budgerigar	**el periquito**
predator	**el depredador**
prey	**la presa**
pet	**el animal doméstico**
puppy	**el perrito**
rabbit	**el conejo**
rabies	**la rabia**
reptile	**el reptil**
it roars	**ruge**
safari park	**el parque de safari**
it squeaks	**chilla**
I stroke	**acaricio**
tortoise	**la tortuga**
I walk *(the dog)*	**paseo**
wildlife park	**la reserva natural**
zoo	**el (jardín / parque) zoológico**

Birds

bird	**el pájaro**
it flies	**vuela**
flock	**la bandada**
it hovers	**permanece inmóvil en el aire**
it migrates	**migra, emigra**
nest	**el nido**
it nests	**anida**
it pecks at	**pica**
it sings	**canta**

Guinea pigs and hamsters are popular pets in Britain.	**Los conejillos de Indias y los hámsteres figuran entre los animales domésticos más populares en Gran Bretaña.**
The campaign to save the whale is increasing in popularity.	**La campaña para salvar la ballena está ganando popularidad.**

Sealife / Waterlife

alligator **el caimán**
anemone **la anémona**
angling **la pesca con caña**
coral **el coral**
crab **el cangrejo**
crocodile **el cocodrilo**
dolphin **el delfín**
fish **el pez**
I fish **pesco**
harpoon **el arpón**
hook **el anzuelo**
marine **marino, marítimo**
mollusk **el molusco**
net **la red**
octopus **el pulpo**
plankton **el plancton**
rod **la caña de pescar**
seal **la foca**
shark **el tiburón**
shoal **el banco**
starfish **la estrella de mar**
it swims **nada**
turtle **la tortuga marina**
whale **la ballena**
whaling **la pesca de ballenas**

Insects

ant **la hormiga**
bee **la abeja**
   queen bee **la abeja reina**
   worker bee **la abeja obrera**
bedbug **el chinche**
beetle **el escarabajo**

bug **el insecto,**
  el bicho
butterfly **la mariposa**
it buzzes **zumba**
caterpillar **la oruga**
cocoon **el capullo**
cockroach **la cucaracha**
cricket **el grillo**
dragonfly **la libélula**
flea **la pulga**
fly **la mosca**
grasshopper **el saltamontes,**
  [el chapulín]
hive **la colmena**
insect **el insecto**
invertebrate **el invertebrado**
ladybug / ladybird **la mariquita**
larva **la larva**
locust **la langosta**
it metamorphoses **metamorfosea**
mosquito **el mosquito**
moth **la polilla**
scorpion **el escorpión**
silkworm **el gusano de seda**
slug **la babosa**
snail **el caracol**
spider **la araña**
it spins (a web) **teje (una tela)**
it stings **pica**
termite **la termita**
tick **la garrapata**
web **la red**
wasp **la avispa**
worm **el gusano**

The panda is in danger of extinction in the wild, because the bamboo, which it eats, inexplicably dies away every fifty years.

Don't forget to walk the dog, feed the cat, and talk to the goldfish!

El panda corre riesgo de extinción en la selva, pues el bambú que come desaparece por completo cada cincuenta años sin que nadie sepa por qué.

¡No olvides de llevar al perro de paseo, de darle de comer al gato y de hablarle al pez de colores!

24c Farming & Gardening

Farm animals

bull **el toro**
cattle **el ganado**
chicken **el pollo**
cow **la vaca**
it crows **canta, cacarea**
dairy (adj) **lácteo**
duck **el pato**
it eats **come**
feed **el alimento**
it feeds **se alimenta**
colt **el potro**
fodder **el pienso, el forraje**
food (for animals) **el alimento de los animales**
it gallops **galopa**
goat **la cabra**
goose **el ganso**
it grazes **pace, pasta**
it grunts **gruñe**
horse **el caballo**
horseshoe **la herradura**
it kicks **da patadas**
kid **la cría**
I milk **ordeño**
it moos **muge**
it neighs **relincha**
ox **el buey**
it pecks **picotea**
pig **el cerdo**
pony **el poni, el caballito**
poultry **las aves**
produce **los productos agrícolas**
it quacks **hace cua-cua**
I ride (a horse) **monto**
rooster / cock **el gallo**

I shear **esquilo**
sheep **la oveja**
sheepdog **el perro pastor de ovejas**
I slaughter **mato, sacrifico**
stallion **el semental**
it trots **trota**

On the farm

agricultural **agrario**
arable **arable, cultivable**
barn **la granja**
combine harvester **la cosechadora, la segadora**
crop **el cultivo**
dairy **la quesería**
farm **la granja**
farmhouse **la casa de la granja**
farm laborer / labourer **el granjero**
farmyard **el patio de la granja**
fence **la valla, el seto, la cerca**
I groom **cepillo al caballo**
harvest **la cosecha**
I harvest **cosecho**
hay **el heno**
bale of hay **la bala de heno**
I irrigate **riego**
milk churn **la lechera**
milking machine **la ordeñadora**
pasture **el pasto**
pen **el corral**
pigsty **la porqueriza, la pocilga**
silage **el silo**
slaughterhouse **el matadero**
stable **el establo**
stud farm **la caballeriza**

In the developing countries, arable land is often owned by rich landlords.	**En los países en desarrollo, la tierra cultivable a menudo es de propietarios ricos.**

Agriculture & gardening

acorn **la bellota**
agriculture **la agricultura**
barley **la cebada**
it blooms **florece**
bloom **la flor**
bouquet **el ramo, el bouquet**
branch **el ramo**
bud **el capullo**
bulb **el bulbo**
bush **el arbusto**
cactus **el cactus**
compost **el abono**
corn / maize **el maíz**
I cultivate **cultivo**
cutting **el esqueje**
I dig **cavo**
ear **la espiga**
I fertilize **abono**
fertilizer **el fertilizante,
   el abono**
fir **el abeto**
flower **la flor**
it flowers **florece**
flowerpot **el tiesto, la maceta, [la
   malera]**
foliage **el follaje**
garden / yard **el jardín**
I gather **recojo**
grain **el grano**
grass **la hierba**
I grow **planto, cultivo**
it grows **crece**
hedge **el seto**
horticulture **la horticultura**
lawn **el césped**
leaf **la hoja**

I mow **corto la hierba**
oats **la avena**
orchard **la huerta**
petal **el pétalo**
I pick **cojo, recojo**
pine **el pino**
pine forest **el bosque de pinos**
I plant **planto**
plant **la planta**
pollen **el polen**
I reap **cosecho, recojo**
ripe **maduro**
it ripens **madura**
root **la raíz**
rotten **podrido**
rye **el centeno**
sap **la savia**
seed **la semilla**
sorghum **el sorgo**
species **la especie**
stalk **el tallo, la caña**
stamen **el estambre**
stem **el tallo**
thorn **la espina**
I transplant **transplanto**
tree **el árbol**
trunk **el tronco**
undergrowth **la maleza, el monte
   bajo**
vegetables **las verduras**
vegetation **la vegetación**
I water **riego**
weeds **las malas hierbas**
I weed **mato las malas hierbas**
wheat **el trigo**
wildflower **la flor salvaje, la flor
   silvestre**
it wilts **se marchita**

Let's go for a walk in the country and stop at the old farmhouse. We'll probably see some newborn lambs in the fields.

Vámonos a dar un paseo en el campo hasta el cortijo viejo. Probablemente veremos unos corderos recién nacidos en los campos.

THE ENVIRONMENT: THE NATURAL WORLD

24d Weather

anticyclone **el anticiclón**
avalanche **la avalancha**
average temperature **la temperatura media**
bad weather **el mal tiempo**
bright **despejado, claro**
bright period **el período despejado**
centigrade **centígrado**
changeable **variable**
climate **el clima**
climatic **climático**
cloud **la nube**
clouded over **cubierto**
cloudless **despejado, sin nubes**
cloudy **nuboso, nublado**
cold **frío**
it is cold **hace frío**
cold front **el frente frío**
it is cool **hace fresco**
cyclone **el ciclón**
damp **húmedo**
degree **el grado**
    above zero **sobre cero**
    below zero **bajo cero**
depression **la depresión**

drizzle **el chirimiri, [la llovizna]**
it drizzles **llovizna**
drought **la sequía**
dry **seco**
dull weather **el tiempo gris**
it's fine **hace buen tiempo**
flash **el relámpago**
fog **la niebla**
it is foggy **está nuboso / nublado**
it's freezing **está helando**
frost **la helada, la escarcha**
frosty **helado**
gale **el vendaval, el ventarrón**
gale warning **el aviso de tormenta**
it's hailing **está granizando**
hail **el granizo**
heat **el calor**
heatwave **la ola de calor**
high pressure **la presión alta**
highest temperature **la temperatura máxima**
it's hot **hace calor**
ice **el hielo**
Indian summer **el verano de San Martín**
lightning **el relámpago, el rayo**

It will be cold over the whole country tomorrow, maximum temperatures four to six Celsius (thirty-nine to forty-three Fahrenheit).

Mañana hará frío en todo el país, con una temperatura máxima de entre cuatro y seis grados Celsius (treinta y nueve a cuarenta y tres Fahrenheit).

Freezing fog patches in the Ebro valley should clear by midday.

Las zonas de niebla helada que se encuentran en la Cuenca del Ebro desaparecerán con toda probabilidad antes de mediodía.

Outlook for the weekend — very warm and sunny.

El pronóstico para el fin de semana — sol y mucho calor.

The whole country will be affected by rain, turning to sleet in the mountains.

El país entero será afectado por la lluvia, que caerá como aguanieve en las zonas montañosas.

low pressure la presión baja
lowest temperature la
    temperatura mínima
mild suave
mist la bruma
misty brumoso
monsoon el monzón
moon la luna
occluded front el frente ocluso
rain la lluvia
it's raining está lloviendo
rainy lluvioso
shade la sombra
it shines brilla
shower el chaparrón
snow la nieve
snowball la bola de nieve
snowdrift la ventisca de nieve
snowfall la nevada
snowflake el copo de nieve
snowman el muñeco de nieve
snow report (for skiing) el
    pronóstico de la nieve
it's snowing está nevando
snowstorm la tormenta de nieve
star la estrella
storm la tormenta
stormy tormentoso

sultry bochornoso
sun / sunshine hace sol
sunny day un día de sol
(daily) temperature la temperatura
    diurna
thunder el trueno
it's thundering hay truenos
thunderbolt el rayo
thunderstorm la tormenta
    eléctrica / de rayos
torrent el torrente
torrential torrencial
tropical tropical
warm cálido
warm front el frente
    cálido
weather el tiempo
weather conditions las
    condiciones climáticas
weather forecast el pronóstico
    del tiempo
weather report el informe del
    tiempo
wet mojado, húmedo
What's the weather like? ¿Cómo
    es el tiempo?
wind el viento
windy ventoso

The monsoon is now well established over southeast Asia.

El monzón ya está bien establecido en la zona sudeste de Asia.

The south of the country will be affected by tropical storms later tonight.

Durante la noche la zona sur del país se verá afectada por tormentas tropicales.

"Did you have a good vacation / holiday?"
"Yes, apart from the weather."
"I thought it was always hot and sunny on the Mediterranean."
"So did I. We must have chosen the one week when it was cold and rainy."

— ¿ Lo pasaste bien en tus vacaciones?
— Sí, aparte del tiempo.
— Creía que siempre hacía sol y calor en el Mediterráneo.
— Yo también. Sin duda escogimos la única semana en que hizo frío y llovió.

THE ENVIRONMENT: THE NATURAL WORLD

24e Pollution

balance of nature **el equilibrio natural**
it becomes extinct **se agota, se extingue**
conservation **la conservación, la preservación**
conservationist **el conservacionista**
I conserve **conservo, preservo**
corrosion **la corrosión, la oxidación**
I consume **consumo**
consumption **el consumo**
I damage **daño, estropeo, perjudico**
damaging **perjudicial, dañoso**
danger (to) **peligro a**
I destroy **destruyo**
disaster **el desastre, el devastamiento**
disposal **el desecho**
I dispose of **desecho, [boto a la basura]**
I do without **no necesito, me arreglo sin**
ecology **la ecología**
ecosystem **el ecosistema**
emission **la emisión**
it emits **emite, desprende**

environment **el medio ambiente**
exhaust pipe **el tubo de escape**
garbage / rubbish **la basura**
harmful **perjudicial**
I improve **mejoro**
industrial waste **los residuos industriales**
I insulate **aíslo**
litter **la basura, los desperdicios**
I poison **enveneno**
poison **el veneno, el tóxico**
pollutant **el contaminante**
I pollute **contamino**
pollution **la contaminación**
I predict **pronostico**
I protect **protejo**
recyclable **reciclable**
I recycle **reciclo**
recycled paper **el papel reciclado**
reprocessing **el reprocesamiento**
residue **el residuo**
it runs out **se agota, se acaba**
I throw away **tiro**
waste *(domestic)* **la basura**
waste disposal unit **el triturador de basuras**
waste products **los productos de desecho, los productos desechables**

The city council / municipality provides facilities for recycling glass, cans, and newspapers.

El ayuntamiento [la alcadía] suministra facilidades para reciclar el vidrio, las latas y los periódicos.

Recent studies suggest the hole in the ozone layer will have serious consequences in the Northern Hemisphere.

Estudios recientes indican que el agujero en la capa de ozono tendrá consecuencias graves para el Hemisferio Norte.

On the earth

artificial fertilizer   **el fertilizante artificial**
biodegradable   **biodegradable**
deforestation   **la deforestación**
garbage / rubbish dump   **el vertedero de basura, [el relleno sanitario]**
nature reserve   **la reserva natural, el parque natural**
natural resources   **los recursos naturales**
nitrates   **los nitratos**
pesticide   **el pesticida**
radioactive   **radioactivo**
radioactive waste   **el residuo radioactivo**
rain forest   **la selva**
refuse   **el desperdicio, la basura, el desecho**
scrap metal   **la chatarra**
soil erosion   **la erosión del suelo**
weedkiller   **el herbicida**

In the atmosphere

acid rain   **la lluvia ácida**
aerosol *(system)*   **el aerosol**
aerosol can   **el tubo de aerosol, la botella de aerosol**
air pollution   **la contaminación del aire**

atmosphere   **la atmósfera**
catalytic convertor   **el catalizador**
CFCs   **los clorofluorocarbonos**
emission (of gas)   **la emisión (de gas)**
incinerator   **el incinerador**
skin cancer   **el cáncer de piel**
I spray   **pulverizo, atomizo, rocío, riego**
unleaded / lead-free gasoline   **la gasolina sin plomo**
waste gases   **los gases residuales**

In the rivers & seas

detergent   **el detergente**
drainage   **el drenaje, el desagüe**
drought   **la sequía**
flooding   **la inundación**
industrial wastes   **los residuos industriales**
oil slick   **la mancha de petróleo**
phosphates   **los fosfatos**
sea level   **el nivel del mar**
sewage   **la depuración de las aguas**
water level   **el nivel del agua**
water supply system   **el sistema de abastecimiento de agua**
water supply   **el suministro de agua**

"Do you think this awful weather is normal? Don't you think it's because of global warming?"

"Not really. It's just the normal cycle."
"Well, I think it's a combination of the greenhouse effect and nuclear testing in the last forty years."

— **¿ Crees que este tiempo horroroso sea normal? ¿ No crees que sea resultado del recalentamiento mundial?**
— **No lo creo. Sólo se trata del ciclo normal.**
— **Bueno, yo creo que se trata de una combinación del efecto invernadero y de las pruebas nucleares que se hacen desde hace cuarenta años.**

Government & Politics

25a Political Life

I abolish **abolo, suprimo una ley**
act (of parliament) **la ley, la disposición parlamentaria**
administration **la administración**
I appoint **nombro, designo**
appointment **el nombramiento**
asylum seeker **el solicitante de asilo político**
it becomes law **cobra fuerza de ley, entra en vigor**
bill **la proposición / el proyecto de ley**
I bring down **derroco, derribo**
citizen **el ciudadano**
civil disobedience **la resistencia pasiva**
civil servant **el funcionario público**
civil war **la guerra civil**
coalition **la coalición**
it comes into effect **entra en vigor, rige**
common **civil**
constitution **la constitución**
cooperation **la cooperación**
corruption **la corrupción**
region **la región**
coup **el golpe de estado**

crisis **la crisis**
debate **el debate**
decree **el decreto**
delegate **el delegado, el diputado**
I demonstrate **participo en la manifestación**
demonstration **la manifestación**
I discuss **discuto**
discussion **la discusión**
I dismiss **destituyo**
I dissolve **disuelvo**
I draw up *(a bill)* **redacto**
duty **el deber**
equal opportunity **la igualdad de oportunidades**
executive **el ejecutivo**
executive *(adj)* **ejecutivo**
foreign policy **la política exterior**
I form a pact with **pacto con**
freedom **la libertad**
freedom of speech **la libertad de expresión**
I govern **gobierno**
government **el gobierno**
I introduce (a bill) **presento (un proyecto de ley)**
judiciary **la judicatura**
law **el derecho, la ley**

The Prime Minister summoned the Cabinet to an emergency meeting.

El Primer Ministro convocó una reunión extraordinaria del Consejo de Ministros.

The Minister of the Interior / Home Secretary said the Government was determined to halt the rise in juvenile crime.

El Ministro del Interior dijo que el Gobierno estaba resuelto a parar la subida en el nivel del crimen juvenil.

I lead **encabezo**
legislation **la legislación**
legislature **la legislatura**
liberty **la libertad**
local affairs **los asuntos internos / locales**
local government **el gobierno local**
long-term **a largo plazo**
majority **la mayoría**
meeting **la reunión**
middle class **la clase media**
ministry **el ministerio**
minority **la minoría**
nation **la nación**
national **nacional**
national flag **la bandera nacional**
Spanish national flag **la bandera de España**
I nationalize **nacionalizo**
I oppose **me opongo**
opposition **la oposición**
I organize **organizo**
I overthrow **derroco**
pact **el pacto**
I pass *(a bill)* **apruebo**
politics **la política**
political **político**
power **el poder**
I privatize **privatizo**
I protest **protesto**
public **el público**
public *(adj)* **público**
public opinion **la opinión pública**
I ratify **ratifico**

reactionary **reaccionario**
I reform **reformo, dimito**
reform **la reforma**
I reject **rechazo**
I repeal *(an act)* **rechazo**
I represent **represento**
I repress **reprimo**
I resign **dimito**
responsible **responsable**
responsibility **la responsabilidad**
reunification **la reunificación**
revolt **la revuelta, el levantamiento**
I rule **rijo, dispongo**
sanction **la sanción**
seat **el escaño**
short-term **a corto plazo**
solidarity **la solidaridad**
speech **el discurso**
state **el estado**
statesman **el hombre de estado**
I support **apoyo**
I take power **tomo el poder**
tax **el impuesto**
taxation **los impuestos**
term of office **la duración del cargo**
I throw out (a bill) **rechazo**
unconstitutional **inconstitucional**
unilateral **unilateral**
unity **la unidad**
veto **el veto**
I veto **veto**
welfare **el bienestar**
working class **la clase obrera**

The Lower Chamber voted on the question of immigration controls.	**La Cámara Baja votó sobre la cuestión del control de inmigración.**
The Treasury promised to cut the proportion of national income taken in taxes to thirty per cent.	**El Ministerio de Hacienda prometió reducir a treinta por ciento la proporción de renta nacional recaudada en impuestos.**

SOCIAL ISSUES 12; THE ECONOMY 14

GOVERNMENT & POLITICS

25b Elections & Ideology

Elections

ballot   **la votación**
ballot box   **la urna electoral /
   de votos**
ballot paper   **la papeleta de voto**
I hold an election   **celebro una
   elección**
campaign   **la campaña**
candidate   **el candidato**
constituency   **la circunscripción
   electoral**
count   **el recuento, la cuenta**
I elect   **elijo**
election   **la elección**
electorate   **el electorado**
I'm entitled to vote   **tengo derecho
   a votar**
floating vote   **el voto flotante**
four-year term of office   **el cargo
   de cuatro años**
general election   **la votación
   general**
I go to the polls   **voto**
I hold *(an election)*   **celebro**
local elections   **las elecciones
   regionales**
majority system   **el sistema
   mayoritario**
off-year elections / by-election   **la
   elección parcial**
opinion poll   **el sondeo de opinión**
party   **el partido**
poll   **el sondeo**
primary   **la primaria**

proportional system   **el sistema
   proporcional**
recount   **el recuento**
I recount   **vuelvo a contar**
referendum   **el referéndum**
right to vote   **el derecho de voto,
   el derecho a votar**
I stand for election   **me presento a
   la elección**
suffrage   **el sufragio**
swing   **el desplazamiento, el
   movimiento**
universal suffrage   **el sufragio
   universal**
vote   **el voto**
I vote (for)   **voto (por)**
voter   **el votante**

Political ideology

anarchist   **el anarquista**
anarchy   **la anarquía**
aristocracy   **la aristocracia**
aristocratic   **aristocrático**
capitalism   **el capitalismo**
capitalist   **capitalista**
center / centre ground   **los partidos
   de centro**
communism   **el comunismo**
communist   **comunista**
conservatism   **el conservadurismo,
   el conservatismo**
conservative   **conservador**
democracy   **la democracia**
democratic   **democrático**

Presidential elections in the
United States occur every
four years.

**Las elecciones presidenciales
en los Estados Unidos se
celebran cada cuatro años.**

The voters went to the polls today;
it was a record turnout.

**Los votantes acudieron a las
urnas hoy; hubo un número
récord de votantes.**

dictator el dictador
dictatorship la dictadura
duke el duque
empire el imperio
emperor/empress el emperador,
  la emperatriz
extremist extremista
fascism el fascismo
fascist fascista
I gain independence me
  independizo
green party el partido verde, el
  partido ecologista
ideology la ideología
imperialism el imperialismo
imperialist imperialista
independence la independencia
independent independiente
king el rey
left la izquierda
loft wing el ala izquierda
liberal liberal
liberalism el liberalismo
marxism el marxismo
marxist marxista
monarchy la monarquía
nationalism el nacionalismo
nationalist nacionalista
patriotic patriótico
patriotism el patriotismo
prince el príncipe
princess la princesa
queen la reina
racism el racismo
racist racista
radicalism el radicalismo

radical radical
republic la república
republicanism el republicanismo
revolutionary el revolucionario
right la derecha
right wing el ala derecha
royal real
royalist monárquico
socialism el socialismo
socialist el socialista

Representatives & politicians

chancellor el canciller, el ministro
congressman/woman el diputado,
  la diputada, el/la congresista
head of state el jefe de estado
leader el líder
mayor el alcalde
minister el ministro
minister of the interior/home
  secretary el Ministro del
  interior
party leader/leader of the party el
  líder del partido político
politician el político
prefect el subsecretario
president el presidente
prime minister el primer
  ministro
secretary of state/foreign minister
  el ministro de asuntos
  exteriores
senator el senador
speaker el presidente de la
  cámara/del Parlamento
spokesperson el/la portavoz

An opinion poll gave the
Democrats a two point lead over
the Republicans.

In the local elections, the Socialist
party won a majority of seats on
the town council.

**Un sondeo atribuyó a los
Demócratas una ventaja de dos
puntos sobre los Republicanos.**

**En las elecciones locales, el
Partido Socialista ganó una
mayoría de escaños en el
concejo municipal.**

Crime & Justice

26a Crime

accomplice **el cómplice**
armed **armado**
assault **el asalto**
assault and battery **el maltrato y
la agresión física**
battered baby **el bebé golpeado,
el bebé maltratado**
burglar **el ladrón**
burglarize / burgle **robo en la casa**
burglary **el robo, el allanamiento
de morada**
car theft **el robo de coche**
theft from car **el robo desde
el coche**
child abuse **el abuso de menores**
I come to blows **me peleo a
golpes**
I commit **cometo**
crime **el crimen, el delito**
crime rate **la tasa delictiva**
crime wave **la ola de crimen,
la ola criminal**
criminal **el criminal,
el delincuente**
criminal (adj) **criminal**
I deceive **defraudo, engaño**
delinquency **la delincuencia**

drug abuse **el abuso de drogas**
drug addict **el drogadicto**
drug barons **los capos de
la droga**
drug dealer / pusher **el traficante
de drogas, el camello**
drugs **las drogas**
drug trafficking **el tráfico de
drogas, el narcotráfico**
I embezzle **desfalco, malverso**
embezzlement **el desfalco, la
malversación**
extortion **la extorsión**
I fight **peleo, lucho, riño**
fight **la pelea, la lucha, la riña**
firearm **el arma de fuego**
I forge (banknote, signature)
falsifico
forged **falsificado**
forgery **la falsificación**
fraud **el fraude**
gang **la banda**
gang warfare **la guerra de las
pandilllas**
grievous bodily harm **los daños
corporales graves**
gun **la pistola**

Members of the public have begun to give information to the police about the rape of two teenage girls by a gang in west Buenos Aires last week.	**Miembros del público han empezado a dar información a la policía con respecto a la violación, la semana pasada, de dos chicas adolescentes por una pandilla en la zona del oeste de Buenos Aires.**

handbag snatching **el tirón del bolso**

handcuffs **las esposas**

Help! **¡Socorro!**

I hijack **secuestro (un avión)**

hijacker **el secuestrador aéreo**

holdup **el atraco, el asalto**

hooker **la prostituta, la fulana**

hostage **el rehén**

illegal **ilegal**

I importune **importuno, molesto**

I injure/wound **hiero, causo heridas**

I joy ride (stolen car) **conduzco un coche robado**

joy riding (stealing a car to go) **el robo de coches para la conducción temeraria**

I kidnap **rapto**

kidnapper **el raptor**

kidnapping **el rapto**

I kill **mato**

killer **el homicida**

knife **el cuchillo**

knifing **matar a cuchilladas**

legal **legal**

mafia **la mafia**

I mug **asalto**

mugger **el asaltador**

mugging **el asalto**

murder **el homicidio**

I murder **mato**

murderer **el asesino, el homicida**

I offend **cometo un delito**

pickpocket **el ratero, el carterista, el bolsista**

pickpocketing **el robo de cartera**

pimp **el proxeneta, el chulo, el alcahuete**

pimping **el proxenetismo, el chuleo**

poison **el veneno**

I poison **enveneno**

procuring **el proxenetismo, el chuleo**

prostitute **la prostituta, la fulana**

prostitution **la prostitución**

I rape **violo**

rape **la violación**

receiver **el receptador/receptor de bienes robados**

reprisals **la represalias**

shoplifting **el hurto en las tiendas**

I steal **robo**

stolen goods **los bienes robados, las cosas robadas**

terrorist **el terrorista**

torture **la tortura**

thief **el ladrón**

trafficking **el tráfico ilegal**

I traffic **trafico**

underworld **los fondos bajos, los bajos fondos**

victim **la víctima**

Pablo Escobar, the world's most infamous drug baron, was killed in a shoot-out with police and the army in Medellín.

Pablo Escobar, el magnate narcotraficante más infame del mundo, resultó muerto en un tiroteo con la policía y el ejército en Medellín.

He was stopped by the police for speeding in a residential area of Lugo.

Fue detenido por la policía por exceso de velocidad en una zona residencial de Lugo.

➤ TRIAL 26b; PUNISHMENT, CRIME PREVENTION 26c

CRIME & JUSTICE

26b Trial

accusation **la acusación**
I accuse **acuso**
accused person **el acusado**
I acquit **absuelvo**
I acquit for lack of evidence
 absuelvo por falta de pruebas
appeal **el recurso**
I appeal **recurro**
awaiting trial (in jail) **en prisión preventiva**
case for the defense **el discurso de la defensa**
compensation **la indemnización**
confession **la confesión**
I confess **confieso**
I convince **pruebo, convenzo**
costs **las costas**
counsel for the defense / defendant **el abogado defensor**
court **el juzgado, el tribunal, la corte**
court of appeal **el juzgado de apelación, la corte de apelación**
courtroom **la sala de juicios**
criminal court **el juzgado criminal, el juzgado (de lo) penal**
I cross-examine **interrogo**
I debate **debato, discuto**
defense / defence **la defensa**
I defend **defiendo**
I defend (myself) **me defiendo**
defendant **el demandado, el acusado**

diminished responsibility **la culpabilidad reducida**
I disagree **disiento**
I discuss **discuto**
district attorney **el fiscal de distrito**
dock **el banquillo de los acusados**
evidence **la prueba**
examining magistrate **el juez de instrucción**
extenuating circumstances **las circunstancias atenuantes**
eyewitness **el testigo ocular / presencial**
I find guilty **declaro culpable**
I give evidence **declaro**
 for the defense **declaro en favor de la defensa**
 for the prosecution **declaro en favor del cargo**
guilt **la culpa**
guilty **culpable**
high court of appeal **el tribunal supremo**
I impeach **acuso**
impeachment **la acusación**
indictment **el procesamiento**
 indictment in court **el procesamiento ante el tribunal**
innocence **la inocencia**

The judge imposed a fine of two thousand pesos and ordered the accused to pay costs.

El juez le impuso al acusado una multa de dos mil pesos y le condenó con costas.

A man will appear in court today charged with the attempted murder of a fourteen-month-old baby boy.

Un hombre comparecerá hoy en el tribunal acusado de tentativa de asesinato de un nene de catorce meses.

innocent inocente
I inquire pregunto
judge el juez
juror el miembro del jurado
jury el jurado
jury box el estrado del jurado
justice la justicia
lawsuit el proceso civil, el pleito, el litigio
lawyer el abogado, el letrado
leniency la clemencia
life imprisonment la condena a cadena / reclusión perpetua
litigation la litigación
magistrate el magistrado
magistrate's court el juzgado correccional / de paz
mercy la misericordia
minor offense la falta menor
miscarriage of justice el error de la justicia
motive el móvil, el motivo
not guilty inocente
oath el juramento
offense el delito
order / writ la orden, el decreto, el mandato
I pass judgment pronuncio sentencia
perjury el perjurio
plea el argumento de la defensa
plea bargaining las negociaciones para los cargos
I plead not guilty me declaro inocente

premeditation la premeditación
I prosecute acuso
prosecution la acusación
public prosecutor el fiscal
public prosecutor's office la fiscalía
I put up / stand bail (for *someone*) garantizo la fianza
I question pregunto
retrial la revisión del proceso
I reward recompenso, indemnizo
speech for the defense / defence el alegato de la defensa
I stand accused estoy acusado
statement la declaración
I sue / I take to court demando
summons la citación
I suspect sospecho
suspicion la sospecha
Supreme Court el tribunal supremo, la corte suprema
sustained! ¡confirmado!
I swear juro
I take legal action empiezo un proceso
trial el juicio, el proceso
unanimous unánime
verdict el veredicto
I witness atestiguo
witness el testigo
witness-box el estrado de los testigos

The case against the accused was dismissed on grounds of insufficient evidence.

El tribunal absolvió al acusado por falta de pruebas.

The accused had strong connections to the underworld.

El acusado tenía fuertes relaciones en el mundo del hampa.

CRIME & JUSTICE

26c Punishment

confinement **la reclusión**
  in solitary confinement **en régimen de aislamiento**
I convict **declaro culpable**
convict **el convicto, el reo**
death penalty **la pena de muerte**
I deport **deporto**
I escape **escapo**
fine **la multa**
I fine **multo**
I free **libero**
hard labor/labour **los trabajos forzados**
I imprison **hago prisionero, meto en prisión**
jailbird **el presidiario**
prison **la prisión, la cárcel**
prisoner **el prisionero**
I punish **castigo**
punishment **el castigo, la pena**
I am out on bail **salgo bajo fianza**
I reprieve a condemned prisoner **indulto**
I sentence to death **sentencio a muerte, condeno a muerte**
I serve a sentence **cumplo una condena**
sentence **la sentencia**

severity **la severidad, la dureza**
suspended sentence **la suspensión de sentencia**

The fight against crime

alarm **la alarma**
  burglar/car alarm **la alarma antirrobo**
autopsy **la autopsia**
arrest **el arresto**
I arrest **arresto**
baton/truncheon **la porra, el bastón**
chief of police **el comisario de policía, el jefe de policía**
civil law **el derecho civil**
clue **la pista**
come quickly! **¡venga rápido!**
crime prevention **la prevención del crimen**
criminal law **el derecho penal**
criminal record **los antecedentes penales**
customs **la aduana**
customs officer **el agente de aduana**
deportation **la deportación**
detective **el detective**
drug raid **la redada de drogas**

"What was the verdict in the trial?"

"The defendant was sentenced to four years imprisonment."
"Will he serve that long?"

"No, nothing like it. He'd already spent eight months awaiting trial."
"Did he plead guilty?"
"Yes, to manslaughter."

— ¿Cuál ha sido el veredicto en el proceso?

— El acusado fue condenado a cuatro años de cárcel.
— ¿Servirá tanto tiempo en la cárcel?

— No, nada de eso. Ya había pasado ocho meses en prisión preventiva.
— ¿Se confesó culpable?
— Sí. Se confesó culpable al homicidio sin premeditación.

drug squad **la brigada antidrogas**
error **el error**
escape **la escapada, el escape**
I escape (to) **me escapo (a)**
examination **el examen, la prueba**
I examine **examino**
I extradite **extradito**
extradition **la extradición**
fingerprints **las huellas dactilares / digitales**
fugitive **el fugitivo**
guard dog **el perro guardián**
handcuff **la esposa**
identikit / photofit picture **el retrato robot**
informer **el informador, el confidente, el informante**
inquiry **el interrogatorio**
interview **el interrogatorio**
I interview **interrogo**
I investigate **investigo**
investigation **la investigación**
investigator **el investigador**
private investigator **el investigador privado**
key **la clave**
law **el derecho, la ley**
lawbreaking **la contravención de la ley, el incumplimiento de la ley**

lock **la cerradura**
I lock **cierro con llave**
padlock **el candado**
plainclothes police **el policía vestido de paisano**
police officer **el policía**
police badge **la placa policial**
police record **el registro policial, los antecedentes penales**
clean record **sin antecedentes penales**
police station **la comisaría [estación] de policía**
policeman **el policía**
policewoman **la mujer policía**
reward **la recompensa**
riot police **la policía antidisturbios [antimotines]**
security **la seguridad**
speed trap **el control de velocidad por radar**
traffic police **la policía de tráfico**
undercover **secreto, clandestino**
warrant **la orden**
arrest warrant **la orden de prisión**
search warrant **la orden de búsqueda**

He was convicted of breaking and entering and given a two-year sentence.

Fue declarado culpable de allanamiento de morada y condenado a dos años de prisión.

The government recommends more custodial sentences for serious offenders.

El gobierno recomienda que haya más condenas a la cárcel para los que son culpables de delitos graves.

Overcrowding is a serious problem in many prisons.

La masificación [superpoblación] es un problema grave en muchas cárceles.

➤ ADDICTION & VIOLENCE 12d

War & Peace

27a War

I abduct **rapto, secuestro, plagio**
aerial bombing **el bombardeo aéreo**
aggressor **el agresor**
air force **las fuerzas aéreas**
I airlift **me transporto por avión**
air raid **el ataque aéreo**
air raid shelter **el refugio antiaéreo**
air raid warning **la alarma antiaérea**
ambush **la emboscada**
antiaircraft **antiaviones**
army **el ejército**
I assassinate **asesino, mato**
assault **el asalto**
atomic **atómico**
I attack **ataco**
attack **el ataque**
barracks **las barracas, el cuartel**
battle **la batalla**
battlefield **el campo de batalla**
blast **la explosión**
I blockade **bloqueo**
blockade **el bloqueo**
I blow up **vuelo, hago explotar**
bomb alert **el aviso de bomba**
bombardment **el bombardeo**
brave **valiente**
I call up **llamo a filas**
camp **el campo**
campaign **la campaña**
I capture **capturo**
causes of war **las causas de la guerra**
I claim responsibility for **pido responsabilidad por**
I commit *(an act)* **cometo**
conflict **el conflicto**
confrontation **la confrontación**
I contaminate **contamino**

conventional *(weapon / warfare)* **convencional**
courtmartial **el consejo de guerra, el consejo militar**
cowardly **la cobardía**
the plane crashes **el avión se estrella**
I crush *(opposition)* **estrello**
I declare *(war)* **declaro**
defeat **la derrota**
I defeat **derroto**
I am defeated **estoy derrotado**
defense / defence **la defensa**
I defend **defiendo**
I destroy **destruyo**
I detain **detengo**
I detect **detecto**
devastating **devastador**
enemy **el enemigo**
espionage **el espionaje**
ethnic cleansing **la limpieza étnica**
I evacuate **evacúo**
evacuation **la evacuación**
I fight a battle **libro una batalla, lucho en una batalla**
I fight off **rechazo**
I flee **huyo, escapo**
front **el frente**
guerrilla warfare **la guerra de guerilleros**
harmful **dañino**
headquarters **los cuarteles generales**
hostilities **las hostilidades**
I interrogate **interrogo**
interrogation **el interrogatorio**
I intervene **intervengo**
intervention **la intervención**
intimidation **la intimidación**

I invade **invado**
invasion **la invasión**
I issue an ultimatum **doy un ultimátum**
I liquidate **liquido**
maneuvers / manoeuvres **las maniobras**
massacre **la masacre**
missing in action **desaparecido en acción**
military service **el servicio militar**
mobilization **la movilización**
I mobilize **movilizo**
morale **la moral**
multilateral **multilateral**
navy **la armada, la marina de guerra**
nuclear **nuclear**
occupation **la ocupación**
I occupy **ocupo**
offensive **la ofensiva**
  offensive (adj) **ofensivo**
I patrol **patrullo**
peace **la paz**
propaganda **la propaganda**
I provoke **provoco**
battle rage **el furor de la batalla**
raid **el ataque, la incursión**
rank **la fila**
reinforcements **los refuerzos**
reprisals **las represalias**
I resist **resisto**
resistance **la resistencia**
I review (troops) **paso revista a, revisto**

I revolt **me rebelo, me sublevo**
revolution **la revolución**
riot **el motín, la sublevación**
rubble **el escombro**
security check **la inspección de seguridad**
shell **el obús, el proyectil, la granada**
shelter **el refugio**
I sink the ship **hundo el barco**
the ship sinks **el barco se hunde**
skirmish **la escaramuza**
I spy **espío**
I start a war **comienzo una guerra**
strategy **la estrategia**
striking power **el poder ofensivo, el poder de ofensiva**
the vessel submerges **la nave se sumerge**
the vessel surfaces **la nave emerge**
survival **la supervivencia**
tactics **las tácticas**
terrorist attack **el ataque terrorista**
I threaten **amenazo**
trench **la trinchera**
underground **bajo tierra, subterráneo**
war **la guerra**
war breaks out **el estallido de guerra**
warmongering **el belicismo**
I win **gano**
wound **la herida**
I wound **hiero**

The Christmas truce was broken when hostilities resumed in Bosnia.

La tregua de Navidad fue infringida cuando se reanudaron las hostilidades en Bosnia.

Civil wars are the bloodiest of all.

Las guerras civiles son las más sangrientas de todas las guerras.

Total war is a concept of the twentieth century.

La guerra total es un concepto del siglo veinte.

27b Military Personnel & Weaponry

archer **el arquero**
assassin **el asesino**
casualty *(dead)* **la baja**
 casualty *(injured)* **el herido**
cavalry **la caballería**
civilian **el civil**
commandos **los comandos**
conscientious objector **el objetor de conciencia**
conscript **el conscripto**
convoy **el convoy**
deserter **el desertor**
division **la división**
foot soldier **el soldado de a pie**
general **el general**
guard **la guardia**
guerrilla **la guerrilla**
hostage **el rehén**
infantry **la infantería**
intelligence officer **el oficial de la inteligencia**
marines **la infantería de marina**
military personnel **el personal militar**
ministry of defense **el ministerio de defensa**
noncommissioned officer / NCO **el suboficial**
officer **el oficial**
orderly **el ordenanza, el asistente**
parachutist **el paracaidista**
prisoner of war **el prisionero de guerra**
rebel **el rebelde**

recruit **el reclutamiento**
regiment **el regimiento**
seaman / sailor **el marino, el marinero**
secret agent **el agente secreto**
sentry **el centinela, el guardia**
sniper **el francotirador**
soldier **el soldado**
spy **el espía**
squadron **el escuadrón**
staff **el personal**
terrorist **el terrorista**
traitor **el traidor**
troops **las tropas**
victor **el vencedor**

Weaponry & its effects

I aim (at) **apunto (a)**
aircraft carrier **el portaviones, el portaeronaves**
ammunition **la munición**
armaments **los armamentos**
armored car / armoured **el coche blindado / acorazado**
arms **las armas**
arms race **la carrera de armas**
artillery **la artillería**
bacteriological **bacteriológico**
barbed wire **el alambre de púas**
bayonet **la bayoneta**
I bomb(ard) **bombardeo**
bomb **la bomba**
bombardment **el bombardeo**
bomber *(aircraft)* **el bombardero aéreo**

In Sarajevo today, a man was shot dead by a sniper.

The explosion was several miles away, but it knocked everyone to the ground. Then the alert sounded for chemical weapons.

Hoy en Sarajevo, un hombre fue matado por un francotirador.

La explosión se produjo a varias millas de distancia, pero derribó a todo el mundo. Luego sonó la alarma de armas químicas.

bullet **la bala**
car bomb **el coche bomba**
crossbow **la ballesta**
chemical **química**
destroyer *(ship)* **el destructor**
I execute **ejecuto**
I explode a bomb **hago explotar una bomba**
explosive **el explosivo**
fighter plane **el caza**
I fire (at) **disparo a**
frigate **la fragata**
gas **el gas**
gas attack **el ataque de gas**
gun **la pistola**
hand grenade **la granada de mano**
H-bomb **la bomba H**
it hits **da contra, impacta, alcanza**
jet *(plane)* **el avión a reacción**
I kill **mato**
knife **el cuchillo, el puñal**
laser **el láser**
launcher **el lanzador**
letter bomb **la cartabomba**
machine gun **la ametralladora**
manufacturer **el fabricante**
minefield **el campo de minas**
minesweeper **el dragaminas**
missile **el misil**
mortar **el mortero**
neutron bomb **la bomba de neutrones**
nuclear test **la prueba nuclear**
nuclear warhead **la cabeza nuclear**

pistol **la pistola**
poison gas **el gas venenoso**
radar **el radar**
radar screen **la pantalla de radar**
radiation **la radiación**
radiation sickness **la enfermedad debida a la radiación**
radioactive **radioactivo**
radioactive fallout **el polvillo radioactivo**
revolver **el revólver**
rifle **el rifle**
rocket **el cohete**
rocket attack **el ataque con cohetes**
I sabotage **hago sabotaje, saboteo**
shell **el obús, el proyectil, la granada**
I shoot dead **mato de un tiro, mato a tiros**
shotgun **la escopeta**
shrapnel **la metralla**
siege **el sitio, el asedio**
I stockpile **formo una reserva**
submachine gun **la metralleta**
submarine **el submarino**
tank **el tanque**
target **el blanco, el objetivo**
torpedo **el torpedo**
torpedo attack **el ataque con torpedos**
I torpedo **torpedeo**
warship **el barco de guerra**
weapon **el arma**

The missile, which had been shot down, scattered debris over a wide area.

El misil que había sido derribado esparció escombros sobre un área extensa.

Six people were wounded when a shell landed in the old town.

Quedaron heridas seis personas al caer un proyectil sobre el barrio viejo del pueblo.

➤ CRIME 26

WAR & PEACE

27c Peace & International Relations

Peace

I ban *(the bomb)* **prohíbo**
cease-fire **el cese al fuego**
control **el control**
I declare peace **declaro la paz**
I demobilize **desmovilizo**
deterrent **la fuerza disuasiva**
I diminish tension **aminoro la tensión**
disarmament **el desarme**
exchanges of information **los intercambios de información**
free **libre**
I free **libero**
human rights **los derechos humanos**
I mediate **medio**
military service **el servicio militar**
negotiable **negociable**
negotiation **la negociación**
neutral **neutral**
neutrality **la neutralidad**
pacifism **el pacifismo**
pacifist **el pacifista**
peace **la paz**
peace plan **el plan de paz**
peace protester **el manifestante por la paz**

peace talks **las conferencias de paz**
peacekeeping force **las fuerzas para mantener la paz**
surrender **el rendimiento, la rendición**
I surrender **me rindo**
test ban **la suspensión de pruebas**
treaty **el tratado**
uncommitted **no comprometido**
victory **la victoria**

International relations

aid **la ayuda, la asistencia**
ambassador **el embajador**
arms reduction **la reducción de armamentos**
attaché **el agregado**
citizen **el ciudadano**
citizenship **la ciudadanía**
consul **el cónsul**
consulate **el consulado**
developing countries **los países en desarrollo**
diplomacy **la diplomacia**
diplomat **el diplomático**

The Spanish government was in danger of being embroiled in a diplomatic dispute.	**El gobierno español corría el riesgo de enredarse en una disputa diplomática.**
The Ministry of Defense announced cuts in the military budget today.	**Hoy el Ministerio de Defensa anunció una reducción en el presupuesto militar.**
Importers continue to take advantage of the low tariff rates.	**Los importadores continúan apovechándose de las tarifas bajas.**

diplomatic immunity **la inmunidad diplomática**
embassy **la embajada**
emergency aid **la asistencia de emergencia**
envoy **el enviado**
famine **el hambre**
foreign affairs **los asuntos exteriores**
foreign aid **la asistencia exterior**
foreigner **el extranjero**
I apply economic sanctions **empleo sanciones económicas**
I join *(organization)* **me afilio, me hago miembro de**
national security **la seguridad interior**
nonaligned **no alineado, neutral**
overseas **en ultramar, en el extranjero**
I ratify *(treaty)* **ratifico**
relief organization **la organización de beneficencia**
relief supplies **las provisiones de auxilio**
I represent **represento**
sanctions **las sanciones**
summit meeting **la cumbre**
Third World **el Tercer Mundo**
underdeveloped countries **los países subdesarrollados**

Trade

agricultural policy **la política agraria**
balance of payments **la balanza de pagos**
balance of trade **la balanza comercial**
common market **el mercado común**
currency **la moneda, la divisa**
customs **la aduana**
customs union **la unión aduanera**
European Union **la unión europea**
exchange rate **el tipo de cambio**
exports **las exportaciones**
floating currency **la divisa flotante**
it floats **flota**
foreign investment **la inversión extranjera**
free-trade zone **la zona franca**
gap between rich and poor **la diferencia entre ricos y pobres**
gross national product/GNP **el producto nacional bruto/PNB**
import controls **el control de importaciones**
imports **las importaciones**
tariff barriers **las tarifas aduaneras**
tariffs **las tarifas**
trade gap *(negative)* **el déficit exterior**

A spokesman for the Spanish Interior Ministry revealed the European Commission is investigating alleged unfair trading practices/practises.

It is hoped that the gap between rich and poor will decrease with the lifting of international trade barriers.

Un portavoz del Ministerio del Interior anunció que la Comisión Europea está investigando presuntas prácticas comerciales injustas.

Se espera que la diferencia entre ricos y pobres disminuya al suprimir las barreras al comercio internacional.

C
APPENDICES

Appendices

3b Clocks & Watches*

alarm clock   **el despertador**
clock   **el reloj**
cuckoo clock   **el reloj de cuco**
dial   **la esfera, la cara, el
cuadrante**
digital watch   **el reloj digital**
egg timer   **el cronómetro para
huevos**
grandfather clock   **el reloj de pie,
el reloj de caja**
hand (of a clock)   **la aguja del
reloj**
   minute hand   **el minutero**
   hour hand   **el horario**
   second hand   **el segundero**
hourglass   **el reloj de arena**
pendulum   **el péndulo**
stopwatch   **el cronógrafo**
sundial   **el reloj de sol**
timer   **el cronómetro
de la cocina, el avisador**
watch   **el reloj de pulsera, el reloj
de mano**
   watch strap   **la pulsera del
reloj, la correa del reloj**
I wind up   **doy cuerda**

4d Mathematical & Geometrical Terms

acute   **agudo**
algebra   **el álgebra**
algebraic   **algebraico**
Arabic numerals   **los números
arábicos**
arithmetic   **la aritmética**
arithmetical   **aritmético**
average   **el promedio**
axis   **el eje**
circumference   **la circunferencia**
complex   **complejo**

constant   **la constante**
cube   **el cubo**
cube root   **la raíz cúbica**
cubed   **al cubo**
decimal   **el decimal**
equality   **la igualdad**
factor   **el factor**
I factorize   **factorizo**
fraction   **la fracción, el quebrado**
function   **la función**
geometry   **la geometría**
geometrical   **geométrico**
imaginary   **imaginario**
integer   **el número entero**
irrational   **el número irracional**
logarithm   **el logaritmo**
mean   **la media**
median   **el medio, el número medio,
el punto medio**
multiple   **el múltiplo**
nine is to three as . . .   **nueve es a
tres como ...**
natural   **natural**
numerical   **numérico**
obtuse   **obtuso**
prime   **primo**
product   **el producto**
probability   **la probabilidad**
I raise to a power   **elevo a una
potencia**
to the fifth power   **a la quinta
potencia**
to the nth power   **a la enésima
potencia**
radius   **el radio**
rational   **racional**
quotient   **el cociente**
real   **real**
reciprocal   **recíproco**
Roman   **romano**
set   **el conjunto**
square   **cuadrado**

* Appendices are numbered according to the most relevant Vocabulary.

square root   la raíz cuadrada
symmetry   la simetría
symmetrical   simétrico
table(s)   las tablas
tangent   la tangente
trigonometry   la trigonometría
variable   la variable
vector   el vector

5b Parts of the Body

ankle   el tobillo
arm   el brazo
back   la espalda
backbone   la columna vertebral
bladder   la vejiga
blood   la sangre
blood pressure   la presión arterial
body   el cuerpo
bone   el hueso
bowel   los intestinos
brain   el cerebro
breast   el pecho, el busto, el seno
buttock   las nalgas
cheek   la mejilla
chest   el pecho
chin   el mentón, la quijada
ear   la oreja
elbow   el codo
eye   el ojo
eyebrow   la ceja
eyelash   la pestaña
face   la cara
finger   el dedo
fingernail   la uña
foot   el pie
forehead   la frente
genitalia   los genitales
gland   la glándula
hair   el pelo, el cabello
hand   la mano
head   la cabeza
heart   el corazón
hip   la cadera
hormone   la hormona
index finger   el dedo índice
jaw   la mandíbula

kidney   el riñón
knee   la rodilla
knuckle   el nudillo
leg   la pierna
lid   el párpado
lip   el labio
liver   el hígado
lung   el pulmón
mouth   la boca
muscle   el músculo
nape of neck   la nuca
neck   el cuello
nose   la nariz
nostril   la ventana de la nariz
organ   el órgano
part of body   la parte del cuerpo
penis   el pene
sex organs   los órganos sexuales
shoulder   el hombro
skin   la piel
stomach   el estómago
thigh   el muslo
throat   la garganta
thumb   el pulgar
toe   el dedo del pie
tongue   la lengua
tooth   el diente
vagina   la vagina
waist   la cintura
womb   la matriz
wrist   la muñeca

6a Human Characteristics

absentminded   despistado
active   activo
adaptable   adaptable, flexible
affectionate   cariñoso
aggression   la agresión
aggressive   agresivo
ambition   la ambición
ambitious   ambicioso
amusing   divertido
anxious   ansioso, nervioso
arrogant   arrogante
artistic   artístico
attractive   atractivo

6a Human Characteristics (cont.)

bad-tempered **mal humorado**
bad / evil **malo, malvado**
boring **aburrido**
brave **valiente**
care **la atención, el cuidado**
careful **atento, cuidadoso**
careless **descuidado**
charm **encanto**
charming **encantador**
cheeky **caradura, fresco**
cheerful **alegre**
clever **listo, espabilado**
cold **frío**
comic **gracioso**
confidence **la seguridad en sí mismo**
confident **seguro de sí mismo**
conscientious **meticuloso**
courage **el valor**
courtesy **la educación, la cortesía**
cowardly **cobarde**
creative **creativo, imaginativo**
critical **crítico, exigente**
cruel **cruel**
cruelty **la crueldad**
cultured **cultivado, educado**
cunning **astuto**
curiosity **la curiosidad**
decisive (in-) **(in)decisivo, firme, tajante, (vacilante)**
demanding **exigente**
dependence (in-) **la (in)dependencia**
dependent (in-) **(in)dependiente**
distrustful **desconfiado**
eccentric **excéntrico**
energetic **enérgico, activo, vigoroso**
envious **envidioso**
envy **la envidia**
extroverted **extrovertido**
faithful (un-) **(in)fiel**
faithfulness **la fidelidad**
friendly (un-) **simpático (antipático)**

frivolous **frívolo**
generosity **la generosidad**
generous **generoso**
gentleness **la amabilidad, la ternura**
good-tempered **amable**
greed **la avaricia**
greedy **avaricioso, avaro**
hardworking **trabajador, laborioso**
helpful **servicial**
honest (dis-) **(des)honesto, (poco) honrado**
honesty (dis-) **la (des)honestidad**
honor / honour **el honor**
humane (in-) **(in)humano**
humble **humilde, modesto**
humorous **gracioso**
hypocritical **hipócrita**
idealistic **idealista**
imagination **la imaginación**
imaginative **imaginativo, creativo**
individualistic **individualista, independiente**
innocence **la inocencia**
innocent **inocente**
inquisitive **inquisitivo**
intelligence **la inteligencia**
intelligent **inteligente**
introverted **introvertido**
ironic **irónico**
kind **amable**
kindness **la amabilidad**
laziness **la pereza, la holgazanería**
lazy **perezoso, holgazán**
liberal **liberal**
likeable **simpático, fácil**
lively **animado**
lonely **solitario**
loveable **encantador**
mad **loco**
madness **la locura**
malicious **malvado**
mature (im-) **(in)maduro**

modest **modesto**
moody **voluble**
moral (im-) **(in)moral**
naive **ingenuo**
natural **natural**
nervous **nervioso**
nice **amable, simpático**
obedience (dis-) **la (des)obediencia**
obedient (dis-) **(des)obediente**
openness **la franqueza**
optimistic **optimista**
originality **la originalidad**
patience (im-) **la (im)paciencia**
patient (im-) **(im)paciente**
pessimistic **pesimista**
pleasant **agradable**
polite **educado, cortés**
politeness **la educación, la cortesía**
possessive **posesivo**
prejudiced **lleno de prejuicios**
pride **el orgullo**
proud **orgulloso**
reasonable (un-) **(poco) razonable**
rebellious **rebelde**
reserved **reservado**
respect **el respeto**
respectable **respetable**
respectful **respetuoso**
responsible (ir-) **(ir)responsable**
rude **maleducado, descortés, grosero**
rudeness **la mala educación, la descortesía, la grosería**
sad **triste**
sarcastic **sarcástico**
scornful **despreciable**
self-confident **seguro de sí mismo**
self-esteem **la autoestima**
selfish (un-) **(no) egoísta**
selfishness **el egoísmo**
self-sufficient **autosuficiente**
sensible **sensato**
sensitive (in-) **(in)sensible**

serious **serio, formal**
shy **tímido**
silent **silencioso**
silly **tonto, bobo**
sincerity **la sinceridad**
skillful **hábil**
sociable (un-) **(in)sociable**
stingy / mean **tacaño, agarrado**
strange **raro, especial**
strict **estricto**
stubborn **cabezota, tenaz, testarudo, terco**
stupidity **la estupidez**
suspicious **suspicaz**
sweet **dulce, cariñoso**
sympathetic (un-) **comprensivo, (in)compasivo**
sympathy **la compasión, la solidaridad**
tactful (-less) **(in)discreto**
talented **dotado**
talkative **hablador, charlatán**
temperamental **temperamental**
thoughtful **pensativo, considerado**
thoughtless **irreflexivo, desconsiderado**
tidy (un-) **(des)ordenado, limpio**
tolerance (in-) **la (in)tolerancia**
tolerant (in-) **(in)tolerante**
traditional **conservador, tradicional**
trust **la confianza**
trusting **confiado**
vain **vanidoso, engreído, vano**
vanity **la vanidad**
violent **violento, agresivo**
virtuous **virtuoso**
warm **cálido**
well-adjusted **equilibrado**
well-behaved **bueno, de buena conducta**
wisdom **la prudencia, la sabiduría**
wise **prudente**
wit **el ingenio**
witty **ingenioso, vivo, ocurrente**

8b Tools

ax / axe **el hacha**
bit **la barrena**
blade **el filo**
bolt **el tornillo**
bucket **el cubo**
chisel **el formón, el cincel**
crowbar **la palanca**
drill **el taladro**
file **la lima**
garden gloves **los guantes de jardinería**
garden shears **las tijeras de jardín**
hammer **el martillo**
hedge clippers **las tijeras podadoras**
hoe **la azada**
hose **la manguera**
ladder **la escalera, la escala**
lawnmower **el cortacésped, [la segadora]**
mallet **el mazo**
nail **el clavo**
nut **la tuerca**
paint **la pintura**
paintbrush **la brocha, el pincel**
pickax(e) **el pico, el zapapico**
plane **el cepillo de carpintería**
pliers **los alicates, las pinzas**
rake **el rastrillo**
sandpaper **el papel de lija**
saw **la sierra**
screw **el tornillo**
screwdriver **el destornillador**
shovel **la pala**
spade **la laya**
spirit level **el nivel de aire**
stepladder **la escalera doble / de tijera**
toolbox **la caja de herramientas**
trowel **el desplantador**
varnish **el barniz**
vise **el torno de banco**
weedkiller **el herbicida**

wrench / spanner (adjustable) **la llave (de tuercas)**

9a Shops, Stores & Services

antique store / shop **la tienda de antigüedades, el anticuario**
bakery / baker's **la panadería**
bank **el banco**
bookmaker's / betting shop **la agencia de apuestas**
bookstore / -shop **la librería**
boutique **la boutique**
butcher's **la carnicería**
candy store / sweetshop **la confitería, [la dulcería]**
car parts / spares store / shop **la tienda de repuestos / recambios**
charity shop / store **la tienda de sociedad benéfica / de caridad**
clothes store / shop **la tienda de modas / de ropa**
cosmetics store / shop **la tienda de estética, [el almacén de cosméticos]**
covered market **la plaza del mercado**
dairy **la lechería**
delicatessen **el delicatessen**
department stores **los (grandes) almacenes, [el centro comercial]**
dress store / shop **la casa de modas**
drugstore / chemist's **la farmacia, la droguería**
dry cleaners **la tintorería, [la lavandería]**
electrical store / shop **la tienda de material eléctrico / de electrodomésticos**
fast-food store / shop **la tienda de fast-food / [de comidas rápidas]**

APPENDIX 9A

fish store / fishmonger's la
  pescadería
fishstall el puesto de pescado
florist's la floristería
furniture store / shop la tienda de
  muebles
garden center / centre el centro de
  jardinería
greengrocer's la verdulería, la
  verdurería, [la tienda de
  verduras]
grocer el tendero (de
  ultramarinos), el mantequero
grocery / grocer's la tienda de
  ultramarinos, la tienda de
  comestibles, [la tienda]
hairdresser el peluquero, la
  peluquera
hairdresser's la peluquería
hardware store / shop la ferretería
healthfood store / shop la tienda
  de alimentos naturales
indoor market la plaza del
  mercado cubierta
insurance agent / broker el agente
  de seguros
jeweler's / jewelry store la joyería
kiosk el quiosco, el kiosco
laundromat / launderette la
  lavandería automática
market el mercado
men's shop / store la tienda de
  ropa de caballero
model shop / store la tienda de
  juguetes / miniaturas
music store / shop la tienda de
  música
newspaper kiosk el quiosco de
  periódicos
newsstand / newsagent's el
  vendedor de periódicos
optician's la (tienda de) óptica
outdoor / open-air market el
  mercado
pastry shop / cakeshop la
  pastelería

petshop / pet store la pajarería
pharmacy la farmacia
photographic shop / store la tienda
  de fotografía
post office Correos, [la oficina de
  correos]
pottery shop / store la tienda de
  cerámica, [la alfarería]
real estate / estate agent el agente
  inmobiliario
shoe repair shop / store el
  zapatero remendón, [la
  remontadora de calzado]
shoe store / shop la zapatería, [el
  almacén de zapatos]
shoemaker's / cobbler's la
  tienda del zapatero remendón,
  [la remontadora de calzado]
shop / store la tienda
shopping mall / shopping center el
  centro comercial, la zona de
  tiendas
souvenir shop / store la tienda de
  recuerdos
sports store / shop la tienda de
  deportes
stationer's / stationery store la
  papelería
store la tienda, el almacén
supermarket el supermercado
superstore / hypermarket el
  hipermercado, [la supertienda]
take-out / take-away food shop /
  store tienda de comidas
  para llevar
tobacconist's / tobacco store el
  estanco, la tabaquería,
  [la cigarrería]
toy store / toyshop la juguetería
travel agent la agencia de
  viajes
vendor el vendedor, la vendedora
vending machine la vendedora
  automática
video store / video-shop la tienda de
  vídeo

215

APPENDICES

9a Currencies

dollar **el dólar**
bolivar **el bolivar**
peso **el peso**
centavo **el centavo**
euro **el euro**
pound sterling **la libra esterlina**
ruble **el rublo**
yen **el yen**

9c Jewelry / Jewellery

bangle **la esclava**
chain bracelet **la pulsera**
brooch **el broche**
carat **el quilate**
chain **la cadena**
charm **el amuleto, [el dije]**
cuff links **los gemelos, [las mancornas]**
earrings **los pendientes**
engagement ring **la sortija de pedida, [el anillo de compromiso]**
jewel **la joya**
jewelry / jewellery **la joyería**
jewelry box **el joyero**
medallion **el medallón**
necklace **el collar**
pendant **el medallón**
precious stone / gem **la piedra preciosa**
real **verdadero**
ring **el anillo, la sortija**
semiprecious stone **la piedra semipreciosa**
tiara **la diadema**
tie pin **el alfiler de corbata**
wedding ring **el anillo de boda**

9c Precious Stones & Metals

agate **el ágata**
amber **el ámbar**
amethyst **la amatista**
chrome **el cromo**
copper **el cobre**
coral **el coral**
crystal **el cristal**
diamond **el diamante**
emerald **la esmeralda**
gold **el oro**
gold plate **la lámina de oro**
ivory **el marfil**
mother-of-pearl **el nácar, la madreperla**
onyx **el ónix**
pearl **la perla**
pewter **el peltre**
platinum **el platino**
quartz **el cuarzo**
ruby **el rubí**
sapphire **el zafiro**
silver plate **la vajilla de plata**
silver **la plata**
topaz **el topacio**
turquoise **la turquesa**

10c Herbs & Spices

aniseed **el anís**
basil **la albahaca**
bay leaf **la hoja de laurel**
caper **la alcaparra**
caraway **la alcaravea**
chives **el cebollino**
cinnamon **la canela**
clove **el clavo**
cumin **el comino**
dill **el eneldo**
garlic **el ajo**
ginger **el jengibre**
marjoram **la mejorana**
mint **la menta**
mixed herbs **las hierbas finas**
mustard **la mostaza**
nutmeg **la nuez moscada**

oregano **el orégano**
parsley **el perejil**
rosemary **el romero**
saffron **el azafrán**
sage **la salvia**
tarragon **el estragón**
thyme **el tomillo**

10d Cooking Utensils

alumin(i)um foil **el papel aluminio / de estaño**
baking tray **la bandeja de horno**
can / tin opener **el abrelatas**
carving knife **el trinchante**
colander **el colador**
food processor **el robot de cocina**
fork **el tenedor**
frying pan / fry-pan **la sartén**
grater **el rallador**
grill **la parrilla**
kettle **el hervedor**
knife **el cuchillo**
lid **la cobertera, la tapa**
pot **la olla**
rolling pin **el rodillo**
saucepan / casserole dish **el cazo, la cacerola**
scale **la balanza**
sieve **la coladera**
skewer **la broqueta**
spatula **la espátula**
spoon **la cuchara**
tablespoon **la cuchara grande**
tablespoonful **la cucharada**
teaspoon **la cucharilla**
teaspoonful **la cucharadita**
tenderizer **el ablandador**
wax paper / greaseproof **el papel apergaminado**

10d Smoking

ashtray **el cenicero**
box of matches **la cajita de cerillas**
cigar **el puro**

cigarette **el cigarrillo**
cigarette butt / stub **la colilla**
lighter **el encendedor**
matches **las cerillas**
pipe **la pipa**
smoke **el humo**
I smoke **fumo**
(no) smoking **(no) fumadores**
tobacco **el tabaco**
tobacconist's **el estanco, la tabaquería, [la cigarrería]**

11b Illness & Disability

AIDS **el SIDA**
angina **la angina**
appendicitis **la apendicitis**
arthritis **la artritis**
asthma **el asma** *(f)*
bacillus **el bacilo**
bacteria **la bacteria**
blister **la ampolla**
boil **el divieso, el furúnculo**
bronchitis **la bronquitis**
bruise **la contusión, el cardenal, la magulladura, el magullón, el moretón**
bubonic plague **la peste bubónica**
cancer **el cáncer**
catarrh **el catarro**
chicken pox **la varicela**
cholera **el cólera**
colic **el cólico**
cold **el resfriado, el catarro**
constipation **el estreñimiento**
corn **el callo**
cough **la tos**
deafness **la sordera**
death **la muerte**
depression **la depresión**
dermatitis **la dermatitis**
diabetes **la diabetes**
diarrhea **la diarrea**
diptheria **la difteria**
disease **la enfermedad**
dizziness **el vértigo, el mareo**
earache **el dolor de oídos**

eczema **el eccema, el eczema**
epilepsy **la epilepsia**
fever **la fiebre**
fit **el ataque**
fleas **las pulgas**
flu **la gripe**
food poisoning **la intoxicación alimenticia, la toxinfección alimenticia**
gallstones **el cálculo biliario**
German measles **la rubéola**
gingivitis **la gingivitis**
gonorrhea **la gonorrea**
graze **el roce, la abrasión, [la raspadura]**
hemorrhoids **las hemorroides**
head louse **el piojo**
headache **el dolor de cabeza**
heart attack **el ataque cardíaco**
hepatitis **la hepatitis**
hernia **la hernia**
high blood pressure **la hipertensión**
HIV positive **(el virus de la inmunodeficiencia humana) VIH positivo**
illness / sickness **la enfermedad**
incontinence **la incontinencia**
influenza **la gripe**
infection **la infección, el contagio**
jaundice **la ictericia**
leukemia **la leucemia**
louse **el piojo**
malaria **la malaria, el paludismo**
measles **el sarampión**
meningitis **la meningitis**
mental illness **la enfermedad mental**
microbe **el microbio**
migraine **la jaqueca**
mumps **las paperas, las parótidas**
nit **la liendre**
overdose **la sobredosis**
piles **las almorranas, las hemorroides**
pneumonia **la pulmonía**

polio **el polio**
pregnancy **el embarazo, la preñez**
rabies **la rabia**
rheumatism **el reumatismo**
salmonella **la salmonelosis**
scabies **la sarna**
seasickness **el mareo**
sickness **la enfermedad, el malestar**
smallpox **la viruela**
stomachache **el dolor de estómago**
stomach upset **el trastorno estomacal**
stroke **el ataque fulminante, la apoplejía**
stye **el orzuelo**
syphilis **la sífilis**
temperature **la calentura, la fiebre**
tetanus **el tétanos**
thrombosis **la trombosis**
tonsillitis **la amigdalitis**
toothache **el dolor de muelas**
tuberculosis **la tuberculosis**
ulcers **las úlceras**
urinary infection **la infección urinaria**
venereal disease **la enfermedad venérea**
whooping cough **la tos ferina**
yellow fever **la fiebre amarilla**

11c Hospital Departments

admissions **la secretaría, las admisiones**
blood bank **el banco de sangre**
casualty **(la sección de) accidentes**
consulting room **el consultorio, la consulta**
coronary care unit **la sección de asistencia cardíaca**
dialysis unit **la sección de diálisis**

emergency **las urgencias**
geriatric **la geriatría**
gynecology **la ginecología**
infectious diseases **las enfermedades infectocontagiosas**
intensive care **la asistencia intensiva**
maternity **la maternidad**
medical ward **la sala médica**
mortuary **el mortuorio, el depósito de cadáveres, la funeraria, [el anfiteatro]**
oncology **la oncología**
operating room / theater **el quirófano, la sala de operaciones**
orthopedic **ortopédico**
outpatient department **el departamento de consulta externa**
pediatrics **la pediatría**
pathology **la patología**
pharmacy **la farmacia**
psychiatric **la psiquiatría**
reception **la recepción**
recovery room **la sala de posoperatorio / recuperación**
surgery **la cirugía**
treatment room **la sala de tratamiento / cura / medicación**
ward **la sala**
X rays **los rayos-X, la radiografía**

13b Holidays & Religious Festivals

All Saints (Nov 1) **el día de todos los santos**
All Souls (Nov 2) **el día de los difuntos**
Ascension Day **el día de la ascensión**
Ash Wednesday **el miércoles de ceniza**

Assumption Day (Aug 15) **el día de la asunción**
Candlemas **el día de la candelaria**
Christmas Day **el día de Navidad**
Christmas Eve **el día de Nochebuena**
Christmas **la Navidad**
at Christmas **en Navidad**
Corpus Christi **el Corpus Cristi**
Easter **la Semana Santa**
Easter Monday **el lunes de Pascua de Resurrección**
Easter Sunday **el domingo de Resurrección**
Eid **el Eid**
festival **el festival**
Good Friday **el Viernes Santo**
Hanukkah **el Hanukkah**
Labor / Labour Day **el día de los trabajadores, el día de San José obrero, el día del trabajo**
Lent **la cuaresma**
New Year's Day **el día de Año Nuevo**
New Year's Eve **el día de Nochevieja**
Palm Sunday **el domingo de Ramos**
Passover **la Pascua judía**
Pentecost / Whitsun **Pentecostés**
Ramadan **El Ramadán**
Sabbath **el sábado**
Shrove Tuesday / Carnival **el martes de carnaval**
Whitsuntide **la semana de Pentecostés**
Yom Kippur **el Yom Kippur**

14b Professions & Jobs

The arts

actor / actress **el actor, la actriz**
announcer **el presentador, el locutor, la presentadora, la locutora**
architect **el arquitecto, la arquitecta**
artist **el / la artista**
bookseller **el vendedor de libros, el librero**
cameraman **el cámara, el camarógrafo**
editor **el redactor**
journalist **el / la periodista**
movie / film director **el director de cine / la directora de cine**
movie / film star **la estrella de cine**
musician **el / la músico**
painter *(artist)* **el pintor, la pintora**
photographer **el fotógrafo / la fotógrafa**
poet **el poeta / la poetisa**
printer **el impresor**
producer (theater / theatre) **el productor / la productora de teatro**
publisher **el editor**
reporter **el reportero, la reportera**
sculptor **el escultor, la escultora**
singer **el cantante, la cantante**
television announcer **el presentador / la presentadora de televisión**
writer **el escritor, la escritora**

Education & research

headteacher / principal **el director, la directora, el rector, la rectora**
lecturer **el profesor universitario, la profesora universitaria**
physicist **el físico, la física**
primary school teacher **el profesor / la profesora de escuela primaria, el maestro, la maestra**

researcher **el investigador, la investigadora**
scientist **el científico, la científica**
secondary school teacher **el profesor / la profesora de escuela secundaria**
student **el / la estudiante**
technician **el técnico, la técnica**

Food & retail

baker **el panadero, la panadera**
brewer **el cervecero, la cervecera**
butcher **el carnicero, la carnicera**
buyer **el encargado / la encargada de compras**
caterer *(supplying meals)* **el abastecedor de comidas**
chemist **el químico, la química**
cook **el cocinero, la cocinera**
farmer **el granjero, la granjera**
fisherman **el pescador, la pescadora**
fishmonger **el pescadero, la pescadera**
florist **el / la florista**
greengrocer **el verdulero, la verdulera, [el vendedor / la vendedora de verduras]**
grocer **el tendero / la tendera (de comestibles)**
jeweler / jeweller **el joyero, la joyera**
pharmacist **el farmacéutico, la farmacéutica**
representative **el representante, el diputado, la diputada**
salesclerk / shop assistant **el dependiente / la dependienta de comercio**
storekeeper / shopkeeper **el tendero, la tendera**
tobacconist **el tabaquero, el estanquero**
waiter **el camarero, la camarera**
winegrower **el vinicultor, la vinicultora**

Government service

civil servant **el funcionario, la funcionaria**
clerk **el / la oficinista**
customs officer **el / la agente de aduanas**
fireman **el bombero, la mujer bombero**
judge **el / la juez**
minister **el ministro, la ministra**
officer **el oficial, la oficial**
policeman **el policía**
policewoman **la mujer policía**
politician **el político, la política**
sailor **el marino, la marino, el marinero**
secret agent **el agente secreto, la agente secreta**
senator / member of Parliament **el senador, la senadora, el diputado, la diputada**
serviceman **el / la militar**
soldier **el / la soldado**

Health care

dentist **el / la dentista**
doctor (Dr.) **el médico, la médica, el doctor, la doctora**
midwife **la comadrona**
nurse **el enfermero, la enfermera**
optician **el / la óptico, [el optómetra]**
physician **el médico**
psychiatrist **el / la psiquiatra**
psychologist **el psicólogo / la psicóloga**
surgeon **el cirujano, la cirujana**
veterinarian **el veterinario, la veterinaria**

In manufacturing & construction

bricklayer **el / la albañil**
builder **el constructor**
carpenter **el carpintero, la carpintera**
engineer **el ingeniero, la ingeniera**

foreman **el / la capataz**
industrialist **el / la industrial**
laborer / labourer **el trabajador, la trabajadora, el obrero, la obrera**
manufacturer **el / la fabricante**
mechanic **el mecánico, la mecánica**
metalworker **el trabajador / la trabajadora del metal**
miner **el minero, la minera**
plasterer **el yesero, la yesera, el enlucidor, el albañil**
stonemason **el cantero**

Services

accountant **el / la contable, el contador, la contadora**
actuary **el actuario / la actuaria de seguros**
agent **el / la agente**
bank manager **el director / la directora de banco**
businessman **el hombre de negocios**
businesswoman **la mujer de negocios**
caretaker **el / la vigilante, el conserje**
cleaner **el limpiador, la limpiadora**
computer programmer **el programador / la programadora de ordenadores [de computadoras]**
counselor **el asesor, la asesora, el consejero, la consejera**
draftsman **el / la delineante**
electrician **el / la electricista**
garbageman / dustman **el basurero, la basurera**
gardener **el jardinero, la jardinera**
gasman **el trabajador / la trabajadora del gas**
guide **el / la guía**

hairdresser   **el peluquero, la peluquera**
insurance agent   **el / la agente de seguros**
interpreter   **el / la intérprete**
job counselor / careers adviser   **el consejero / la consejera profesional**
labor / trade unionist   **el / la sindicalista**
lawyer / solicitor   **el abogado, la abogada, el letrado / la letrada**
librarian   **el bibliotecario, la bibliotecaria**
mail carrier / postman   **el cartero, la cartera**
mover / furniture remover   **el empleado / la empleada de la mudanza**
office worker   **el / la oficinista**
painter and decorator   **el pintor, la pintora, el decorador, la decoradora**
plumber   **el fontanero, la fontanera**
priest   **el sacerdote**
receptionist   **el / la recepcionista**
servant   **el criado, la criada**
social worker   **el / la asistente social**
stockbroker   **el / la agente de bolsa**
surveyor   **el topógrafo, la topógrafa**
tax inspector   **el inspector / la inspectora de impuestos / hacienda**
translator   **el traductor, la traductora**
travel agent   **el agente de viajes**
typist   **el mecanógrafo, la mecanógrafa**
undertaker   **el director de pompas fúnebres**

Transportation

bus driver   **el conductor / la conductora de autobuses**
driver   **el conductor, la conductora**
driving instructor   **el profesor / la profesora de autoescuela / conducción**

pilot   **el / la piloto**
stewardess / air hostess   **la azafata**
taxi driver   **el / la taxista**
ticket inspector   **el revisor, la revisora**
truck / lorry driver   **el camionero, la camionera**

14b Places of Work

blast furnace   **el alto horno**
branch office   **la sucursal**
brewery   **la cervecería**
business park   **el centro de negocios**
construction site   **la obra**
distillery   **la destilería**
factory   **la fábrica**
farm   **la granja**
foundry   **la fundición**
head office   **la oficina principal**
hospital   **el hospital**
mill   **el molino**
  paper mill   **la fábrica de papel**
  rolling mill   **el taller de laminación**
  sawmill   **el aserradero**
  spinning mill   **la hilandería**
  steel mill   **la fábrica de acero, la fábrica siderúrgica, la fundidura**
  weaving mill   **la fábrica de tejidos**
mine   **la mina**
office   **la oficina**
plant   **la planta**
public company   **la empresa pública**
steel plant / steelworks   **la fábrica de acero, la fábrica siderúrgica**
store / shop   **la tienda, el almacén**
sweatshop   **taller de trabajo afanoso y poco sueldo**
theme park   **el parque temático**
vineyard / winery   **la viña**
warehouse   **el almacén, el depósito**
workshop   **el taller**

14b Company Personnel & Structure

accounts department **el departamento de cuentas / contabilidad**
apprentice **el aprendiz, la aprendiza**
assistant **el ayudante, el asistente**
associate **el asociado, el socio**
board of directors **el consejo directivo, la junta de directores**
boss **el jefe**
colleague **el colega, el compañero de trabajo**
department **el departamento**
director **el director**
division **la división**
employee **el empleado**
employer **el empresario, el patrón / la patrona**
executive **el ejecutivo**
foreman **el capataz**
labor / labour **el trabajo**
line manager **el encargado de sección**
management **la dirección, la gestión, la administración, la gerencia**
manager **el director, el encargado, el gerente**
manager (f) **la directora, la encargada, la gerente**
managing director / CEO **el director / la directora general**
marketing department **el departamento de márketing / mercadeo**
personal assistant **el asistente personal**
president **el presidente**
production department **el departamento de producción**
sales department **el departamento de ventas**
secretary **el secretario, la secretaria**

specialist **el especialista**
staff / personnel **el personal**
team **el equipo**
trainee **el empleado en período de aprendizaje, el aprendiz**
vice president **el vicepresidente**

15c Letter-Writing Formulae

Dear . . . **Querido / a ...**
Dear Madam **Muy señora mía, Estimada**
Dear Mr. and Mrs. . . . **Estimados Señores ...**
Dear Peter **Querido Pedro, Mi querido amigo Pedro**
Dear Sir **Muy señor mío, Estimado señor**
greetings from **recuerdos de**
I am pleased that **Me alegro de**
I enclose **Remito adjunto / a**
All the best to **Recuerdos para**
Best wishes from **Saludos de**
Love from **Besos, Un abrazo de ..., Un cariñoso saludo de ...**
With best wishes from **Saludos de, Un cordial saludo de**
With kind regards **Con muchos recuerdos**
Yours faithfully **Lo / La saluda atentamente**
Yours sincerely **Lo / La saluda atentamente / cordialmente**

15d Computer Hardware

adaptor **el adaptador**
backlit screen **la pantalla a iluminación trasera**
battery **la pila, la batería**
brightness **el brillo**
brightness control **el botón de ajuste del brillo**
charger **el cargador**
central processing unit **la unidad procesadora central**

chip **el chip, la micropastilla, el microplaquete, el circuito integrado**

computer **el ordenador, la computadora**

computer system **el sistema de ordenadores**

delete key **la tecla de borrado**

desktop **... de escritorio**

disk / disc drive **la unidad de disco, el disk drive**

disk / disc **el disco**

diskette **el disquete, el diskette, el disco flexible**

display **la visualización, el despliegue**

double density disk / disc **el disco de densidad doble**

drive **la unidad de disco, el disk drive**

escape key **la tecla de escape**

exit key **la tecla de salida**

flat screen monitor **la pantalla plana**

floppy disk **el disco flexible, el floppy, el disquete, el diskette**

floppy drive **la unidad de disco, el disk drive**

function key **la tecla de función**

hard disk **el disco duro**

hard drive **la unidad del disco duro**

hardware **el hardware, el material informático**

high density disk **el disco de densidad alta**

integrated circuit **el circuito integrado**

interface **la interfaz, el interface**

keyboard **el teclado**

laptop **el ordenador portátil plegable**

liquid crystal display **el visualizador de cristal líquido**

local area network / LAN **la red de área local**

Macintosh **Macintosh, una Mac**

mainframe computer **la computadora central, el ordenador central**

microprocessor **el microprocesador**

minicomputer **el miniordenador, el minicomputador**

modem **el módem**

dial-up **marcar**

DSL **DSL**

cable **cable**

monitor **el monitor**

mouse **el ratón**

network **la red**

personal computer / PC **el ordenador personal, el computador personal**

plug-in drive **la unidad de disco enchufable**

port **la puerta, el puerto, el port**

portable **portátil**

processor **el procesador**

random access memory / RAM **el RAM / la memoria de acceso directo**

resolution **la resolución, la definición**

return key **la tecla de retorno**

screen **la pantalla**

scroll bar **la barra de desplazamiento**

space bar **el espaciador, la espaciadora**

terminal **la terminal**

touch screen **la pantalla de toque**

visual display unit / VDU **la unidad de presentación visual, la unidad de despliegue visual**

viewdata system **el sistema de videodatos**

wide area network / WAN **la red de área amplia**

15d Computer Software

algebraic **algebraico**
algorithm **el algoritmo**
bug **el duende, el fallo, el error**
byte **el byte, el octeto**
coding **la codificación**
command **el comando**
compatible **compatible**
compatibility **la compatibilidad**
computer aided design / CAD **el diseño asistido por ordenador / DAO**
computer aided learning / CAL **la instrucción asistida por ordenador / IAO**
computer aided language learning / CALL **la enseñanza de lenguas asistida por ordenador**
computer animation **la animación por ordenador**
computer graphics **las gráficas por ordenador**
computer language **el lenguaje de ordenador**
computer literacy **la competencia en la informática**
computer literate **competente en la informática**
copy **la copia**
corrupted **degradado**
data **los datos**
data capture **la formulación de datos**
data entry **la entrada de datos**
data processing **el tratamiento de datos**
database **la base de datos**
default option **la opción por defectos**
double clicking **el doble pulsar, el doble clic (del ratón)**
drive **la unidad de disco**
escape **el escape**
exit **la salida del sistema**
file **el fichero**
flowchart **el diagrama de flujo, el organigrama, el ordinograma**
format **el formato**
function **la función**
graphical **gráfico**
graphical application **la aplicación gráfica**
graphics **los gráficos**
graphics accelerator **el acelerador de gráficos**
help **ayuda, asistencia, auxilio**
help menu **el menú de asistencia**
incompatible **incompatible**
information technology / IT **la informática**
language **el lenguaje**
logic circuit **el circuito lógico**
low / high density **la densidad baja / alta**
macro **macro**
memory **la memoria**
menu **el menú**
operating system **el sistema de explotación, el sistema operativo**
on-line **on-line, en línea**
output **la salida, el output**
output unit **la unidad de salida, el dispositivo de salida**
password **la contraseña de acceso**
program(me) **el programa**
programmable **programable**
programmer **el programador**
programming **la programación**
pulldown menu **el menú desplegable**
reference archive **el archivo de referencias, el archivo de consulta**
return **el retorno**
software **el software, los elementos de programación**
software package **el paquete de programas**
sort **la ordenación**
space **el espacio**
spreadsheet **la hoja electrónica,**

la hoja de cálculo
statistics package **el paquete estadístico**
update **la actualización**
user friendly **fácil de utilizar**
virus **el virus**

15d Computer Printing

continuous paper **el papel continuo**
font **la fuente, el tipo de letra**
hard copy **la copia impresa**
ink cartridge **el cartucho / el recambio de tinta**
inkjet **la impresora de chorro de tinta**
laser printer **la impresora (por) láser**
paper feed **el alimentador de papel**
paper tray **la reserva de papel**
ribbon **la cinta (de impresora)**
roller **el rodillo**
sheetfeeder **el alimentador de papel**
style **el estilo**
toner **el virador**

16a Hobbies

angling **la pesca con caña**
archeology **la arqueología**
archery **el tiro con arco**
ballroom dancing **el baile de salón**
beekeeping **la apicultura**
birdwatching **la ornitología, la observación de aves**
carpentry **la carpintería**
collecting antiques **la colección de antigüedades**
collecting stamps **la colección de sellos / [estampillas]**
dancing **bailar**

fishing **la pesca**
gambling **el juego**
gardening **la jardinería**
going to the movies / cinema **ir al cine**
knitting **el tejido de punto**
listening to music **escuchar música**
photography **la fotografía**
playing chess **jugar al ajedrez**
reading **la lectura**
sewing **la costura**
spinning **hilar**
walking **pasear**
watching television **mirar la televisión**

17b Architectural Terms

alcove **el hueco, el nicho**
arch **el arco**
architrave **el arquitrabe**
atrium **el atrio**
bas relief **el bajorrelieve**
battlement **la almena**
buttress **el contrafuerte**
capital **el capitel**
caryatid **la cariátide**
colonnade **la galería**
column **la columna**
  doric **dórica**
  ionic **jónica**
  corinthian **corintia**
concave **cóncavo**
convex **convexo**
cornerstone **la piedra angular**
cupola **la cúpula**
diptych **el díptico**
drawbridge **el puente levadizo**
eaves **el alero**
facade **la fachada**
fanlight **el montante de abánico**
frieze / dado **el zócalo, el friso**
gable **el frontón**
gargoyle **la gárgola**
half-timbered **con entramado de madera**

haut relief **el altorrelieve**
headstone **la lápida**
herringbone *(adj)* **de espinapez**
molding / moulding **el zócalo**
nave **la nave**
ogive **la ojiva**
oval **ovalado**
overhanging **sobresaliente, voladizo**
pagoda **la pagoda**
pilaster **la pilastra**
pinnacle **el pináculo**
plinth **el plinto**
porch **el pórtico, la entrada**
portico **el pórtico, la arcada**
rear arch **el arco trasero**
roof **el tejado**
rosette **el rosetón**
rotunda **la rotonda**
sacristy **la sacristía**
spire / steeple **la aguja**
triumphal arch **el arco triunfal, de triunfo**
tryptych **el tríptico**
vault **la bóveda**
vaulted **abovedado**
volute **la voluta**
wainscot **el revestimiento**

17c Publishing

abridged version **la versión abreviada**
acknowledgment **el agradecimiento**
appendix **el apéndice**
artwork **la obra de arte**
author **el autor**
best-seller **el best-seller, el libro de más venta**
bibliography **la bibliografía**
book fair **la feria del libro**
catalogue **el catálogo**
chapter **el capítulo**
contents **el contenido**
contract **el contrato**
copy **la copia**

copyright **el derecho de autor**
cover *(of book)* **la cubierta, la tapa**
deadline **el plazo**
dedicated to **dedicado a**
edition **la edición**
  first edition **la primera edición**
  latest edition **la última edición**
editor **el redactor**
  literary editor **el redactor literario**
footnotes **las notas a pie de página**
illustrations **las ilustraciones**
manuscript **el manuscrito**
paperback **la cubierta rústica, el libro en rústica**
preface **el prefacio**
proofreading **la corrección de textos**
publication date **la fecha de publicación**
publisher **el editor**
publishing house **la casa editorial**
quote **la cita**
review **la revisión, la revista**
reviewer **el crítico, el reseñante**
subtitle **el subtítulo**
translation **la traducción**
version **la versión**
with a foreword by **con prólogo escrito por**

17d Musicians & Instruments

accordionist **el acordeonista**
alto *(singer)* **el contralto**
bagpipe **la gaita**
baritone **el barítono**
bass *(singer)* **el bajo**
bass clarinet **el clarinete bajo**
basset horn **el cuerno de bajo**
bassoon **el fagot**
bassoonist **el fagotista**
bells **las campanas tubulares**
bugle **la corneta, el clarín**
castanets **las castañuelas**

celeste   la celesta
cellist   el violoncelista
cello   el violoncelo
cembalo   el cémbalo
chorister   el corista
clarinet   el clarinete
clarinetist   el clarinetista
clarion   la trompeta
classical guitar   la guitarra clásica
clavicord   el clavicordio
conductor   el director de orquesta
contralto   el contralto
cornet   la corneta
cymbal   el cimbal
double bass   el contrabajo
double bassoon   el contrafagot
drum   el tambor
drummer   el batería
dulcimer   el salterio, el dulcémele
flautist   el flautista
flute   la flauta
French horn   el cuerno francés
grand piano   el piano de cola
guitar   la guitarra
guitarist   el guitarrista
harmonica/mouth organ   la armónica
harmonium   el armonio
harp   el arpa (f)
harpist   el arpista
harpsichord   el clavicordio
horn   el cuerno
hurdy-gurdy   el organillo
instrumentalist   el instrumentalista
jews' harp   el birimbao
librettist   el libretista
lyre   la lira
mandolin   la mandolina
mezzo-soprano   la mezzosoprano
oboe   el oboe
oboe player   el oboe
orchestra leader   el primer violín
orchestra players   los músicos de la orquesta
organ   el órgano
organist   el organista
percussion   los instrumentos de percusión

percussionist   el percusionista
pianist   el pianista
piano   el piano
pipe   la gaita, el tubo
recorder   la flauta dulce, la flauta de pico
saxophone   el saxofón
saxophonist   el saxofonista
soprano   el/la soprano
spinet   la espineta
accordion   la concertina
string instruments   los instrumentos de cuerda
strolling musician/busker   el músico ambulante
synthesizer   el sintetizador
tenor   el tenor
tin whistle   la flauta metálica
triangle   el triángulo
trombone   el trombón
trumpet   la trompeta
tuba   la tuba
tuning fork   el diapasón
timpani   los tímpanos
viol   la viola
viola   la violeta, la viola
viola player   el músico de viola
violin   el violín
violinist   el violinista
violoncello   el violoncelo
vocalist   el cantante
Welsh harp   el arpa (f) galesa
xylophone   el xilófono

17d Musical Forms

aria   el aria (f)
ballad   la balada
cantata   la cantata
canzonetta   la canzoneta
chamber music   la música de cámara
choral music   la música coral
concerto   el concierto
    piano concerto   el concierto para piano
duet   el dúo

fugue   la fuga
madrigal   el madrigal
march   la marcha
music drama   el drama musical
musical (comedy)   la comedia
   musical
nocturne   el nocturno
octet   el octeto
opera   la ópera
operetta   la opereta
oratorio   el oratorio
overture   la obertura
piano trio   el trío de piano
plainsong   el canto llano
prelude   el preludio
quartet   el cuarteto
quintet   el quinteto
recitative   el recitativo, el recitado
requiem Mass   la misa de réquiem
sacred music   la música sagrada
serenade   la serenata
sextet   el sexteto
septet   el septeto
sinfonietta   la sinfonieta
sonata   la sonata
song cycle   el ciclo de canciones
suite   la suite
symphony   la sinfonía
string quartet   el cuarteto de cuerda
trio   el trío

17d Musical Terms

accompaniment   el acompañamiento
accompanist   el acompañante
arpeggio   el arpegio
bar   el compás
beat   el compás, el ritmo
bow   el arco
bowing   la técnica del arco
cadence   la cadencia
chord   el acorde
clef   la clave
   bass   de bajo
   treble   de soprano
discord   la disonancia
improvisation   la improvisación

key   la clave, la nota
   major   mayor
   minor   menor
note   la nota
   breve   la breve
   half note / minim   la blanca
   quarter note / crotchet   la negra
   eighth note / quaver   la corchea
   sixteenth note / semiquaver   la
      semicorchea
mute   sorda
scale   la escala
score   la partitura
sharp   sostenido
sheet (of music)   la partitura

17e Movie / Film Genres

adventure movie / film   la película
   de aventuras
animation   la animación
black and white   blanco y negro
black comedy   la comedia negra,
   el cine negro
cartoons   los dibujos animados
comedy   la comedia
documentary   el documental
feature movie / film   el largometraje
horror movie / film   la película de
   terror
low-budget   de bajo presupuesto
sci-fi   la ciencia ficción
short film   el corto de cine
silent movies / cinema   el cine mudo
tearjerker / weepie   la película
   lacrimosa
thriller   la película de intriga
video clip   el vídeo-clip
war movie / film   la película de
   guerra
western   la película del oeste

19a Means of Transportation

by air   por aire, por avión
in an ambulance   en una
   ambulancia

by bicycle **en bicicleta**
by bus **en autobús**
by cable car **en teleférico**
by car **en coche**
by coach **en autobús**
in a dinghy **en barca**
by ferry **en ferry**
by helicopter **en helicóptero**
by hovercraft **en hidrodeslizador /
aerodeslizador**
by hydrofoil **en hidroala**
by jumbo jet **en jumbo**
by plane **en avión**
by ship **en barco, en buque**
by subway / underground **por metro**
by taxi / cab **en taxi**
by trolley / tram **en tranvía**
by trolleybus **en trolebús**
in a truck / lorry **en camión**

19b Ships & Boats

aircraft carrier **el porta(a)viones**
canoe **la canoa**
cargo ship **el barco de
mercancías, el buque mercante**
dinghy **el bote**
ferry **el ferry**
hovercraft **el hidrodeslizador**
hydrofoil **el hidroala**
lifeboat **el bote salvavidas**
merchant ship **el barco mercante**
ocean liner **el transatlántico**
oil tanker / petrol tank **el tanque de
petróleo**
rowing boat **el bote de remo**
sailing boat **el barco de vela**
ship **el barco, el buque, la nave**
speedboat **la lancha rápida**
submarine **el submarino**
towboat **el remolcador**
warship **el buque de guerra**
yacht **el yate**

19c Parts of the Car

air conditioning **la
climatización**
alternator **el alternador de
corriente**
automatic gear **la marcha
automática, el cambio
automático**
back wheel **la rueda de atrás, la
rueda trasera**
battery **la batería**
bodywork **la carrocería**
brake **el freno**
bumper / tender **el parachoques**
carburetor **el carburador**
catalytic converter **el convertidor,
el catalizador**
choke **el obturador, el estárter**
clutch **el embrague**
dashboard **el cuadro de
mandos, el tablero (de
instrumentos)**
door **la puerta**
　front **delantera**
　passenger **del pasajero**
engine **el motor**
exhaust pipe **el tubo de escape**
front seats **los asientos
delanteros**
front wheel **la rueda delantera**
gearbox **la caja de marchas / de
cambios**
headlights **los focos, los faros**
horn **la bocina, el pito**
hood / bonnet **la capota, el capó**
indicator **el indicador de
dirección, el intermitente**
license / number plate **la matrícula**
lights **las luces**
motor **el motor**
passenger seat **el asiento de
pasajero**
pedal **el pedal**
　accelerator **el pedal de
aceleración, el acelerador**

brake el pedal de freno, el freno
clutch el pedal de embrague, el embrague
rearview / rear mirror el espejo retrovisor
registration number el número de matrícula, [las placas]
roof el techo
roof rack la baca, la canasta
safety belt el cinturón de seguridad
spares las piezas de repuesto
spare wheel la rueda de repuesto
spark plug la bujía
speedometer el velocímetro, el cuentakilómetros
starter el arranque
steering wheel el volante
tank el depósito de gasolina
throttle valve la válvula reguladora
tire / tyre la cubierta, la llanta, la neumática
back tire / tyre la cubierta / llanta trasera
front tire / tyre la cubierta / llanta delantera
spare tire / tyre la cubierta / llanta de repuesto
tire / tyre pressure la presión de las ruedas
trunk / boot el maletero
wheel la rueda
windshield / windscreen el parabrisas
windshield / windscreen wiper el limpiaparabrisas

19c Road Signs

Cross now cruzar ahora
Danger! ¡peligro!
Detour / Diversion la desviación
End of detour / diversion fin de la desviación
End of roadworks fin de las obras de la carretera
End of speed zone fin de la regulación / señalización
Free parking aparcamiento gratuito, parqueadero gratis
Highway / Expressway entrance acceso a la autopista
Junction cruce de autopistas
Keep clear dejar libre el paso
Loading bay la zona de carga y descarga
Maximum speed la velocidad máxima
No entry prohibida la entrada
No parking no aparcar
Pedestrians crossing el cruce de peatones
Residents only sólo residentes
Road closed carretera cerrada
Roadworks carretera en obras
Stop stop, parar
Toll el peaje

20a Tourist Sights

abbey la abadía
playground el parque infantil
amphitheater / amphitheatre el anfiteatro
aquarium el acuario
art gallery la galería de arte
battlefield el campo de batalla
battlements las almenas
boulevard el bulevar
castle el castillo, el alcázar
catacombs las catacumbas
cathedral la catedral
cave la cueva
cemetery el cementerio
city la ciudad
chapel la capilla
church la iglesia
concert hall la sala de conciertos
convent el convento

APPENDICES

downtown / town centre **el centro de la ciudad**
exhibition **la exhibición**
fortress **la fortaleza**
fountain **la fuente**
gardens **los jardines públicos**
harbor / harbour **el puerto**
library **la biblioteca**
mansion **la mansión**
market **el mercado**
monastery **el monasterio**
monument **el monumento**
museum **el museo**
opera **la ópera**
palace **el palacio**
parliament building **el edificio de las Cortes / [del Parlamento]**
pier **el embarcadero**
planetarium **el planetario**
ruins **las ruinas**
shopping area **la zona de tiendas**
square **la plaza**
stadium **el estadio**
statue **la estatua**
temple **el templo**
theater / theatre **el teatro**
tomb **la tumba**
tower **la torre**
town hall **el ayuntamiento, [la alcadía]**
university **la universidad**
zoo **el parque / jardín zoológico**

20a On the Beach

beach **la playa**
beach ball **la pelota de playa**
cabana / bathing hut **la cabina, la cabaña, la caseta de playa**
deck chair **la silla de lona**
I dive **me tiro al agua**
diver **el buceador**
pail and shovel / bucket and spade **el cubo y pala**
sand **la arena**
  grain of sand **el grano de arena**

sandcastle **el castillo de arena**
sandy (beach) **arenoso**
scuba diving **la natación submarina**
sea **el mar**
seashore **la costa**
snorkel **el tubo snorkel, el esnórquel**
I snorkel **nado respirando por un tubo**
suntan lotion **la loción solar / bronceadora**
sunshade (umbrella) **la sombrilla**
I surf **hago surf**
surfboard **la tabla deslizadora**
surfboarder **el surfista**
surfing **el surf, el acuaplano**
I swim **nado**
waterskiing **el esquí acuático**
windsurfing / sailboarding **el windsurf, el surf a vela**
I go windsurfing **practico el windsurf**

20a Continents & Regions

Africa **Africa**
Antarctica **Tierras Antárticas**
Arctic **Ártico**
Asia **Asia**
Australasia **Australasia**
Balkans **los Balcanes**
Baltic States **los estados bálticos**
Central America **América Central**
Eastern Europe **Europa del este**
Europe **Europa**
European Union **la Unión Europea**
Far East **el Extremo Oriente**
Middle East **el Medio Oriente**
North America **América del Norte**
Oceania **Oceanía**
Scandinavia **Escandinavia**
South America **América del Sur**
former Soviet Union **la ex-Unión Soviética**
West Indies **las Antillas Occidentales**

former Yugoslavia **la ex-Yugoslavia**

20a Countries

Afghanistan **Afganistán**
Albania **Albania**
Algeria **Argelia**
Argentina **Argentina**
Austria **Austria**
Belgium **Bélgica**
Bolivia **Bolivia**
Bosnia **Bosnia**
Brazil **Brasil**
Bulgaria **Bulgaria**
Canada **el Canadá**
Chile **Chile**
China **China**
Colombia **Colombia**
Costa Rica **Costa Rica**
Croatia **Croacia**
Cuba **Cuba**
Cyprus **Chipre**
Czech Republic **la República Checa**
Denmark **Dinamarca**
Ecuador **Ecuador**
Egypt **Egipto**
England **Inglaterra**
Estonia **Estonia**
Finland **Finlandia**
France **Francia**
Germany **Alemania**
Great Britain **Gran Bretaña**
Greece **Grecia**
Guatemala **Guatemala**
Hungary **Hungría**
Iceland **Islandia**
India **India**
Indonesia **Indonesia**
Iran **Irán**
Iraq **Irak**
Ireland **Irlanda**
Israel **Israel**
Italy **Italia**
Japan **el Japón**
Jordan **Jordania**

Kampuchea **Kampuchea**
Kenya **Kenia**
Korea (North / South) **Corea (del Norte / del Sur)**
Kuwait **Kuwait**
Latvia **Letonia**
Lebanon **Líbano**
Libya **Libia**
Lithuania **Lituania**
Luxembourg **Luxemburgo**
Malaysia **Malasia**
Mexico **México**
Mongolia **Mongolia**
Morocco **Marruecos**
Netherlands **los Países Bajos**
New Zealand **Nueva Zelandia**
Nicaragua **Nicaragua**
Norway **Noruega**
Pakistan **Pakistán**
Palestine **Palestina**
Paraguay **Paraguay**
Peru **el Perú**
Philippines **las Filipinas**
Poland **Polonia**
Portugal **Portugal**
Romania **Rumania**
Russia **Rusia**
Saudi Arabia **Arabia Saudita**
Scotland **Escocia**
Serbia **Serbia**
Slovakia **Eslovaquia**
Slovenia **Eslovenia**
South Africa **Africa del Sur**
Spain **España**
Sri Lanka **Sri Lanka**
Sudan **Sudán**
Sweden **Suecia**
Switzerland **Sulza**
Syria **Siria**
Taiwan **Taiwán**
Tanzania **Tanzania**
Thailand **Tailandia**
Tibet **el Tibet**
Tunisia **Túnez**
Turkey **Turquía**
Uganda **Uganda**
Ukraine **Ucrania**

United States   **los Estados Unidos**
Uruguay   **Uruguay**
Venezuela   **Venezuela**
Vietnam   **Vietnam**
Wales   **el País de Gales**
Zaire   **Zaire**
Zimbabwe   **Zimbabue**

20a Oceans & Seas

Adriatic Sea   **el Mar Adriático**
Arctic Ocean   **el Océano Glacial Ártico**
Atlantic Ocean   **el Océano Atlántico**
Baltic Sea   **el Mar Báltico**
Bay of Biscay   **la Bahía de Vizcaya**
English Channel   **el Canal de la Mancha**
Gulf of Mexico   **el Golfo de México**
Indian Ocean   **el Océano Indico**
Mediterranean Sea   **el Mar Mediterráneo**
Pacific Ocean   **el Océano Pácifico**

21a Main Language Families

Afro-Asiatic   **afroasiático**
Altaic   **altaico**
Austronesian   **austronesiano**
Australian   **australiano**
Caucasian   **caucasiano, caucásico**
Central and South   **central y del sur**
Eskimo   **esquimal**
Indo-European   **indoeuropeo**
  Baltic   **báltico**
  Celtic   **céltico**
  Germanic   **germánico**
  Hellenic   **helénico**
  Indo-Iranian   **indoiraní**
  Italic   **itálico**
  Romance   **romance**
  Slavic   **eslavo**
Independent   **independiente**
North American Indian   **indio norteamericano**

Paleo-Asiatic   **paleoasiático**
Papuan   **papúa**
Sino-Tibetan   **sino tibetano**
Uralic   **urálico**

21a Languages & Nationalities*

Afrikaans   **el africano**
Albanian   **el albanés**
Arabic   **el árabe**
Armenian   **el armenio**
Basque   **el vasco**
Bengali   **el bengalí**
Breton   **el bretón**
Bulgarian   **el búlgaro**
Burmese   **el birmano**
Catalan   **el catalán**
Chinese   **el chino**
Coptic   **el copto**
Czech   **el checo**
Danish   **el danés**
Dutch   **el holandés**
English   **el inglés**
Eskimo   **el esquimal**
Estonian   **el estonio**
Finnish   **el finés, el finlandés**
Flemish   **el flamenco**
French   **el francés**
Gallegan   **el gallego**
German   **el alemán**
Greek   **el griego**
Hebrew   **el hebreo**
Hindi   **el hindú**
Hungarian   **el húngaro**
Icelandic   **el islandés**
Indonesian   **el indonesio**
Irish Gaelic   **el gaélico irlandés**
Italian   **el italiano**
Japanese   **el japonés**
Korean   **el coreano**
Kurdish   **el kurdo**
Latin   **el latín**
Majorcan   **el mallorquín**
Mongolian   **el mongol**
Norwegian   **el noruego**
Persian   **el persa**

➤ *Where applicable, the adjective of nationality (masculine form) is the same as the language.

Polish **el polaco**
Portuguese **el portugués**
Punjabi **el punjabí**
Rumanian **el rumano**
Russian **el ruso**
Scottish Gaelic **el gaélico escocés**
Slovak **el eslovaco**
Somali **el somalí**
Spanish **el español**
Swahili **el swahilí**
Swedish **el sueco**
Thai **el tailandés**
Tamil **el tamil**
Tibetan **el tibetano**
Turkish **el turco**
Urdu **el urdú**
Valencian **el valenciano**
Vietnamese **el vietnamita**
Welsh **el galés**

Latin American languages

Aztec **el azteca**
Guarani **el guaraní**
Inca **el inca**
Nahuatl **el nahuatl**
Pampa **el pampa**
Quechua **el quechua**

Other nationalities

Algerian **argelino**
American **americano**
American Indian **indio, indígena**
Argentinian **argentino**
Australian **australiano**
Austrian **austríaco**
Belgian **belga**
Bolivian **boliviano**
Brazilian **brasileño**
Canadian **canadiense**
Chilean **chileno**
Colombian **colombiano**
Costa Rican **costarricense**
Ecuadorean **ecuatoriano**
Egyptian **egipicio**
French Canadian
  francocanadiense

Guatemalan **guatemalteco**
Indian **indio**
Iraqi **iraquí**
Iranian **iraní**
Irish **irlandés**
Israeli **israelí**
Lebanese **libanés**
Mexican **mexicano, mejicano**
Moroccan **marroquí**
New Zealander **neozelandés**
Nicaraguan **nicaragüense**
Pakistani **pakistaní**
Palestinian **palestino**
Panamanian **panameño**
Paraguayan **paraguayo**
Peruvian **peruano**
Puerto Rican **puertorriqueño**
Saudi **saudí, saudita**
Scottish **escocés**
South African **sudafricano**
Swiss **suizo**
Syrian **sirio**
Uruguayan **uruguayo**

21b Grammar

accusative **el acusativo**
  accusative *(adj)* **acusativo**
adjective **el adjetivo**
adverb **el adverbio**
agreement **la concordancia**
it agrees with **concuerda con**
article **el artículo**
  definite article **el artículo
  definido**
  indefinite article **el artículo
  indefinido**
case **el caso**
case ending **la terminación del
  caso**
clause **la cláusula**
comparative **el comparativo**
conjunction **la conjunción**
dative **el dativo**
definite **el definido**
demonstrative **el demostrativo**
direct object **el objeto directo**

APPENDICES

ending **la terminación**
exception **la excepción**
gender **el género**
genitive **el genitivo**
indefinite **el indefinido**
indirect object **el objeto indirecto**
interrogative **el interrogativo**
negative **el negativo**
nominative **el nominativo**
noun **el nombre, el sustantivo**
object **el objeto**
phrase **la frase, la oración**
plural **el plural**
  plural *(adj)* **plural**
possessive **el posesivo**
prefix **el prefijo**
preposition **la preposición**
pronoun **el pronombre**
  demonstrative **el pronombre demostrativo**
  indefinite **el pronombre indefinido**
  interrogative **el pronombre interrogativo**
  personal **el pronombre personal**
  relative **el pronombre relativo**
  subject **el pronombre sujeto**
reflexive **el reflexivo**
  reflexive *(adj)* **reflexivo**
rule **la regla**
sequence **la concordancia, la sucesión**
singular **el singular**
suffix **el sufijo**
superlative **el superlativo**
  superlative *(adj)* **superlativo**
word order **el orden de las palabras**

Verbs

active voice **la voz activa**
auxiliary **auxiliar**
compound **compuesto**
conditional **el condicional**
defective **el defectivo**

formation **la formación**
future **el futuro**
gerund **el gerundio**
imperative **el imperativo**
imperfect **el imperfecto**
impersonal **el impersonal**
infinitive **el infinitivo**
intransitive **el intransitivo**
irregular **irregular**
passive voice **la voz pasiva**
participle **el participio**
past **el pasado**
  past *(adj)* **pasado**
perfect **el perfecto**
present **el presente**
reflexive **el reflexivo**
  reflexive *(adj)* **reflexivo**
regular **regular**
sequence **la concordancia, la sucesión**
simple **simple**
strong **fuerte**
subjunctive **el subjuntivo**
system **el sistema**
tense **el tiempo**
transitive **el transitivo**
use **el uso**
verb **el verbo**
weak **débil**

21b Punctuation

apostrophe **el apóstrofe**
asterisk **el asterisco**
bracket **el corchete**
colon **los dos puntos** *(pl)*
comma **la coma**
dash **el guión**
exclamation mark **el signo de exclamación / admiración**
quotation marks **las comillas**
(in) parentheses **(entre) paréntesis**
period / full stop **el punto final**
question mark **el signo de interrogación**
semicolon **punto y coma**

22b Stationery

adhesive tape la cinta adhesiva, el papel celo, [la cinta pegante]
blackboard eraser el borrador de la pizarra
carbon paper el papel carbón
card index el fichero, el tarjetero
chalk la tiza
clipboard la tablilla con sujetapapeles
compasses el compás
correction fluid el líquido corrector
diary / datebook la agenda
envelope el sobre
eraser / rubber la gomma de borra, la gomita
felt-tip pen el rotulador
file la carpeta archivadora
filing cabinet el archivador
fountain pen la pluma
glue el pegamento, [el pegante]
highlighter el rotulador fluorescente, el marcador
hole punch la taladradora, el taladro, [la perforadora]
ink la tinta
ink refill la mina de bolígrafo
in tray / out tray la bandeja de entradas / de salidas
label la etiqueta
letter opener / scalpel el escalpelo
marker el rotulador
note book el cuaderno, el block
overhead projector / OHP el proyector de transparencias
paper el papel
paper clip el clip, el sujetapapeles
paper cutter / guillotine la guillotina
pen el bolígrafo
pencil el lápiz
photocopier la fotocopiadora
pocket calculator la calculadora de bolsillo
protractor el transportador de ángulos

ring binder la carpeta de anillos
rubber band / elastic band la gomilla, la gomita
ruler la regla
scissors las tijeras
screen la pantalla
T- / set square el juego de escuadra y cartabón, el cartabón, la escuadra
sheet of paper la hoja de papel
shredder la trituradora de papel, el desfibrador
stamp el sello, el tampón, la estampilla
stapler la grapadora, la cosedora
staple remover el quitagrapas
textbook el libro de texto
thumbtack / drawing pin la chincheta, el chinche
typewriter la máquina de escribir
typewriter ribbon la cinta de la máquina de escribir
transparency la transparencia
wastepaper basket la papelera
whiteboard la pizarra blanca
workbook / exercise book el cuaderno de ejercicios

23a Scientific Disciplines

applied sciences las ciencias aplicadas
anthropology la antropología
astronomy la astronomía
astrophysics la astrofísica
biochemistry la bioquímica
biology la biología
botany la botánica
chemistry la química
geology la geología
medicine la medicina
microbiology la microbiología
physics la física
physiology la fisiología
psychology la psicología
social sciences las ciencias sociales

technology la tecnología
zoology la zoología

23b Chemical Elements

aluminum / aluminium el aluminio
arsenic el arsénico
calcium el calcio
carbon el carbono
chlorine el cloro
copper el cobre
gold el oro
hydrogen el hidrógeno
iodine el yodo
iron el hierro
lead el plomo
magnesium el magnesio
mercury el mercurio
nitrogen el nitrógeno
oxygen el oxígeno
phosphorus el fósforo
platinum el platino
plutonium el plutonio
potassium el potasio
silver la plata
sodium el sodio
sulfur el sulfuro
uranium el uranio
zinc el zinc, el cinc

23b Compounds & Alloys

acetic acid al ácido acético
alloy la aleación
ammonia el amoniaco
asbestos el amianto, el asbesto
brass el latón
carbon dioxide el dióxido de carbono
carbon monoxide el monóxido de carbono
copper oxide el óxido de cobre
hydrochloric acid el ácido clorhídrico
iron oxide el óxido de hierro
lead oxide el óxido de plomo

nickel el níquel
nitric acid el ácido nítrico
it oxidizes oxida, se oxida
ozone el ozono
propane el propano
silver nitrate el nitrato de plata
sodium bicarbonate el bicarbonato de sodio
sodium carbonate el carbonato de sodio
sodium chloride el cloruro de sodio
sulfuric acid el ácido sulfúrico
tin el estaño

23c The Zodiac

Aries Aries
Taurus Tauro
Gemini Géminis
Cancer Cáncer
Leo Leo
Virgo Virgo
Libra Libra
Scorpio Escorpión
Sagittarius Sagitario
Capricorn Capricornio
Aquarius Acuario
Pisces Piscis

23c Planets & Stars

Earth Tierra
Venus Venus
Mercury Mercurio
Pluto Plutón
Mars Marte
Jupiter Júpiter
Saturn Saturno
Uranus Urano
Neptune Neptuno
North star la Estrella Polar
Big Dipper / Great Bear la Osa Mayor
Halley's comet el Cometa Halley
Southern Cross la Cruz del Sur

24b Wild Animals

baboon   el mandril
badger   el tejón
bear   el oso
beaver   el castor
bison / buffalo   el búfalo
camel   el camello
cheetah   el leopardo cazador
chimpanzee   el chimpancé
cougar   el puma
coyote   el coyote
deer   el ciervo, el venado
elephant   el elefante
elk   el alce, el anta
fox   el zorro
frog   la rana
giraffe   la jirafa
gorilla   el gorila
grizzly bear   el oso pardo
hare   la liebre
hedgehog   el erizo
hippopotamus   el hipopótamo
hyena   la hiena
jaguar   el jaguar
leopard   el leopardo
lion   el león
lizard   el lagarto
lynx   el lince
mink   el visón
mole   el topo
monkey   el mono
moose   el alce de América
mouse   el ratón
otter   la nutria
panther   la pantera
polar bear   el oso polar
puma   el puma
rat   la rata
reindeer   el reno
rhinoceros   el rinoceronte
snake   la serpiente, la culebra
squirrel   la ardilla
tiger   el tigre
toad   el sapo
whale   la ballena
wildcat   el gato montés

wolf   el lobo
zebra   la cebra

24b Birds

albatross   el albatros
blackbird   el cuervo
bluetit   el herrerillo
chaffinch   el pinzón
crow   el grajo, la corneja
dove   la paloma
eagle   el águila (f)
   golden eagle   el águila real
emu   el emú, el dromeo
hawk / falcon   el halcón
heron   la garza
hummingbird   el colibrí, el picaflor
kingfisher   el martín pescador
magpie   la urraca
osprey   el águila (f) pescadora
ostrich   el avestruz
owl   el búho, la lechuza, el mochuelo
parrot   el loro
peacock   el pavo real, el pavón
pelican   el pelícano
penguin   el pingüino
pigeon   la paloma
robin   el petirrojo
seagull   la gaviota
sparrow   el gorrión
starling   el estornino
swallow   la golondrina
swan   el cisne
swift   el vencejo
thrush   el tordo
woodpecker   el pájaro carpintero
wren   el troglodito

24b Parts of the Animal Body

beak   el pico
claw   la garra, la zarpa
comb   la cresta
feather   la pluma
fin   la aleta
fleece   la lana, el vellón

fur **el pelo**
gills **la branquia, la agalla**
hide **el pellejo, la piel**
hoof **la pezuña**
mane **la melena, la crin**
paw **la pata, la garra**
pelt **el pelo, el pelaje**
scale **la escama**
shell *(oyster, snail)* **la concha**
  shell *(tortoise, crab)* **el caparazón**
tail **el rabo, la cola**
trunk **la trompa**
tusk **el colmillo**
udder **la ubre**
wing **el ala**

24c Trees

apple tree **el manzano**
ash **el fresno**
beech **la haya**
cherry tree **el cerezo**
chestnut **el castaño**
cypress **el ciprés**
eucalyptus **el eucalipto**
fig tree **la higuera**
fir tree **el abeto**
fruit tree **el árbol frutal**
holly **el acebo**
maple **el arce, el maple**
oak **el roble**
olive tree **el olivo**
palm **la palmera**
peach tree **el melocotonero**
pear tree **el peral**
pine **el pino**
plum tree **el ciruelo**
poplar **el chopo, el álamo**
redwood **la secoya**
rhododendron **el rododendro**
walnut tree **el nogal**
willow **el sauce**
yew **el tejo**

24c Flowers & Weeds

azalea **la azalea**
cactus **el cactus, el cacto**
carnation **el clavel**
chrysanthemum **el crisantemo**
clover **el trébol**
crocus **la flor del azafrán**
daffodil **el narciso**
dahlia **la dalia**
daisy **la margarita**
dandelion **el diente de león**
fern **el helecho**
flax **el lino**
foxglove **la dedalera**
geranium **el geranio**
hydrangea **la hortensia**
lily **la azucena**
nettle (stinging) **la ortiga**
orchid **la orquídea**
poppy **la amapola**
rose **la rosa**
snowdrop **la campanilla de invierno, la flor de nieve**
sunflower **el girasol**
thistle **el cardo**
tulip **el tulipán**
violet **la violeta**

25b Political Institutions

assembly **la asamblea**
association **la asociación**
cabinet **el gabinete**
  shadow cabinet *(UK)* **el gobierno en la sombra**
confederation **la confederación**
congress **el congreso**
council **el consejo, la junta**
federation **la federación**
House of Representatives **la cámara de los representantes**
local authority **la autoridad local**
Lower House / Lower Chamber **la cámara baja**
parliament **el parlamento**
party **el partido político**

Senate **el senado**
town council **la junta local, el consejo de gobierno local**
town hall **el ayuntamiento, [la alcadía]**
Upper House **la cámara alta**

27b Military Ranks

admiral **el almirante**
air marshal **el mariscal de aire**
brigadier **el brigadier, el general de brigada**
captain **el capitán**
  captain *(Naval)* **el capitán de navío**
commander **el capitán general del ejército**
  commander *(Naval)* **el capitán de fragata**
commanding officer **el comandante**
corporal **el cabo**
field marshal **el mariscal de campo**
general **el general**
lieutenant **el teniente**
lieutenant commander **el capitán de corbeta**
major **el comandante**
private **el soldado raso**
rear admiral **el contraalmirante**
sergeant **el sargento**
sergeant major **el sargento mayor, el brigada**
sergeant major *(US)* **el primer sargento**

27c International Organizations

ASEAN / Association of South-East Asian Nations **ANSA / Asociación de Naciones del Sudeste Asiático**
Council of Europe **el Consejo de Europa**

EC / European Community **CE / la Comunidad Europea**
EU / European Union **UE / la Unión Europea**
IMF / International Monetary Fund **FMI / el Fondo Monetario Internacional**
NATO / North Atlantic Treaty Organization **OTAN / la Organización del Tratado del Atlántico Norte**
OECD / Organization for Economic Cooperation and Development **OCDE / la Organización de Cooperación y Desarrollo Económico**
OPEC / Organization of Petroleum Exporting Countries **OPEP / la Organización de Países Exportadores de Petróleo**
Security Council **el Consejo de Seguridad**
UNO / United Nations Organization **ONU / la Organización de las Naciones Unidas**
WHO / World Health Organization **OMS / la Organización Mundial de la Salud**
World Bank **el Banco Mundial**

D

SUBJECT INDEX

Subject Index

SUBJECT INDEX